MY SPIRITUAL GARDEN

with

A BUNCH OF HOMILIES

and

A POSY OF POEMS

Foreword by Rt. Rev Cormac Murphy-O'Connor
Bishop of Arundel and Brighton

HILARY PARSONS

Hellipar Publications
Chichester

Published in 1996 by Hellipar Publications
7 Elsaw Court, Cawley Road, Chichester PO19 1XF

ISBN 0 9527090 0 7

Acknowledgements
The author wishes to express his gratitude to:
DIANA BOWEN
for permission to reproduce a photograph
of her painting *"Les Peupliers, St John, Jersey"*
on the front cover of this book.

"HIS FRIENDS PICTURED WITHIN"
or their nearest surviving relatives, for permission
to mention them by name.

PHILIP STIBBE
for permission to quote from his book *'Return via Rangoon'*

Quotations from the works of Carlo Caretto are published
by permission of Burns & Oates.

The Scripture quotations are taken from The Jerusalem Bible,
published and copyright © 1966, 1967 and 1968 by
Darton, Longman & Todd Ltd and Doubleday & Co Inc,
and used by permission of the publishers

Typeset and Printed by Brenco Printing Services
2 Wilbury Crescent, Hove BN3 6FL

Bound by Biddles Limited, Guildford, Surrey

Distribution through WORDS Ink
PO Box 97, Chichester PO18 8AY

British Library Cataloguing in Publication Data.
A catalogue record for this book is available
from the British Library.

CONTENTS

FOREWORD

Among the many gifts of ministry in my diocese is that of the Permanent Diaconite. Deacon Hilary Parsons has been writing and preaching regularly for over ten years and he has now compiled a collection of his homilies and other writings for wider readership. The homilies seem to me to be full of the sense of gratitude to God that Hilary Parsons experiences in his Catholic Faith and which permeates the whole of the book. So I believe that these writings are not only to the 'greater glory of God' but will also help succeeding generations to persevere in giving witness to Christ. I warmly commend this book and sincerely hope it will gain a wide readership within my diocese and beyond.

Rt. Rev Cormac Murphy-O'Connor

Bishop of Arundel and Brighton

PREFACE

Since my ordination on the Feast of Saints Peter and Paul in 1984 I have been asked on many occasions to print some of my homilies and writings so that people might be able to read and reflect on them at their leisure. I never did any thing about it until November 1994. In that month I was cut down by a sudden severe heart condition. This made me realize that if ever I was going to do something about these requests I had better get cracking. So I went through my files and extracted what I thought were among the better things I had said and written. I offer them now *ad majorem Dei gloriam* to anyone kind enough to read them.

I dedicate this little work to my long-suffering wife, Helen, who has supported me lovingly and loyally throughout nearly fifty years of marriage, and to my sons and grandchildren. It is my dearest wish that those who follow me in the succeeding generations will continue to practise the Catholic faith which has been in our family for at least 200 years to my certain knowledge and which was handed down to me as a sacred trust by my own parents. If this book helps to strengthen other Catholics in their faith, or brings anyone outside the Catholic Church into it, then that will be a providential bonus.

Hilary Parsons
Deacon of the Diocese of Arundel & Brighton

Feast of St Ignatius Loyola

ERRATA (My Spiritual Garden)

Page 5, line 2: for 'Diaconite' read 'Diaconate'
Page 67,heading: for 'FIRST READING' read 'SECOND READING'
Page 125, line 22: for 'page 35' read 'page 39'
Pages 132 and 133: for 'Mother Theresa' read Mother Teresa'
Page 157, line 2: for 'Ihave been' read 'I had been'
Page 203, lines 2 & 4: for 'Fleet Arm' read 'Fleet Air Arm'
Page 212, line 22: for 'contact' read 'contract'

A YEAR
IN
MY SPIRITUAL GARDEN

INTRODUCTION

I want to take you for a walk around my spiritual garden. First let me give you a brief general description.

My garden has a cultivated area, like one of those walled gardens you find in the grounds of stately homes. In this part of my garden I try to see that the flowers and the vegetables and the fruit trees are properly tended and fertilized. I try to follow the teachings to be found in the *Guide to Good Horticulture* and put into practice the wisdom of those renowned gardeners who have gone before me. But outside the walled garden is an area where cultivated trees and plants are all jumbled up with wild flowers and untamed undergrowth. I keep telling myself I really must do something about this area and bring some sort of order into chaos, but despite the occasional foray I never seem to manage to get round to making any real impression. In fact I am ashamed to have to confess that when I start to tackle the briars and get my arms and legs well and truly lacerated I turn my back on them and try to pretend they are not there, or at least to convince myself that the wild part of my garden is exotically attractive in a romantic kind of way. Mind you, even within the walled garden the weeds soon spring up if I'm not constantly at them. On the other hand, I have managed to produce some nice flowers and healthy vegetables and succulent fruits in due season; in fact the Squire up at the Big House has complimented me from time to time on the produce of my garden. So it's not all gloom and doom, all briars and thistles. There are happy times when the sun shines, the bees are busy, the flowers are in bloom and the fruits ripen.

As we go along I will explain to you how things alter quite markedly in my spiritual garden as the seasons change. We'll also have a look inside my greenhouse and the tool shed, and I'll try to arrange for you to meet the Squire. He's a wonderful person to work for, full of wisdom and kindness and encouragement, though he's quite definite about what he wants and what he doesn't want.

I am sure, dear Reader, you have got the idea by now. The garden is my soul: the flowers, vegetables and fruits are the different virtues and blessings; the undergrowth and the weeds are faults, sins and weaknesses; the Guide to Good Horticulture is the Bible; the Squire is Jesus Christ, Our Lord.

See you next month. Be sure to have your winter woollies on and bring a good overcoat and head scarf!

JANUARY

MY SPIRITUAL GARDEN IN WINTER

It's winter now in my spiritual garden. The beautiful summer flowers (those happy times and blessings) are no more than a memory: the annuals (those one-off blessings unlikely to recur) have long ago been pulled up and thrown on the bonfire: the perennials look forlorn and lifeless. I think the frost has done for some of my best hydrangeas and my favourite apple tree died just before Christmas, like my very dear friend who died last week. We had shared many happy times together and when I was ill or feeling depressed he somehow had the knack of making me laugh and lifting my spirits. But now he's dead and a light has gone out of my life. Up at the Big House the Squire is away, the blinds are drawn and the furniture is covered with dust sheets.

There's not much I can do now in my spiritual garden beyond sweeping up the leaves and doing a bit of hedge trimming. The ground is like a rock and plant life is dormant. The skies are grey and leaden and mostly I feel depressed. It is difficult to believe that spring will come, and last summer seems a long time ago. However, last week we had a heavy snowfall. It looked so pretty and one evening there was a glorious red sunset which cast a deep crimson glow across the landscape which gave me a nice warm feeling and brought back happy childhood memories. But today it has rained all day. Sometimes I feel like quitting my job here and moving to the town where life is more comfortable and not dependent on the weather. But is the grass really greener on the other side of the fence?

I don't know about you, but in my spiritual life I find that from time to time I have to suffer a spiritual winter. Some people refer to the spiritual desert, but there are cold deserts as well as hot deserts. Life is difficult to sustain in either. In the spiritual winter God seems to have abandoned me. I find prayer difficult and meaningless. When I go to church I get nothing out of it, as they say. I come away feeling as cold inside as the temperature inside the church froze my outside and as bored with religion in general as I was by the sermon. Usually at times like this my personal relationships seem to go awry. I feel more than usually hurt by criticism and find myself easily irritated by others. Why doesn't God do something about it and help me? Dash it all, I've done enough for Him over the years! Perhaps I'll jack it all in. After all, plenty of people seem to get along all right without God and His religion. I would have more time to do the things I want and could stop worrying about the commandments and things like that. I feel like Peter, about to sink beneath the waves. *"Lord, save me. I'm perishing".*

But even in the depths of a spiritual winter I know in my heart of hearts that I could never really be happy without God, however alluring the bright lights of permissive materialism might appear on a dark winter's evening. In any case, God usually gives me just enough encouragement to keep me going, like that glorious sunset over the snow. And then, when I think about things rationally, past experience tells me that spring always does follow winter. If I hang on, my Master, my Lord, my Love (the Squire) will return. *"O ye of little faith"*, He would say. *"Have mercy on me, God, I place all my trust in You"*, I must reply.

FEBRUARY

WINTER OCCUPATIONS

Last month I described the winter scene in my spiritual garden. Let's now go and have a chat in my tool shed. It's a bit warmer in there. There's a little log fire and I can show you some of my spiritual tools while we talk.

Even though the frost has made the ground rock-like there are always things to be done in a garden, most especially a spiritual one. It is at this time of the year that I give some attention to that wild area outside the walled garden. It's there, you will remember, that the briars and weeds have a real hold, those sins and character defects I find so difficult to shift and alter. To make inroads into the undergrowth I sharpen the sickle, the shears and the secateurs, I put on my gauntlets and go to work. When the ground is soft enough I also get busy with the spade and pickaxe in an effort to root out the worst offenders. In spiritual terms this means fasting, alms-giving and penances of various kinds. Different tools for different jobs – horses for courses.

But the winter also provides an opportunity to get away for a break. We all need a break from time to time. I try to make a short retreat each year when I can look back over the past season and assess the mistakes I made, find out where I went wrong, so that looking ahead I can plan how to make my garden more productive and eliminate more of the destructive weeds and pests.There are also courses one can attend which enable one to find out how other gardeners are coping with the same problems one faces oneself and keep up to date with biblical scholarship and new ideas of marketing (spreading the Good News) and encouraging better spiritual growth.

You'll notice over in that corner I've started getting in next season's stock of fertilizer, and on the shelf above are the packets of seeds I shall need. It's too early to plant them but one has to get ready. If you don't have a system for regularly preparing the ground, re-seeding and developing new growth in a spiritual garden, the weeds quickly take over and the life of the Spirit is gradually extinguished. And, of course, plants need nourishment, hence the need for food, water and fertilizer. The life of the soul needs the food of the Eucharist and the living water of prayer in the Spirit. Over the years I have learnt that the same fertilizer and the same amount of water does not suit all plants alike. I know now more or less what and how much to give each kind. This attention to the specific needs of individuals is indispensable in the pastoral ministry. So in my tool rack you will notice I have several forks and rakes, each with differently spaced tines, and I have a number of roses for my watering-can and hose.

Some people who don't understand these things imagine that when I sit in my shed and huddle over my little fire, like we are doing now, I'm just idling my time away. In fact it's during these periods of tranquillity and silence that I do a lot of my thinking and planning. The monks of old used to refer to it as meditation and prayer. The townies don't understand things like peace and quiet: they're all rush and pother. But here in the country things don't change much. We have to work with nature, you see. And quite often when he's at home the Squire pops in here and has a chat with me. He understands. I always look forward to these visits of his. He's so wise and has such a wide experience that I always gain some new insight and feel encouraged and happy in his presence. "Praise the Lord".

See you next month – same time, same place!

MARCH

SPRING A-COMETH IN

It's been a long hard winter in my spiritual garden, but Spring does come eventually. It doesn't always come at the same time each year in our unpredictable British climate, of course, but it's usually round about Easter that things start happening. While digging up the ground ready for planting, with your mind miles away, you find yourself by an apple tree and notice the first bud peeping through the end of a twig, laughing at you.Then, as if by magic, everything seems suddenly to spring to life. Next morning you become more aware of the bird-song; the plants in the herbaceous border shake off that dull grey look and put on their bright spring clothes. The wild area outside the walled garden goes berserk with trees, bushes and brambles all putting out leaves like mad.

I have suddenly to do a mental about-turn. From feeling dozy and depressed I have to jump to it. If I don't get the seeds planted and the seedlings ready in the greenhouse the plants won't fruit at the right time. I still have some ground to prepare and, of course, my old sparring-partners, the weeds, are galloping ahead hoping to beat me to it yet again. There's no time to think about myself and my woes now. "Tide and time wait for no man". If I don't get cracking I shall soon be left behind by Mother Nature. She's in a hurry. And up at the Big House they're getting ready for the Squire's return.

Soon all my blues are gone and I get caught up in the expectancy and the excitement of it all. God is coming back into my life in a way I can feel and appreciate. New life is all around me. The birds are rearing their young in the nests, the first lambs have been born up at the Home Farm, the trees are covered in their bright green foliage, there's blossom on the fruit trees, Spring flowers seem to be everywhere. God is not only definitely in His heaven but He's also mighty busy down here on earth.

When the Master returns all is well. I feel the warmth of His presence. I experience new zest in my spiritual life. Now I want to pray. I am eager to visit His house (the church) now that 'He lives in me and I in Him'. All those thoughts about leaving Him and going to the godless city – how stupid can you be! I really ought to have known better. It's when Spring comes to my spiritual garden that I turn again to Gerard Manley Hopkins:

The world is charged with the grandeur of God.
It will flame out, like shining from shook foil;
It gathers to a greatness, like the ooze of oil
Crushed. Why do men then now not reck his rod?
Generations have trod, have trod, have trod;
All is seared with trade; bleared, smeared with toil;
And wears man's smudge and shares man's smell: the soil
Is bare now, nor can foot feel, being shod.

And for all this, nature is never spent;
There lives the dearest freshness deep down things;
And though the last lights off the black West went
Oh, morning, at the brown brink eastward, springs
Because the Holy Ghost over the bent
World broods with warm breast and with ah! bright wings.

"God's Grandeur." Gerald Manley Hopkins

APRIL

BEATING THE BOUNDS

Every year round about this time, just before the new season begins, the Squire gathers his grandchildren and the young people from the estate at the Big House and takes them on a tour of the grounds. There used to be an old English custom called "Beating the Bounds". At this annual ceremony the boys of the town or village were taken by the parish councillors, led by the Beadle, on a tour of the parish or town boundary, and at strategic points the boys had their bottoms beaten so that they would remember where the boundary was and be discouraged from going outside it. Well, the Squire doesn't beat anybody and the purpose of his annual tour is somewhat different, but the idea is the same. He expects people to discipline themselves and to avoid getting into trouble because they trust him and want to please him, though it has to be said that even common sense ought to be enough to make people see the wisdom of following the Squire's advice.

He begins his tour by showing his young retinue all the beauties of the gardens and the estate and telling them that when they are free during holiday times they can enjoy themselves to their hearts' content. Everything that is his is theirs – within certain limitations, and about these he is very clear and warns that he will be strict. For instance, there is a large and beautiful lake in the main park. The young people can swim in it, sail their boats and picnic on the banks – but a swift stream enters the lake at one end and leaves it in a strong current over a steep and rocky waterfall at the other. The latter is extremely dangerous, so no one is to go beyond the 20 yard barrier. Then again there are several lovely woods – but one is a known haunt of poisonous snakes and must on no account be entered. The Squire encourages the children to talk to the craftsmen and groundsmen on the estate and to learn about their work – but no child is ever to touch a piece of machinery without the express permission of an adult. The plants and wild life must be respected and the Squire will be very cross if they are wantonly damaged or destroyed.

So the Squire stakes out the danger areas, not to destroy the children's enjoyment and spoil their fun, but to protect them and teach them how to respect his property, to be considerate of other people and to learn to live at peace with the whole of his creation. He doesn't call his instructions "commandments" but that is what they are. And, of course, he expects visitors to observe them too. Unbridled selfishness, "doing your own thing" without consideration for other people and their property, not only provokes anger and leads to unhappiness, but it causes chaos and destroys what is fine and beautiful. So, having shown his young friends the beauties of this his 'Garden of Eden', he takes them to each of the danger points and explains why they are dangerous and to be avoided. Only the foolish disobey. He has always taught us that God is our Father, who loves us with an everlasting love, and who restricts us as little as possible, and then only for our own good,

MAY

A SPECIAL LADY COMES TO STAY

We always look forward to May on our estate because that is the month when our Squire's mother arrives to spend the summer with him. I haven't told you about her yet but she's someone very special. Somehow the whole place takes on a kind of glow when she's around. In some ways she reminds me of the Queen Mother, Queen Elizabeth – everyone loves her. She's not at all stuck up and has the knack of being able to put everyone at their ease, no matter who they are. She is loved especially by young people. Towards the middle of the month, just about now, they come up to the Big House and on "The Square" (the big lawn in front of the house) they erect a maypole and in the evening they dance and sing for her. Like several events or feasts in the christian calendar, the maypole originated in a pagan festival, but the Spring Festival (like the mid-winter festival, now Christmas) has long been christianised and is now an opportunity for honouring Our Lady. They prepare all winter for this annual occasion which is probably the happiest and most carefree event of the whole year. People come to it from all over the district.

I said that in some ways the Squire's mother reminds me of our Queen Mother, but she had a much tougher time in her early life. She was not born with a silver spoon in her mouth. Far from it. She (her name's Mary, by the way) came from simple country folk and within weeks of the Squire's birth she, her husband, Joseph, and her baby had to flee their native land because the dictator who was in power at that time got it into his head that among the new-born male babies was one who would one day take his place, so he decided to slaughter the lot. In exile Joseph managed to scrape a living somehow by doing odd jobs as a carpenter but he and his family knew all about poverty. Mary often wondered where the next meal would come from and how she was going to rear her baby son. Of course, things are different now but she has never forgotten those hard times and has a very special understanding of people who are in trouble, any sort of trouble. Even if they have brought their troubles on themselves they know instinctively that they can take their problems to her and receive a sympathetic reception. No one has ever asked her help and been turned away. She somehow manages to be everyone's mother.

She also has an amazing memory. She knows every family on the estate and makes sure she visits each one during the summer. She remembers when their babies were born, if any were ill the last time she called, and if she feels they are in real trouble she has a quiet word in the Squire's ear and, as far as I am aware, he's never been known to refuse a request from her.

But what about my spiritual garden? Well, Mary is a frequent visitor. When there are no outsiders around she loves to come and find a quiet corner where she will sit, often for quite a long time, just listening to the birds, contemplating the beauty of the flowers or the blossom and praying silently. As a matter of fact she is a floral expert and much of what I know about flowers (virtues) I have learnt from her. She knows exactly the colours and the perfume of each, how to raise even the most delicate and advises me how to mix the colours so that we are able to produce most beautiful variegated beds. The Squire is very good on vegetables and fruit which keep us alive but how dull life would be without flowers!

Often on a May evening, when the sun has gone down below the trees, I sit on the bench outside my tool shed and thank God for allowing me to work for Him in His garden and for giving me the consolation of knowing His Mother, Mary. I recall that lovely prayer of Robert Southwell who was martyred at Tyburn in 1595:

Greetings, Mary.
God's favour overflows in you
His special friend.
Of all women you are most blessed.
For Jesus. your Son, is truly God's Holy One.
Star of the Sea.
Whisper a word for us now
And in the moment of our greatest need.
Sinners He saves.   Amen.

She began her own prayer, the Magnificat, with the words: "My soul magnifies the Lord". The function of a magnifying glass is to make clear some writing or drawing which without its assistance is hazy and difficult to decipher. Mary brings God into focus and enables us to know and understand Him with a reality which is difficult to comprehend without her aid. I hope she will soon visit my garden again.

JUNE

THE REAL PURPOSE OF MY SPIRITUAL GARDEN

If you have been joining me these past months in my periodic jaunts round my spiritual garden you may have gained the impression that we have a somewhat cosy set-up on our estate and that everything is rather inward looking and perhaps a bit self-satisfied? Well, if you have, perhaps that's the way I have presented things, but in fact you would have been much mistaken.

You may remember that I said on my introductory walk that although the Squire (Christ, our Lord) is a super person to work for he has very definite ideas about what he wants and doesn't want. He has always insisted, for instance, that what we do here is not just for ourselves but must be for the benefit of the wider community, the villages and the little market town on our borders, and he places an absolute priority on giving assistance to the poor, the sick, the lonely and anyone in trouble, particularly if they are strangers who have come looking for help. He has converted the old stables into a refuge where someone without shelter can get a free bed for the night, and every morning he provides a free hot meal for people on the road. If any who turn up at the refuge are obviously sick he takes them into the Big House and sees that they are properly cared for until they are better. He always talks to those who call and if he finds someone who has no work and no home, but who genuinely wants to work, he does his best to find them a job. If there are no vacancies on his own estate he will try all his friends. Sometimes he will create a job, if there is no other solution, so that he can help a person over a bad patch by giving them a wage instead of a charitable handout, thereby enabling them to retain their human dignity.

As for the produce from my garden, some of it goes to the Big House and the staff, some to the refuge, but quite a lot is taken round the villages and sold at very low prices to people who have fallen on hard times. We all know that if it ever came to it, and there was a major shortage of food, the Squire would see to it that the poor and the sick got enough for their needs even if that meant us going without. Whenever he engages a new member of staff he makes it perfectly clear that he sees his role and that of his estate as serving the local community. His basic rule for all of us is that we must love our neighbours as ourselves, and that means making sure that other people are cared for before we start feathering our own nests. In all of this the Squire takes his full part and sets us a fine example.

In consequence of this philosophy the Squire shares his possessions. I mentioned during our last walk that the Squire's mother, Mary, is an expert where flowers (virtues) are concerned. Amongst other things she has an unerring eye for colour and artistic floral arrangements. Working by her advice we usually manage to produce each year flower beds and borders which are a riot of colour and people come from all around to see them. The Squire welcomes visitors, believing that the beautiful things of nature are his father's (God's) gift to all people and are not just for himself and his friends. Hence he has resisted pressure to charge an entrance fee. Other estate owners think he is a fool, and inevitably there are some visitors each year who take advantage of him and abuse his generosity, but he refuses to alter his policy. By and large the example of his kindness and liberality does far more good than the vandals do harm. He's no absentee landlord, you see. He is always around looking after his guests and the many people who thus meet him are in some way changed for the better by the magnetic effect of his personality. It's not so much what he says, it's just being in his presence which makes all the difference.

So I hope you will be able to appreciate that, as a community, we are outward looking and we all try to follow our Squire's lead. I have to admit that I find it difficult sometimes to keep my patience when visitors get in the way of what I am doing in my garden, and I am afraid I cannot equal the Squire when it comes to forgiving the person who picks some of my choicest flowers or vandalises one of my precious fruit trees. But at least I try, and as a community we are trying to care for those in need. We are aware that cosy self-preservation ought not to be the purpose of our labours.

JULY

THE IMPORTANCE OF "CHOOSING THE BETTER PART"

July is a busy and exciting month in my spiritual garden. The summer flowers are in full bloom, the vegetables are cropping, the early fruits are ready and the later ones filling out on the trees. We are at full stretch keeping everything in order. Besides starting to gather the fruits of our earlier labours we have to keep the weeds down, try to control the pests which attack our plants and, of course, we have lots of visitors to cope with, especially once the school holidays start. It's all go, go, go.

In my earlier years in the spiritual garden I used to like all the activity and throve on the hard manual work involved. I was fit and eager. It was only when I was promoted to under-gardener and assumed responsibility for certain parts of the garden that I came to realize that activity of itself does not ensure a good garden nor make it produce what the Squire (Christ our Lord) wants from it. The successful gardener, I came to discover, is the one who finds time to ponder and observe, who learns from past mistakes and plans ahead for future seasons. Successful gardeners know their plants and what each needs to grow to best advantage; they have studied the weather and know how to respond to differing conditions. Moreover, they know how to deal with all manner of weeds and pests. Of equal importance is man management – the ability to work harmoniously with bosses, colleagues and visitors.

As I have suggested before, the spiritual life has a lot in common with gardening. If we are not careful activity can become a substitute for holiness. It is possible to spend every minute of our waking lives attending committee meetings, counselling those in trouble, organising church services and parish programmes, singing in the choir, running fetes and engaging in all manner of charitable works, but leaving no time for prayer and silent contemplation. In fact we can come to believe that the maintenance of God's kingdom depends on our own efforts and that we are indispensable. Apart from the fact that this is the surest way to a nervous breakdown, it is a bit of an insult to God, implying that it is He who can be dispensed with; He can leave it all to us. This mental attitude results from a fundamental misunderstanding of the christian faith. We depend on God far more than He depends on us. If we don't give Him the opportunity to guide us and bless our work we are like a car roaring down the road without a driver. We may be very capable and energetic in human terms, but the Kingdom of God far transcends human affairs and only the power of the Holy Spirit is adequate in the spiritual garden.

This may all seem very obvious and eminently sensible but the 'activity trap' is such an easy one to fall into. Many a parish priest and parish worker has discovered this to their cost. This is not to say that we can just sit back and let God get on with it (sloth is among the deadly sins); in His humility and His desire to be one with us He has ordained that the work of His kingdom needs our co-operation. But there is a necessary balance between activity and prayer. Down the ages all truly holy people have realized and understood this. Jesus Himself pointed to it in His famous remark at the house of Martha and Mary – *"Martha, Martha, you worry and fret about so many things, and yet few are needed. It is Mary who has chosen the better part; it is not to be taken from her."* Prayer, contemplation and meditation on the scriptures are essential elements in the following of Christ. Men and women who at different times have founded congregations or religious orders nearly all wrote a rule of life to ensure that their followers would keep a balance between spirituality and activity. If the spiritual element is allowed to falter history proves that the congregation or order begins to decline and may ultimately become so corrupt that it dies. These examples should serve as a warning to us. Activity without spirituality is like a building which has an impressive facade but nothing behind it. When the wind blows and the earth shakes it quickly collapses into a heap of rubble.

AUGUST

A COUNTRYMAN'S SPIRITUAL SUMMER

August is the month of harvest and holiday; the month of maturity and fullness; the month when those who work on the land gather in the fruits of their labours and those who work in towns try to 'get away from it all' and relax with their families and friends in unaccustomed pastures. Harvest, pastures, holidays – I am reminded every year of the summer holidays I spent as a lad on a farm deep in the countryside on the border between Worcestershire and Gloucestershire. In those days (before World War II) there were parts of England where there was no distant roar of traffic and in the part where I went there were no tractors either; the farms still used heavy horses. A passing aeroplane was a rarity and transistor radios and 'ghetto-blasters' had not been invented. The only sounds were those of the farm at work and the wild life. In the evenings only the wild life.

I remember warm balmy Sunday afternoons when, lying among the grasses in a meadow near the top of a bank with the leaves of a tree fluttering occasionally on an overhanging branch, I watched the cows grazing and listened to the birds, many different kinds of bird. I soaked up the English countryside right into my innermost consciousness. I recall lying, weary, against a stook of corn during the midday break in the harvest field with a couple of horses next to me enjoying their nosebags and lazily swishing their tails to keep the flies at bay. Occasionally one would stamp his foot. It is the smells I remember so clearly – horse sweat, freshly cut corn, the scent of wild flowers. Streams were not polluted then. You could pick watercress and eat it and cup the cold clear water in your hands and drink it quite safely.

It was in those days that I pondered the meaning of it all. There was time to ponder then, and in the evenings to talk and discuss with country folk (there was no TV and only farm owners had a car; the rest of us walked or went on bikes, so our roaming was restricted). Like Wordsworth I had "Intimations of Immortality" which later I lost as the hurly-burly of adult life swept me away in its flood.

There was a time when meadow, grove and stream,
The earth, and every common sight, to me did seem
Apparelled in celestial light,
The glory and the freshness of a dream.......
Whither is it fled the visionary gleam?
Where is it now. the glory and the dream?.....

Heaven lies about us in our infancy!
Shades of the prison-house begin to close
Upon the growing Boy ....
At length the Man perceives it die away,
And fade into the light of common day.

("Intimations of Immortality
from Recollections of Early Childhood"
by William Wordsworth)

But those who have faith in Jesus and His vision do not share Wordsworth's pantheistic pessimism. It is perfectly possible in adulthood to rediscover that *"first fine careless rapture"* of childhood, though now no longer so naive and simplistic as once it was, but deeper and richer, more mature, more comprehending. Last month I drew attention to the need for recollection, quiet and meditation in the spiritual garden. In August, because the vegetables, fruit and flowers have come full term, there is not so much to be done, so I can usually find time to sit in a quiet corner of my garden and just watch and listen and pray. As I watch a flock of rooks wheeling in a summer thermal, or a hawk hovering in the shimmering sky, I recall again that evocative poem of Gerard Manley Hopkins which he called "The Windhover":

I caught this morning morning's minion, king-
dom of daylight's dauphin, dapple-dawn-drawn Falcon, in his riding
Of the rolling level underneath him steady air, and striding
High there, how he rung upon the rein of a wimpling wing
In his ecstacy! then off, off forth on swing.
As a skate's heel sweeps smooth on a bow-bend: the hurl and gliding
Rebuffed the big wind. My heart in hiding
Stirred for a bird.–the achieve of, the mastery of the thing!

(The Windhover:
to Christ our Lord – by Gerald Manley Hopkins)

O God, my friend, my lover, my master, my Squire, how wonderful You are ! You are Creator, Supreme Artist. How complex and yet how simple is Your creative work, from the exquisite cameo to the vast canvas! Your world is full of marvels and delights – "the achieve of, the mastery of the thing"! We praise You and thank You, and ask that we may conform to Your designs for each one of us and be faithful to the parts You have scripted for us so that we may enhance Your creation and not spoil it by our wilfulness, our selfishness or our refusal to be bidden by You, our loving Father, who longs only for what is best for us.

SEPTEMBER

A TIME FOR THANKSGIVING

Season of mists and mellow fruitfulness !
Close bosom-friend of the maturing sun;
Conspiring with him how to load and bless
With fruit the vines that round the thatch-eaves run;
To bend with apples the moss'd cottage-trees,
And fill all fruit with ripeness to the core;
To swell the gourd, and plump the hazel shells
With a sweet kernel; to set budding more,
And still more, later flowers for the bees,
Until they think warm days will never cease,
For summer has o'er-brimmed their clammy cells.
("To Autumn" – by John Keats)

Thus wrote John Keats. Although in September there can be an Indian Summer, a late period of warm weather which can cheat plants into a final burst of activity, on most farms and gardens the harvest has been gathered in and at some point in the month people assemble for a party at which to reminisce about the season just past before battening down the hatches for the winter. September is the month of harvest festivals. In days gone by in every village and market town a central feature of the harvest festival was a service of thanksgiving in the local church. This custom is still observed in many places although the local community may now no longer have any real connection with the land, and fewer people attend.

On our estate the 'Squire' has always made a particular feature of the harvest festival. He has a closeness with his Father in heaven which surpasses any human relationship. He often mentions his Father and tries to make us understand that all good things come from Him, indeed that his Father is the Creator of all things, inanimate as well as animate. Hence the importance the Squire attaches to the giving of thanks. He has taught us to appreciate the kindnesses we receive from others and not to take for granted the good things of life.

I fear we live in an age when many people do take things for granted and too easily grumble when they are deprived (even temporarily) of what they have been used to or what they think they are entitled to. Compared to the poverty endured by people in other parts of the world ours is a land 'flowing with milk and honey', and yet how easily we are dissatisfied and begin to grumble. Sometimes the 'Squire' reminds us of what his Father had to put up with from His 'Chosen People' who frequently forgot all He had done for them and instantly blamed Him when things went wrong. Nothing hurts our 'Squire' more than ingratitude among his own folk.

If this had been done by an enemy
I could bear his taunts.
If a rival had risen against me,
I could hide from him.
But it is you, my own companion,
My intimate friend.
How close was the friendship between us.!
We walked together in harmony
In the house of God. (Psalm 55)

Each day before I start work in my Spiritual Garden I try to remember all the good things I have had in my life and the happy times I have enjoyed. I also recall the successes I have had in my garden. I give thanks for all these things. I find this puts the coming day into perspective and helps me to cope when things go wrong. At the day's end when I have shut my shed and am wending my way home I go briefly over the day in my mind. Even if it's been a bad day I can always find at least something to be thankful for. After all I know that the Squire and his Mother love me and that his Father in heaven cares for me even if no one else seems to! Perhaps there is no better prayer with which to end the day than that of our own St Richard:

Thanks be to you, my Lord Jesus Christ,
For all the benefits which you have given me,
For all the pains and insults which you have borne for me.
O most merciful Redeemer, Friend and Brother,
May I know you more clearly,
Love you more dearly,
And follow you more nearly.

OCTOBER

THE AUTUMN OF LIFE

By October, in my Spiritual Garden, Nature is going into retirement. The annuals have faded and are dying off; in the perennials the sap is draining back into the roots. The deciduous trees are showering their golden leaves over beds, lawns and paths alike in indiscriminate profusion. Many plants are dropping their seeds so that some at least will germinate and continue the species into another generation. All around there are signs of ageing. Mother Nature is withdrawing into hibernation so as to survive another winter. Yet one more life-cycle is ending.

As I gather up the leaves in my spiritual garden and generally tidy up at the season's end I reflect that I am myself subject to this natural life-cycle. The spring and summer of my own life are over and I am now in the autumn of life. I am in what nowadays they call the 'Third Age'. Experts in the field of anthropology tell us that there are four ages in the human life-cycle. The 'First Age' is a period of dependence when, as children, we need our parents and other adults if we are to survive and grow. The 'Second Age' is a period of independence when, as adults, we belong to the productive community. The 'Third Age' is the time when we have retired from our principal careers but are sufficiently healthy to retain our independence and can continue to make at least some contribution to the well-being of society. The 'Fourth Age' is like the 'First', a phase of dependence when, because of senility or ill health, we have to rely on others to keep us alive.

Some people fear retirement. They cannot accustom themselves to having left the activity and excitement of their working careers; they feel cut off and lonely. Others look forward to retirement as an opportunity to do the things they have always wanted to do but have never had the time. As with many other things, much in retirement depends on our mental attitude. Most of us have to accept a reduced income (in some cases very much reduced!) and, if we are wise, we realize that our bodies require us gradually to slow down the pace of life. But for some, retirement never comes, or only very late in life. For instance, children, themselves of normal retirement age, who still have elderly parents to care for; wives caring for disabled husbands or husbands for disabled wives; parents, long past retirement age, caring for mentally handicapped children; grandparents caring for grandchildren whose parents have died or abandoned them. These are the heroes of the 'Third Age' whose charity and whose contribution to society often goes unrecognized and unsung by the rest of us, though not by God.

As I stand in my Spiritual Garden I find the autumn has a richness and a beauty all its own. The colours are not as bright as in spring or summer, and the bursting energy is not there, but the golden tints of the leaves and the occasional golden sunsets in the West give me a feeling of comfort and satisfaction no other season provides and leads me to a longing for my heavenly home, without the fear which once accompanied thoughts of departure (death). Sometimes when the Squire comes to have a look around my Spiritual Garden we talk of his Father's house (heaven). He tells me about the many rooms in it, one of which is being kept for me. *"Do not let your hearts be troubled. Trust in God still, and trust in me. There are many rooms in my Father's house; if there were not, I should have told you. I am going now to prepare a place for you, and after I have gone and prepared you a place, I shall return to take you with me; so that where I am you may be too." (John 14: 1-4).* He makes it sound so attractive and I begin to prepare, not just for the winter, but for my eventual departure to another land. In days gone by when a bishop was moved from one bishopric to another they used the word 'translation'. I like that word. It suggests an ease of transfer, something in the natural order of things. That's how I think of death: not something traumatic to be dreaded, but a perfectly normal progression from one home to another, from one world to another. Having moved house 27 times in the course of my married life, what's so remarkable about one more move! In the meantime there is still plenty to be done in my Spiritual Garden.

NOVEMBER

NOVEMBER'S SILVER LINING

In November autumn gives way to winter once more. Gardens enter the period of hibernation and on the surface at least life seems to have stopped. Those of you who have visited my spiritual garden regularly since January will realize that we have nearly come full circle – from winter back to winter.

November is also the month when Roman Catholics remember their dead. They pray for the Holy Souls. Our Church divides Christ's followers into three categories: the Church Militant (those on earth engaged in the battle of life), the Church Suffering (those who have died but have not yet been admitted to God's presence) and the Church Triumphant (those who have begun an eternity of happiness in the fellowship of God and His angels). I know that not all christians share the Roman Catholic belief in a period of cleansing between earth and heaven (Purgatory) but a word of explanation might help to dispel some misunderstandings. Perhaps some people are baffled by Cardinal Newman's poem "The Dream of Gerontius" set to such haunting music by Sir Edward Elgar.

If a person steals some property or embezzles a sum of money, he/she may afterwards be truly sorry and may be truly forgiven by the injured party, but the matter does not end there. Justice demands that the erstwhile thief makes every effort to restore the ill-gotten wealth. We tend to forget that our sins often have long-term consequences. If I have destroyed a person's reputation by uncharitable or spiteful references to their hidden faults, can I be sure that I can ever fully repair the consequences? *The evil that men do lives after them*, said Shakespeare. Scripture says: *Nothing unclean can enter heaven* (Rev 2127). So even though a person may die penitent and forgiven by God so that his place in heaven is assured, there may yet be need for reparation. Presumably, therefore, a further cleansing is necessary before the person can enjoy the fullness of God's presence. Thus Catholics pray for their deceased loved ones that, through the merits of Christ's sufferings and death, the period of cleansing, or purging (hence 'Purgatory') may be shortened and that they may soon be united with the angels and saints around the throne of God.

Praying for the dead was a major point of controversy at the Reformation and I have no wish to revive that controversy now. I have no quarrel with Christians who believe that at death a person is judged and goes straight to heaven or hell, but if we are to accept one another as brothers and sisters in the Lord it can be helpful to know what we each believe even if on certain points we continue to disagree.

For myself I think of death and bereavement in the context of what Jesus revealed to us about God's mercy and unconditional love, and of the long held christian belief in the Communion of Saints which is enshrined in the creeds. I think there are very few really evil people (though undoubtedly there are some) who consciously and deliberately, with full knowledge of what they are doing, hate God and would destroy everything connected with Him if they could. The sins which most of us commit are due to human weakness and fallibility in one form or another. Jesus made it very clear that his Father longs for the return of the prodigal and I suspect that everyone, believer or not, when at the gates of death is given an opportunity to apprehend the truth, and that few refuse God's loving offer of forgiveness. Surely, too, the whole court of heaven must be praying that no soul will be lost, because God's Son gave His life for the redemption of the whole world.

To mourn and weep at the loss of a dear one is a natural human response (Jesus wept for His friend Lazarus), but I believe the Communion of Saints embraces us all and that one day we shall all be united in heaven as members of one family, freed from all the weaknesses which bedevil our relationships on earth, and purged of all our sins. I have no doubt that after my death I shall be reunited with my relatives and friends who have gone before me. At last I shall be shown to that room which is being kept for me in my Father's house. So November, far from being a gloomy month, is for me a time of great hope and expectancy.

DECEMBER

A VERY SPECIAL BIRTHDAY

The yearly cycle of the seasons would not be complete in any christian country, and especially in any spiritual garden, without Christmas – our Squire's birthday. Of all the times of the year Christmas is the time for home-coming and home-making: the time of love, of hearth and warmth and good cheer. Even the garden tries to join in. There are scarlet berries on the holly and white berries on the mistletoe. There are winter roses and winter pansies. Even when our spiritual lives are dull and wintry and depressing and we feel spiritually dead, we shall find, if we look hard enough, that there are little virtues and graces growing on our spiritual plants and peeping out at us from beneath the snow-covered leaves to remind us that God hasn't forgotten us and is there all the time. In "the bleak mid winter" He comes to enlighten and enliven the greyness of our lives in the most appealing and most vulnerable of forms – that of a little baby.

Innocence has an appeal all its own. It is not just that anything new has a pristine look and feel about it, whether it be the young of a living species (a baby, a lamb, a chick, for instance) or even a material object (a house, a car, a dress), but it is the knowledge that this person, this animal, this object is unsullied and has not yet been damaged by the buffeting, the wear and tear, and the dirt of usage. This is in fact (whether realized or not) a recognition that the biblical story of Adam and Eve in the Garden of Eden contains a profound truth – that the created world as conceived by God is perfect but that it is often sullied and damaged by sin. There is a wilfulness and potential cruelty in all of us, the most intelligent of the living creatures on the earth, which, if not controlled, can destroy for ourselves and others so many of the good things God has provided for us during our mortal pilgrimage. Jesus impressed on his disciples the obligation of adults to guard the innocence of children. His condemnation of those who scandalize children was uncompromising. Innocence is not the same as inexperience. 'Innocence' means 'without guilt'. It is possible to be experienced yet innocent, as indeed was Jesus himself. In the Christmas festivities at the big house the Squire invites all the estate workers and their families, and all the homeless and lonely who come to the door, to join him and his Mother and the angelic visitors who come from his Father's house. This is earth joined to heaven, and the love of God made visible. Of course, this foretaste of heaven cannot last because it is only a foretaste; the reality of the cold wintry world outside remains. Nevertheless this mid-winter interlude warms the hearts and strengthens the spirits of all who take part and enter into the innocent festivities which the Squire provides. His friends enter the new year with optimism and joy in their hearts. "All is well: all manner of things is well."

To conclude this little walk around my 'Spiritual Garden' I invite you to join me in thanking and praising God for all the blessings He has given me, and I am sure to you too. The life cycle in the Spiritual Garden continues and I am content to leave the Garden's future in the hands of those who will come after me. No doubt they will make it more productive than I have. I shall, I hope, look down from heaven and rejoice in their progress. May God bless them, and you dear Reader, through the merits of Jesus Christ, our Lord. Amen.

A SELECTION OF SUNDAY HOMILIES

Author's note: If readers are fully to understand this section they will need a copy of the New Testament at hand to look up the references at the beginning of each homily.

FOURTH SUNDAY OF ADVENT

GOSPEL READING – MATTHEW 1:18-25

If we are to have some understanding of the immensity of God's love manifested in the Incarnation of His Son: if we are to get some measure of the vital part played by Mary in this world-shattering event, we need to ponder on the events described in today's gospel and supplement it with the parallel account in St Luke Chap 1.

It is perhaps difficult for people today to appreciate the circumstances which prevailed in first century Palestine. Today we live in a permissive society. The cohabiting of couples outside marriage is socially acceptable. Single parenthood is recognised by the State as qualifying for special financial assistance. I suppose the situation is roughly summarised by the current use of the word 'partner' which covers everything from marriage to prostitution. Equality of the sexes is accepted as the ideal even if the removal of discrimination against women has not gone far enough for some people. But it was not ever thus, and certainly was not the case at the time of the incarnation.

The Jewish theocracy was almost completely male dominated. For a woman convicted of adultery the punishment was death by stoning. An unmarried woman found to be with child was ostracized and had to eke out a meagre existence on the margins of society. Religious belief was minutely codified and strictly controlled by the priestly caste. Imagine, therefore, the shock, the terror, the disbelief which must have been felt by Mary on first hearing the message brought by Gabriel. In what form the angel appeared we do not know. The idea of angels as comely sexless beings with wings, haloes and white robes is a concept of medieval artists. Maybe Gabriel approached Mary in human form as a stranger. But whatever the means chosen by God, his message was at first sight preposterous. Mary was a country girl and would certainly have known the facts of life. How could she conceive without intercourse with a man? And then to say that her child would be the son of God! It was like someone bringing me a message to tell me that I was to be the father of the next king of England! Did Mary signify her acceptance straightaway or was she given time to think it over? The gospels are very economical with words, as we know. Imagine the thoughts going through her mind. Was this a joke? Was it some form of cruel hoax? If it was true, and if she accepted, how was she going to convince Joseph of so unlikely a story? If he decided she had deceived him and had made up the whole story, what was her future? Death by stoning? A life of degradation as an outcast? Even if Joseph could be convinced, whatever would being the mother of God entail? The references to the Messiah in the scriptures were not exactly encouraging. Nonetheless, we know that Mary responded positively to God. Has there ever been a greater act of faith on the part of a human being in all history? Was there ever a more stupendous act of trust by God in one of his creatures, the trusting of his own Son to a mortal woman?

How long did it take Mary to summon up the courage to tell Joseph? When she did he reacted as most men would if they found the girl they were intending to marry was pregnant by someone else, he decided to break off the engagement. But that was not quite as simple as in our society. Under the then Jewish law a betrothal was a legal contract which could only be broken by an official divorce. In our culture when two people get engaged it is a purely personal arrangement which can be broken by mutual agreement without recourse to the courts. Not so for Mary and Joseph. Joseph proposed to go about it as tactfully as possible but that did not let Mary off the hook of the eventual disclosure of her condition. But God protected the mother of his Son and intervened to convince Joseph of the truth of Mary's story and of the part he was himself to play in this mighty drama.

As we prepare for Christmas during these next few days, let's ponder on these things. We live in a world where so many things seem to be going wrong – where there is confusion in many people's minds about what is morally right and morally wrong – where siren voices tell us that religion is an irrelevant myth, or worse, the cause of most of the violent conflicts around the globe. Now is the time to steady our religious nerves: to take encouragement from the example of Mary and Joseph and the providence of God who protected them and kept His promise. Christmas should convince us that God has come among us in a form we can understand and relate to: that He has visited His people to reassure them that He can be trusted and that all will be well in the end.

SECOND SUNDAY OF THE YEAR

GOSPEL READING - JOHN 1: 35-42

At the time of Jesus the high road from what is now Syria and Iraq, which includes what geographers call 'The Fertile Crescent' which was one of the great granaries of the Ancient World, passed down the east side of the Jordan valley but crossed over the river to the west at a ford roughly opposite Jericho. Thence it wound its way up the western escarpment, past Jerusalem and then southwards to Egypt. It was a great commercial highway. Along it you would have seen trains of camels (the juggernauts of the Ancient World), drovers with their herds of cattle and flocks of sheep and goats, a cohort or two of Roman soldiers marching from one strong point to another, perhaps a few chariots (the Porsches of the Ancient World), caravans of people going to or from Jerusalem, individuals or families on their donkeys: in other words, a cross-section of people, both rich and poor, whom Jesus moved among. The Jordan ford was a natural stopping place for the watering of animals, for replenishing water bags and having a rest. To it, therefore, came local people selling all manner of things travellers might need – bread, fruit, coffee, wine, hay, kindling, etc. The banks on either side were the ancient equivalent of our motorway service areas. May I ask you for a minute to apply your imaginations? Imagine the sounds: the water rippling over the rocks and stones, the snorting of camels and the braying of donkeys, the cries of vendors, the jingle of harness and the buzz of human conversation. Now the smells: the animal smells, the smell of human sweat, the smell of fruits, of smouldering wood fires and the contents of cooking pots. Then the feel of damp riverside grass, of cool water flowing over tired feet, and at night the sudden drop in temperature experienced in desert lands which causes people to reach for their blankets and roll themselves up for sleep. What a wonderful pitch the ford made for a preacher who wanted to spread his message far and wide! To it came John the Baptist, a strange figure clothed in animal skins, from out of the desert as if from nowhere.

As John began to preach and baptize he quickly attracted crowds of the curious, and travellers soon took news of his appearance and his teaching up the escarpment to Jerusalem. Both the Jewish and Roman authorities became interested: the Jews because he might be teaching false doctrine and challenging their hold on the people; the Romans because here might be the instigator of yet another politico/religious revolt. So both establishments sent agents to listen and to ask questions. At that time any Jewish man over 30 years of age and with sufficient knowledge could call himself a rabbi and begin to teach. There were a number of such itinerant rabbis and they each collected round them a group of disciples. This was how John began his mission, and so did Jesus. When John was at the ford his disciples would camp out with him. In his teaching he frequently referred to a man who was to come after him, for whose appearance he was preparing the way. Then one day he saw this man coming down the road towards him. He called his disciples.You can imagine the intense excitement and interest as John went forward to greet Jesus and then Jesus asked John for baptism. St Matthew and St Luke record that as Jesus came out of the water the heavens opened, a dove appeared and a voice was heard which said: "This is my beloved son: my favour rests on him". Whether the voice was heard by everyone who was present or only by John and his disciples we do not know. What we do know is that two of John's disciples, a younger John and Andrew, were mightily impressed.

On the following day John was again at the ford and again he saw Jesus coming up the road. He immediately called his disciples and, pointing to Jesus said: "There is the Lamb of God". Curiosity got the better of John and Andrew and, on the impulse, as Jesus crossed the ford to the other side, they decided to follow him, no doubt at a respectable distance. After a while Jesus turned round and asked them what they wanted. No doubt flummoxed at the sudden question they blurted out the first thing that came into their heads: "Rabbi, where do you live?" Being far from home Jesus was probably camping out somewhere peaceful along the river bank. Poor travellers often camped out as do poor people, and not-so-poor back-packers, to this day, especially in hot countries. At all events Jesus replied; "Come and see", and the gospel tells us that they spent the rest of the day with him. We are not told what Jesus said to them, but we do know that it had a profound effect, because the following day Andrew went to find his brother, Peter, and told him: "We have found the Messiah." Thus began the calling of the Apostles, those ordinary working men on whom the personality of Jesus Christ made such a powerful impact that they left everything to follow him.

Perhaps the reason why there are so many lukewarm and half-hearted Christians is because too few of us spend sufficient time with Jesus to be influenced by the magnetism of His personality. No relationship can flourish unless the parties to it spend time with each other. "Absence" does not always "make the heart grow fonder". If we seldom come to Him in private prayer or in church we cannot expect to know much about Him, still less come to know Him as a real living person. But if once we encounter Him and spend more and more time with Him we shall be drawn, like the Apostles, to make Him the centre and driving force of our lives. So where do we find Him, and how do we spend time with Him? It is easy enough to see how that could have happened when Jesus in His humanity lived in Palestine, but how now? The first thing we must realize and reflect upon is that Jesus rose from the dead and is therefore alive now. He is here. For this we have His own assurance. *"Where two or three are gathered together in My name I will be in their midst"*. We can find Him in our churches, in the Blessed Sacrament, in our liturgies and small groups when we "gather together". But equally we can find Him in private prayer. He Himself spent long hours in private prayer; as the gospels relate, sometimes "all night". His heavenly Father was indeed the centre of His life, and the prayer He taught us is addressed to His Father whom He said we should call our father. A habit of daily prayer is essential for progress in the spiritual life, and this requires discipline in our personal lives. It is all too easy to allow the way to daily prayer to be paved with good intentions but little reality. We have to be honest with ourselves. If we have not really begun, then we must make a start, not tomorrow, or next week, or when the holidays come, but today. If we did make a start but have since fallen away, then we, too, must re-start. Whatever our situation, however busy we are, we must set aside a little time for prayer today – this afternoon or this evening perhaps – but definitely today.

THIRD SUNDAY OF THE YEAR

GOSPEL READING - LUKE 4:14-21

Many of our young people today complain that the Church is irrelevant to their lives and to the world they live in. On the whole the only thing they see the Church doing is what happens in their local parish church when they go to Mass on a Sunday, which many do with reluctance, if indeed they still go at all. Could it be that the Church has ceased to follow its Founder by carrying out his manifesto?

There was a time, within my own lifetime, when the Church could be seen to be doing what Jesus talks about in today's gospel. I remember, for instance, the Little Sisters of the Poor and other Congregations who ran houses where they cared for the destitute and the elderly poor. I recall the hospitals and nursing homes run by Religious Congregations where they healed the sick, looked after the blind and cleansed the lepers. I recall the schools run by Religious Orders to provide a good education for those who could not afford it in the days when you had to pay. So good was the education they provided that non-catholics clamoured to get their children into Catholic schools. And I remember the great Missionary Orders who sent men and women to bring the good news to people in places where the gospel had never been preached nor the downtrodden set free. In those days there was no lack of vocations. The seminaries were full as were the noviciates of the religious orders and congregations. So what has happened since?

After the Second World War the state took over the welfare services in most European countries and professionalised them. The former missionary lands began to produce their own priests and nuns. Is the day of the religious order over? In God's providence are priests meant to be in short supply today for some reason as yet undisclosed?

I think we sometimes miss an important point. If you look at the social works performed by humanists, atheists and christians, superficially they seem remarkably similar. The philosophy of the atheist Karl Marx, for instance, had something in common with the gospels before Lenin and Stalin got hold of it. The following words from the magnificat are a case in point: *"He casts the mighty from their thrones and raises the lowly. He fills the starving with good things and sends the rich empty away"* Likewise the welfare state which in this country is largely humanistic in its philosophy. But there is a fundamental difference between the motivation of the humanist or the atheist and the christian. The humanist and the atheist are concerned solely with this world, and it makes sense to be kind and caring to one's neighbour and makes for a better world to live in than one in which there is conflict and cruelty. The Christian's motive is quite different. Christians care for their neighbours because they see in their neighbours the face of Christ made in the image and likeness of God. They want to follow Jesus: to give and not count the cost. They are not concerned whether they are paid for their services well or not at all, because they are not set on piling up treasure and kudos in this world, rather they feel called to follow Christ who chose to be poor.

Why is it that Mother Teresa has not only caught the imagination of an agnostic and materialist world, but has drawn volunteers around her of all ages and classes? Her Congregation has no lack of recruits; indeed they have more applicants than they can cope with. Why is it that every year the Diocesan pilgrimage to Lourdes attracts many young people who happily work all hours without a thought of pay packets or conditions of service? Why is it that in our very small way here in Chichester the Christian Care Association has attracted volunteers from all the denominations and stirred people to send donations in cash and in kind without being asked? Of the one hundred and twelve volunteers on the roster for the Night Refuge almost all are under forty. Could the answers to these questions have any connection with today's gospel?

I have a feeling that the present malaise of Christianity, in the West at least, is because the challenge has been removed from it. Young people will respond to a challenge. Indeed the more you ask of them the more they will give. If what is on offer is all rather easy and bland and stale, they become disinterested, disheartened and bored – a word much too frequently heard.

The welfare system founded on atheism in Russia has, after seventy years, collapsed in astonishing and spectacular manner. The system founded on humanism in this country is coming apart at the seams as the cost escalates beyond the ability of the exchequer to bear the burden. Perhaps the call of Christ to labour without counting the cost, to volunteer out of love for Him, is in the end the only enduring way to help the lame to walk, to give new sight to the blind, to set the downtrodden free, to bring the good news to the poor. As the sick and destitute begin once more to appear on the streets not just of this country but right across Europe and the USA, not to mention the Third World, I think the Holy Spirit is calling us to put the challenge back into Christianity. Whether the day of the Religious Order is over I know not. Perhaps a new form of fellowship is called for. What I do know is that if we fail to challenge our young people they will continue to be bored and to drift rudderless on the tide. So let's hoist the sails, catch the pentecostal wind, and get under way. Then our liturgy will reflect our deeds in the wider community. Relevance will be restored. As they said of Jesus when He was in Galilee, so they will say again: "A great prophet has risen among us; God has visited His people".

FOURTH SUNDAY OF THE YEAR

GOSPEL READING - MARK 1:21-28

In the Jewish State of Our Lord's day, the scribes and pharisees and the priestly caste generally, held the positions of authority inherited from the prophets and kings with all the external trappings of power. Yet the ordinary people who crowded round Jesus recognised that He taught with an authority which relied on no human establishment or structure. He wore no special clothes or religious emblems; He had no headquarters or palace or church. True, He attended the nearest synagogue on the Sabbath as the Law demanded, but He did much of His teaching in the open air. Though they disapproved of His activities, even His enemies admitted that He had a charisma which drew the crowds.

This authority, which He said was given Him by His Father, He passed on to His apostles, and through them to the Church He founded. But when He gave Peter the keys He made no promise that His successors would be perfect: indeed, the men He Himself chose were far from perfect and not even well educated, yet they, too, taught with authority as the crowds at Pentecost acknowledged, and as the Epistles of Paul make clear. Ever since, authority has been the distinguishing mark of the Church which claims direct descent from the Apostles.

I have recently been reading about the Oxford Movement and its sequel. Of its major figures Newman and Manning are the best known among Catholics today. Both were born into the Church of England and as young men were among the most brilliant scholars of their day, marked out for rapid preferment. The Church of England was at a low ebb in the first decades of the last century and the young divines at Oxford, led by Newman, sought to rejuvenate the Church by proving that it was an integral part of the universal Catholic Church. The further in their quest their study of theology, scripture and of the early fathers took them, the less certain of their position they became. Despite all the things which, as Protestants, they disliked about Roman Catholicism (excesses of piety, sentimental mariology, the corruption of the Renaissance Popes and papal triumphalism), and after desperate battles of conscience, they found themselves forced to concede that only in the Roman Catholic Church could they find the authority they believed Christ had promised. Newman was the first to leave for Rome, but others soon followed: the Wilberforce brothers, later the Benson brothers, sons of an Archbishop of Canterbury, then Chesterton, Belloc and Ronald Knox. The latest addition to that long line of distinguished people is, of course, the Duchess of Kent.

The controversy over the ordination of women, which is currently agitating the Church of England, despite what the media would have us believe, is not about sexism and misogyny, but about authority. Those Anglicans who oppose the ordination of women do so because they do not believe the Church of England has the authority unilaterally to overturn a tradition which has existed since apostolic times; unlike Newman and Manning, high church Anglicans still see themselves as part of the universal Catholic Church which includes the Roman Catholic and the Orthodox Churches.

Authority is not a popular concept today, largely because it implies discipline of some sort. In a degenerate age the popular thing is to throw off the shackles of discipline, whether self-imposed or imposed by others. And yet there is an innate longing in everyone for an ordering of society which enables people to live in peace and security and freedom. But human nature being what it is, there is a price to pay which involves surrendering some personal freedom so that right ordering can prevail. It just is not possible for everyone to do their own thing without friction and chaos resulting. Where spiritual matters are concerned the same principle applies: we may have to surrender part of our will if the truth is to prevail in us.

When people revolt against authority, in most cases what they dislike is the way it is exercised rather than the idea of authority itself. Those in positions of authority can be very unjust and cruel, very insensitive and selfish, using their power for self-aggrandisement and greed. If we want to learn how those in authority should behave, we must, as usual, study the life and teaching of the Master who was "meek and humble of heart" and "full of compassion", while at the same time being unshakable in upholding the honour of His Father and uncompromising with the truth. Jesus never disputed the right of the Jewish hierarchy, or indeed of the Romans, to govern and dispense the Law, but He openly rebuked them in the strongest terms for the way they did it. Following his Master's teaching, St Paul calls on his christians to obey their employers and the civil authorities, while at the same time calling on employers and governors to act with justice and charity. He applies the same principles when instructing the early christian communities in spiritual matters.

In today's world the whole concept of authority is much in dispute, and the institutions where traditionally authority has resided, both in Church and State, are under threat. I suggest that in the first paragraph of today's gospel reading there is much for us to think about and pray about. I also suggest that anyone who holds a position of authority in the Church or in the world, but particularly in the Church, should read frequently what Jesus said to His apostles about leadership as recorded in St Luke's gospel, chapter 20: *"You know that among the pagans the rulers lord it over them, and their great men make their authority felt. This is not to happen among you. No; anyone who wants to be great among you must be your servant, and anyone who wants to be first among you must be your slave, just as the Son of Man came not to be served but to serve, and to give His life as a ransom for many."*

FIFTH SUNDAY OF THE YEAR

MATTHEW 5: 13-16

This Sunday is being kept as a Day of Prayer for World Peace, and the Pope has suggested that we should consider especially young people, as this year (1985) is International Youth Year. Young people in particular, he thinks, are very sensitive about issues affecting peace, justice and the environment. Certain it is that they would have to fight any war which might occur, and they don't want their predecessors to hand them a world in ruins, especially a nuclear ruin.

I am sure we all, no matter what our age, hope that the wars going on at present in the Middle East, Afghanistan, Central America and elsewhere can be brought to a speedy end and that war can be avoided in the future. All of us ought to be praying daily for world peace. So these international events, like a Day of Prayer for World Peace, are good as they focus our attention on the great issues of the day, but they also, in my opinion, contain a danger. By concentrating our attention on events largely outside our control, they can divert us from doing the things which are very much within our control nearer home.

When we talk about 'the world' in this sense we mean the world which consists of people. The world will become more peaceful when people become more peaceful: and that means you and me. Unfortunately the pace and conditions of modern life tend to produce aggression more than peace. Many of us become too abrasive, too waspish. Let me suggest a few homely examples.

If you are a teenager living at home and your bedroom bears a distinct resemblance to a tip, when your Mum asks you to tidy it up, what is your reaction? Do you treat her quite cheerily but condescendingly as though Mums have to say that sort of thing from time to time, but then totally ignore her request? Do you accept criticism and acknowledge that your Mum has the right to tell you what to do in her own house, and tidy up your room without fuss? Or do you take the line that the state of your room is your own affair and make it jolly plain that you have no intention of clearing it up, and perhaps go into a sulk and for good measure slam the door on your way out?

And what if you are the Mum? Instead of getting up on time you take that extra 5 minutes, 10 minutes, even 15 minutes in bed. The result is that you concertina the time between getting up and going off to work, with the result that everything has to be rushed, everyone gets in everyone else's way, and by the time you get into the car to take the kids to school and then go on to the office, everyone is thoroughly bad tempered. So you roar off down the road until you get to the T junction, and there you meet a long queue of traffic trying to get into town. You try to edge your way in but the other drivers are equally late and will not give way. Your temperature is rising by the second. By the time you get to the office you are like a loaded gun ready to go off. When the supervisor greets you with a mild rebuke for being late, instead of apologising you adopt the old military principle that attack is the best form of defence and counter her rebuke by letting her know in no uncertain terms that you are aware of her own shortcomings. For some reason we imagine that if we point out the other person's shortcomings that somehow excuses our own.

And what if I am the Dad? When someone attempts to jump the queue at the supermarket checkout, is it I who lead the angry battalions into the fray to make sure the wretched miscreant doesn't get away with it? Or, when I bring home my latest purchase and find it doesn't work, am I the sort who storms down to the shop, calling down anathemas on all manufacturers and shopkeepers, and when I get there thump the counter and demand justice? It is, of course, possible to see that justice is done without raising the roof and causing a great commotion. There's a phrase which is often used half-jokingly but is in fact a kind of arrogant perverted boast. "I've got a short fuse", you will hear people say (as though that will excuse their behaviour), "so don't push me too hard, ha, ha". What that means in plain language is "I cannot control my temper and I have no intention of being responsible for the consequences".

'Blessed are the peacemakers'. Oh, dear, how desperately the world needs peacemakers at all levels, from the home to international affairs. I am sure we all know people, or at least have met some, who always seem to have an inner peace which enables them to keep calm when everyone around them is in a tizzy. The sort of person who, when there is a row in the family, or open warfare at work, people will say: "Go and get John. He knows how to pour oil on troubled waters". Such people have the knack of being able to smooth ruffled feathers, to cool people down and restore things to normality. Sure, peacemakers get trampled on at times, and Jesus was trampled on a great deal. By contrast the attitude of the world is: "If anyone is going to be trampled on it is certainly not going to be me. Out of my way, boy."

All such everyday incidents (and I am sure you can all think of many more) raise the level of tension and aggression in society. The sort of touchiness which starts arguments in the family circle and destroys peace in the home, is exactly the same as that which destroys the peace of nations. People seldom change character just because they become presidents or prime ministers, or trade union leaders or captains of industry. Aggression is aggression. Listen to a debate in the House of Commons or an angry exchange in the boardroom!

On average about 800 people attend Mass in this parish every weekend. Just imagine what a calming effect it would have, not only in Chichester, but wherever we fan out to during the working week, if all 800 of us were peacemakers who spread calm and gentleness and peace around us. Even more, imagine the fantastic effect on the world if all Christians were peacemakers like the Son of God they profess to follow. Were that so there would be no need for a special Day of Prayer for World Peace. The world would be at peace.

SIXTH SUNDAY OF THE YEAR

GOSPEL READING – MARK 1: 40-45

The Sunday readings are full of good things but seldom, I guess, do we pay much attention to the Entrance Antiphon. Often enough we are still settling into our seats when it is read, or as we process to the altar we are looking at the congregation. So for a change this morning I want to suggest a few thoughts about today's Entrance Antiphon. Let me remind you what it said:

"Lord, be my rock of safety, the stronghold that saves me. For the honour of your name, lead me and guide me."

There is something primaeval and indestructible about a mass of rock. Watch the seas pounding against a rocky coast. Time and again they come thundering in and crash against the rocks, only to be thrown back upon themselves shattered into a myriad droplets of spray. Think of those huge granite massifs in the Highlands, on Dartmoor or in Wales where I was last week. For thousands and thousands of years they have stood against all types of weather – wind, rain, sun, frost, snow – and all the puny quarryings of men, their great bulk scarcely scratched. This is how the Old Testament prophets thought of God; Christ used the same imagery when founding His Church; and perhaps you remember that grand christian hymn we said in the Divine Office last week: "Immortal, invisible, God only wise". We are going to sing it at the end of Mass today. The second verse, you may remember, goes like this:

"Unresting, unhasting, and silent as light,
Nor wanting nor wasting, thou rulest in might;
Thy justice like mountains high soaring above
Thy clouds which are fountains of goodness and love".

We live today in a shifting world full of change; a world full of threats, foreboding and disasters on a colossal scale (think of the famine sweeping Africa). Even the Catholic Church has not been exempt. In the years after the Second Vatican Council many catholics, as you will remember, felt that the foundations of the Church they had been brought up in had been undermined. The tremors of that spiritual earthquake have not yet entirely died down. People the world over are searching for something that holds, for ground that does not shift when you throw the anchor out. They are looking for certainties beyond the ephemeral ebb and flow of human affairs, for reassurance. Philosophies and theories abound; the media are continually telling us that this or that new idea, this or that new product, is the panacea we are all looking for. It is the evident failure of these things, the unreliability of human wisdom, which explains the popularity of eastern religions, strange cults, spiritualism and the born-again hot gospellers. Some of these born-again evangelists are well-meaning, sincere people, but they can be dangerous, because they teach that instant answers are to be found to all the world's problems in the words of the Bible which often they select at random and interpret literally. Young people particularly are attracted by such people because they like categorical answers to straight questions. But real life is not always like that. There are not always simple answers, even to straight questions. The faith which has been handed down to us, the faith we have to give the world, is not of that simplistic type. The faith we have is much deeper; it goes beyond the daily incidents of life and holds firm when, humanly speaking at least, there are no answers. What explanation can you give a man dying from a terminal disease? What answers can you give his distraught widow when he dies? It is the faith which holds in those black periods, when the dark night settles upon the soul, that is the faith which is worth having. That is the faith the world is groping for but cannot give; that is the faith we have.

What the world needs are christians who have the self-confidence born of this faith to proclaim God's truth by the example of their lives and the conviction with which they speak of God and holy things. The christian faith is proof against all that the powers of evil can throw against it, just as rocks repel the raging seas.

I have a long-standing friend who is not a catholic; though he has been nibbling at Catholicism. Last Christmas we were out for a walk together when he brought up a number of current topics and asked me what the Catholic Church had to say about them. I am not very good at that sort of thing so I simply told him where I, at least, thought the Church stood. After a bit he suddenly stopped me and said: "Hilary, it's no good. You have faith and I haven't. That's the difference between us. I envy you your faith, I really do, and I long for something solid to hang on to, but I don't have any faith like yours. Please pray for me". I am sure that man will eventually find the faith he is looking for, and in passing I would ask you to join me in praying for him and for all who are searching.

I've not told you that little incident in any self-congratulatory sense because faith, we must always remember, is a gift which we have done nothing to deserve. My point is that people can detect faith, even if they don't possess it : even if they react violently against it as did the unclean spirits in last Sunday's gospel. All of us here, thank God, have this gift of faith, but it has been given us not for ourselves alone but that we might spread it around us. You don't need to be clever or learned (I am neither). In fact, as we know, God often hides His truth from the clever and learned. All we need is to root ourselves on the rock of God: to hold confidently to the rock of Peter on which our Church is built. Neither principalities nor powers, nor, let it be said, false prophets who misinterpret Vatican 2, can shake us if we hold fast to Peter's successor. "Fear not, little flock", Jesus told us, "I have overcome the world".

Cardinal Hume has said that the Church in Britain will start gaining ground when Catholics regain their self-confidence. When they are confident of what they believe; confident to teach their children; confident to face the world. Let's be proud of our birthright and, drawing strength from the Blessed Eucharist which is inexhaustible because it is God Himself present among us, let us go forth from Mass this morning to spread the knowledge of our God around us, confident in our faith because –

"Lord, you are my rock of safety, the stronghold that saves me.
For the honour of your name, lead me and guide me."

EIGHTH SUNDAY OF THE YEAR

FIRST READING - ISAIAH 49:14-15

RESPONSORIAL PSALM -- PSALM 61

GOSPEL READING – MATTHEW 6:24-34

Today's First Reading is, I think, the shortest in the Lectionary, but it contains a profound truth which is reflected in the Responsorial Psalm and reinforced by Our Lord's own inimitable words in the Gospel. The truth is this: God never forgets anything He has made and He cares for all His creatures, which includes us. As the Psalmist says: *"In God alone is my soul at rest; my help comes from Him. He alone is my rock, my stronghold, my fortress: I stand firm"*. And the consequence of this is that we should put all our trust in God with a rocklike faith. In the Gospel Jesus says: *"That is why I am telling you not to worry about your life and what you are to eat, nor about your body and how you are to clothe it...Can any of you, for all your worrying, add one single cubit to his span of life?...So do not worry about tomorrow: tomorrow will take care of itself."*

Now all this comes very hard to a generation which has been taught to believe that man is in control of himself and his environment, and which is obsessed by insurance. Most of us think in our heart of hearts that unless we control our own lives things will go wrong. We are like people learning to swim: we cannot let go from the side of the bath and trust the water to keep us afloat. And as for insurance, we insure everything; indeed in some cases we are bound by law to do so. We insure our houses and their contents; we insure our cars and their contents; we insure our lives and our health; we insure our holidays and our hobbies. In fact, come to think of it, there's not much we don't insure. The insurance industry is among the most extensive and wealthiest in the world. I suggest this says something about our civilization: about the value we attach to material things and about the level of crime and the prevalence of greed and dishonesty. I recall that when I went to live in Norway in the late 60s I was astounded that the Norwegians seldom bothered to lock their houses or their cars. Burglary, I discovered, was scarcely known among them. May be it is different now, I don't know. Certain it is that the prevalence of crime makes people defensive and wary. But there's more to this gospel than that.

Those people I have known who have manifestly been followers of Jesus Christ have sat lightly to their material possessions, and the poor, of course, have little to lose anyway. You do not find burglar alarms on the houses of the poor. In the gospel Jesus tells us: *"You cannot be the slave both of God and money"*. When He sent His disciples on a mission He did not tell them what to say but He gave them precise instructions on how to conduct themselves. *"Carry no purse, no haversack, no sandals"*. When people came to Him and said they wanted to follow Him, He rejected those who wanted to hang onto their wealth or to go back and settle their affairs. He took those who were willing to leave all things, even their jobs. He Himself, of course, led from the front. When He began His mission He left the security of Nazareth where He had a home and a job, and set out as an itinerant rabbi with "nowhere to lay His head", as He put it. In His teaching, He had a lot to say about the corrupting influence of worldly riches and the importance of storing up incorruptible riches in heaven. Ever since then those who have followed Him most closely, the people we call 'saints', have embraced poverty themselves, even those born into princely and wealthy families, and have been in the forefront of providing succour for the deprived, the sick and the outcasts of society.

But clearly we have a problem. We are perfectly at liberty to do what we want with our own money and possessions (such as they are), but with many of us our wealth is not entirely our own. Husbands and wives must care for each other and provide for their children. It would not be right for me, for example, to give all my money to the poor and go off and preach the gospel, because that would leave Helen destitute and without support. A few years ago there occurred the case of a parish priest in another diocese who gave so generously to everyone who begged at his presbytery door that he soon got the reputation as a soft touch. In the end his bishop had to step in because the chap had brought the parish to the edge of bankruptcy. Under Canon Law parish funds belong to the parishoners, although the parish priest has the administration of them. So this good priest was giving away too much of what was not strictly his own. Where other people are involved we must be responsible and not be foolhardy, even for the best of intentions. The point is, I think, that we have to cultivate what Jesus called "poverty of spirit", which means seeing money and material possessions for the passing ephemeral things they are. It means leaning towards poverty and simplicity of lifestyle rather than yearning for greater wealth and more and more possessions. It means being generous and open-handed and erring on the side of being over-generous as against being tight fisted and mean. It means making sure that other people have what they need as against making sure that we get what we need and want first. It means spoiling people sometimes. I can say truthfully that these things have been characteristics of all the nicest people I have known. I also have to say that in my experience such characteristics are more likely, though not exclusively, to be found among people of modest or scanty means than among the better off.

We need to take to heart what Jesus says in today's gospel: *"Do not say, 'What are we to eat? What are we to drink? How are we to be clothed?' It is the pagans who set their hearts on all these things. Your heavenly Father knows you need them all. Set your hearts on His kingdom first, and on his righteousness, and all these other things will be given you as well."* The advertising media apply every pressure they can think of to push us in the opposite direction and make us believe that material possessions are essential and that unless we conform to the latest fashion and purchase the most up-to-date gadgets life really is not worth living. And how successful they are! We must not fall for their blandishments. If we follow Jesus, not only will we make progress in the spiritual life and store up treasure in heaven, but we shall save ourselves a lot of worry and heartache if things go wrong and we lose our wealth and become poor. 'Insure for heaven' should be our slogan. Now that is something really worth insuring for!

FIRST SUNDAY OF LENT

GOSPEL READING - MARK 1:12-15

Jesus opened the campaign of His public life with a simple, unmistakable call: *"Repent and believe the Good News"*, a call He was to repeat many times. Later He told us that He had not come to destroy the Old Law and the Prophets but to fulfil them. Periodically throughout the history of the Old Testament Jews God had raised up prophets to confront His chosen people with the sins of society and call them to repentance. Jesus was following in that tradition, and in our own day Our Lady has made the same call in each of her appearances, "repent, do penance if God's anger is to be averted".

Jesus's assessment of the age in which He lived was that it was "a wicked and adulterous generation". My Brothers and Sisters in Christ, we too live in a wicked and adulterous generation.

The people who organize the drug traffic for immense profits and push drugs onto unsuspecting and innocent young people to get them hooked are wicked. We have produced a generation, in the West at least, a very significant number of whom consider sex outside marriage to be perfectly acceptable, indeed would probably argue fiercely in its favour. It is more than likely that more people have met violent deaths in this century than in any previous one. Two world wars wiped out literally millions of people; the Nazis set about the systematic annihilation of an entire race; how many people have been liquidated in Soviet Russia and China probably no one will ever know; but think, too, of the slaughter at the time of Indian independence and of the wars in Vietnam, Cambodia and Afghanistan. The terrible famines in Africa have not been due entirely to the unpredictability of the weather: power-hungry and greedy men have had a hand in them too. Divorce in the West is now so common that some of the Christian Churches have bowed before the storm and remarry divorced people in church (let's recall in passing that divorce itself is not wrong, it never was, it is remarriage after divorce which is). In Britain alone, with the full blessing of the State, an average of 200,000 abortions are performed each year. Think, too, of the wholesale destruction of the innocence of children, of the brutal muggings of elderly people, of the prevalence of rape. One could go on. But yes, indeed, we live in "a wicked and adulterous generation".

You will hear it said that this sort of talk is scare-mongering; that all these things went on in the past and that its just that the mass media make us more aware of them. We shall not be judged by what went on in the past but by what goes on now in our own times. The script-writers of Dallas once gave JR a memorable line. He said: "Once you have thrown integrity out of the window the rest is easy". The same can be said of God. "Once you have thrown God out of the window the rest is easy" because then you are free to make up your own code of ethics to suit yourself – and that is precisely what the modern world has done. But it is then that things begin to go wrong: and things are going very wrong indeed.

Repent, but not just for ourselves. We are liable to think that our sins are a private matter between ourselves, God and the priest who hears our confession. But no man is an island unto himself, and no woman is an island unto herself. My bad temper affects other people. My uncharitable tongue affects other people, as do my lies, my deceit and my dishonesty. Illicit sexual relationships require the cooperation of two people, but may involve more if children and marriage partners are involved. How can I cry out against the blood-letting in Northern Ireland; how can I say, "Stop! Can't you forget the hurts and wrongs of the past and live together in harmony"; how can I say that if in my own life there is someone I have not forgiven, or won't forgive? Every sin we commit adds to the sum total of wickedness in the world. Sin is not a private matter only.

The whole human family is inexorably linked. What I do affects my neighbour: what happens in Britain has repercussions abroad. If that needs bringing home, we would do well to remember that if, which God forbid, there were ever to be a major nuclear war it would not make much difference whether you were in London, Liverpool, Paris or Moscow, whether you were a catholic, a protestant, an agnostic or an atheist, we should all perish together. God told Ahraham that he would spare Sodom if Abraham could find even 10 just men. But Abraham couldn't, and Sodom was destroyed. So it is that we have to do penance not just for ourselves but for those too who do not know God or perhaps hate Him.

Because we are human, as Lent proceeds we tend to fall down on the resolutions we began with. If only we could bring ourselves to a better understanding of sin and evil we would rather increase our commitment and bring it to a climax in Holy Week when we see in stark and grisly reality what sin really means. On Good Friday we are witnesses to the price. The price was the killing of the innocent God-Man. Repent and believe the Good News!

To end on a positive note, let's turn the coin over. On the other side we find that to all those who do repent and who are really honest with God and admit their weaknesses and faults, God has nothing but mercy, understanding, forgiveness and love. But if we want His love we must repent and do penance, so as to fill up, as St Paul puts it, what is wanting in the sufferings of Christ. Jesus told us that if we want to follow Him we must deny ourselves and take up our crosses daily. "Now is the acceptable time", today's gospel tells us. "Now!"

THIRD SUNDAY OF LENT

GOSPEL READING - JOHN 4:5-42

Samaria lay between Galilee to the north and Jerusalem to the south. At the time of Jesus the Samaritans were considered by orthodox Jews to be heretics and half-castes because in the course of their history they had inter-married with other peoples and their religion had become infected by paganism. As the parable of the Good Samaritan reminds us, self-respecting Jews would have nothing to do with Samaritans. Prostitutes and promiscuous women were also outcasts. So in today's gospel we find Jesus breaking two taboos. The woman who is the other central figure in the story is both promiscuous and a Samaritan.

Let us set the scene. Jesus and His disciples were on their way back to Galilee after a visit to Jerusalem, a journey of several days on foot, and they had chosen the highland route which took them through Samaria. When they reached the little hill town of Sychar they needed a rest and refreshment. Jesus sent His disciples into the town to buy supplies while He Himself stayed by the well which was a little way out of the town. Opposite the town across the valley was Mount Garizim which was sacred to the Samaritans who traced their lineage to Jacob who offered sacrifice on that mountain. The well was the well where Jacob had drunk. St John mentions the time when Jesus met the woman; around midday. This is important. In those days women would not normally go out during the day. If they needed to get water or go to the fields they would go in groups either in the early morning or the evening. So the fact that this woman came to the well alone and at midday immediately tells us something about her. She was the sort of woman other women would not associate with, so she had to come to the well alone when other women would not be going.

As I have said, self-respecting Jewish men would have shunned such a woman, as much for their own reputation as from principle, but Jesus engages her in conversation. Notice how He gradually gains her confidence and leads her on to the fullness of faith in Him. We have here a perfect example of spiritual direction.

First Jesus attracts the woman's attention by a perfectly ordinary human request; "Give me a drink". Then He offers her a spiritual gift: "If only you knew what God is offering you." but she totally misses the point. Nevertheless she is sufficiently intrigued to pursue the conversation. Jesus continues the spiritual theme and elaborates the efficacy of the "living water" He is offering her. Although she still does not understand what He is getting at, she realizes she is dealing with no ordinary man. There is something about Him which causes her to address Him as 'Sir'. He then tells her to go and get her husband, knowing perfectly well that she is living with a man out of wedlock. This offers an entry into her private life, an offer she can take up or refuse. In fact she is taken aback when He reveals that He already knows her situation. She knows for certain now that this man before her is not only unlike any other man she has had dealings with but that He has extraordinary powers. "I see you are a prophet, Sir", she says. She realizes that Jesus is getting very near to unmasking her sinfulness altogether. So she does what most of us do when we realize that our defences are about to be breached, she tries to change the subject; "Our fathers worshipped on this mountain...". Jesus then reveals who He is; the woman gives in; the boil is lanced: her conversion is complete. She runs back to the town in relief and joy and goes round telling every one what has happened to her. The result is that the people want to hear more from this man and ask Jesus to stay, which He does for two days and makes many converts.

There are many lessons we can learn from this story. Here are a couple. In Jerusalem which was the centre of the Jewish religion with its temple and its hierarchy, where He had come from, Jesus found only hardness of heart. Here in despised Samaria He found people willing to listen to Him and to follow Him. Could an impartial observer, do you think, notice any similarity at all between the attitude of the Jerusalem Jews vis-a-vis the Samaritans in Our Lord's day and the attitude of Catholics vis-a-vis non-Catholics in our own day?

Secondly, the christian religion is not concerned primarily with book knowledge, is not simply a matter of intellectual conviction, it is about knowing Jesus Christ as a real living person, and this is a matter of revelation. *"Jesus exclaimed: 'I bless you, Father, Lord of heaven and earth, for hiding these things from the learned and the clever and revealing them to mere children...' No one knows the Son except the Father, just as no one knows the Father except the Son and those to whom the Son chooses to reveal him."* (Matthew 11:25-30). For the Son to reveal the Father to us requires conversion on our part, and conversion involves dropping all our defences before the Son, Jesus Christ, and acknowledging our weakness, our faults and our innermost sins – those sins we hardly dare admit even to ourselves. In other words we have to become "mere children". But then, as the Samaritan woman discovered, colossal spiritual and emotional relief follows as the unconditional love and mercy comes flooding in and we experience, perhaps for the first time, that God is a true father and we His true children. This is not something fanciful and pretty-pretty, the stuff of children's story-books: on the contrary it is through this relationship that our Father imparts to us a deep adult understanding of the profoundest truths. Moreover, everyone who has experienced this conversion is filled with a joy which is uncontainable. Like the Samaritan woman they feel impelled to tell all their friends what has happened to them. Indeed the change in the person becomes apparent to everyone who knows them. Thus are others inspired and the Kingdom spread. Conversion and the grace which follows is "the spring of water, welling up to eternal life."

FOURTH SUNDAY OF LENT

GOSPEL READING –JOHN 3:14-21

As the reading from St John's gospel has just reminded us evil men have always tried to hide their deeds. We are all aware that crooks inhabit the murky corridors of the underworld. Murderers try to cover up their crimes, drug pushers flit from place to place to avoid being caught, swindlers and embezzelers plan their operations in secret, thieves aim to strike at their victims in a flash and then disappear into the night or the crowd or up the nearest alley. These examples of wrongdoers shunning the light are obvious. Can we close the Lectionary with a happy conscience and go on our way thinking that at least that part of the gospel message does not apply to us. Perhaps we should take another look at it, because things are not always what they seem.

Most marriages that go wrong start to go wrong at the point when one or other of the partners begins to conceal something important from the other. I can recall a couple who always seemed to be arguing. They got quite a name among the circle in which they moved. You could more or less bet on it that when you called to see Mike and Rosemary they would be having a row. In fact that marriage was rock solid and lasted until death did them part. The reason was that their disagreements were always out in the open, they didn't hide their differences, they quickly made up and their love prospered. I can recall other couples who when you met them you would have thought well adjusted; they didn't appear to have any serious differences. One was greatly shocked when later one heard that they had split up. In every case, when the story was told, there had been a long history of concealment; it might be infidelity, it might be resentment, jealousy, neglect, but whatever it was it festered until it killed the marriage.

The same can happen in religious life. When the inside stories have been told of men and women religious who have left their Orders or of priests who have abandoned the priesthood, the start of the parting of the-ways can be traced to the day when they began a line of thought or started on a course of action which they no longer were prepared to discuss with their superiors or share with their colleagues. What they were doing might on the surface have been quite innocent but in their heart or hearts they knew that they had begun to play with fire. There is a fascination about fire because it warms but it can also burn. There is always something exciting and stimulating about operating outside the legal framework. It gets the adrenaline moving. The devil is a pastmaster at covering the hook with which he catches people with attractive beguiling bait. It is only when the hook is well bedded in that he begins to pull on the line and his victims begin to pay the price.

You young people listening to me, if you are tempted to do something which you think your parents would not like or might disapprove of, stop and think. I am not saying that you must agree with your parents all the time and never do anything they might not like, but I am saying keep it out in the open. Be prepared to fight your corner if necessary. So long as people can discuss things, benefits can accrue to both sides. Your parents may come to see that they are being a bit fuddy-duddy or over-restrictive; you may come to see that they have a point or two after all. But once you slink off and start doing things secretly which you try to hide from them, then all sorts of troubles can follow. So long as what you do is done in the open "that all men may see", you can be pretty certain that you will not go far wrong. Once people start turning in on themselves, once guilt begins to take hold, then Satan has an opportunity to strike. There are, of course, perfectly legitimate areas of confidence. In this context I suppose the most obvious is confession. The seal of confession is absolute. But in general the right kind of confidences concern other people. It is when I come to deal with myself that I must be careful. Once I stamp 'Confidential' on my own affairs, which means everyone else keep out, then I must seriously examine my motives.

All this is easy enough to talk about but I am sure we all know from our own experience it can be extremely difficult to practise. There are times when to keep our affairs out in the open takes a very great deal of moral courage, because the consequence may be a pretty rough time. And indeed there may be times when we fail and scurry off into the darkness. That is when we need to hang on to God for dear life. He will not let us down. He said of Himself that He is the light of the world. There is no darkness about God. He is also the truth: "I am the way, the truth and the life". Satan is the spirit of darkness, of hate, of deceit; he is also ruthless and without mercy. Our Saviour, Jesus Christ, by contrast is the source of all spiritual light, of truth, of mercy, but above all of love, and it is because He loves us that He will not let us down. If we hang onto Him He will drag us back into the light when we have fallen into the darkness of sin.

So let's finish with the advice St Peter gave to his converts in his Second Letter. It is a bit dramatic but perhaps we shall remember it all the better. He says: "Be calm (don't get agitated about things) but be vigilant (be always on your guard), for your enemy the devil is prowling round like a roaring lion looking for someone to eat. Stand up to him, strong in faith". That is the answer -- our faith in the strength and the mercy and love of God.

"I love you, Jesus my love, above all things. I am sorry for ever having offended you. Never permit me to separate myself from you again. Grant that I may love you always, and then do with me what you will".

THE FOURTH SUNDAY AFTER EASTER

"GOOD SHEPHERD SUNDAY"

On this Sunday in the liturgical calendar each year the gospel readings are taken from Chapter 10 of St John's Gospel in which Jesus likens Himself to a good shepherd and His followers to the sheep whom He cares for and eventually lays down His life for. This year (1995) we are commemorating the end of the Second World War and the anniversary has brought powerfully to my mind a friend of mine who served with General Wingate's Chindits in the Burma Campaign. Those of you who were around at the time will recall that the Chindits were a brigade specially selected and trained to operate in the jungle behind the Japanese lines. Their job was to destroy objectives vital to the Japanese war effort. Because they were isolated from their base for weeks and even months at a time their missions were among the most hazardous and uncomfortable of the entire war.

On operations the brigade moved in independent columns, each consisting of up to 200 men, mostly British but including some Burmese riflemen. They also had some mules for carrying heavy equipment and they were dependent on air drops for re-supply. On this occasion the column in which my friend Philip Stibbe was a platoon commander was returning to the safety of India after a successful mission when, owing to faulty intelligence, they entered a village which was thought to be friendly but turned out to be occupied by a Japanese company. In the fierce engagement which followed the Japanese were routed, but not before several Chindits had been killed and Philip very severely wounded. The fighting had, of course, disclosed the Chindits' presence in the area and they knew that as soon as word reached the nearest Japanese headquarters reinforcements would be sent. Their only hope of survival was to get out of the area with the greatest possible speed, which meant avoiding roads and paths and taking off through the jungle. Philip was too badly wounded to walk so they tied him to the remaining mule. Because of their size mules cannot move as quickly as men through thick forest, and after a few hours march it was clear that Philip and his mule were hindering the progress of the column, so the commander took the difficult decision to leave Philip behind to his almost certain death in order that the rest of his men might have a better chance of reaching safety. At the very last moment a Burmese rifleman stepped forward and volunteered to stay behind with Philip. His name was Maung Tun.

Maung Tun dressed Philip's wounds, cared for him tenderly and mounted guard over him, but after 24 hours the two of them had used up their meagre rations and were desperately short of water. Maung Tun decided to find the nearest village and persuade one of his countrymen to give him some supplies. He succeeded in his mission and a rendezvous was arranged for the following day. When he got there it transpired that he had been betrayed and the Japs were waiting for him. By now they knew that there was a wounded British officer in the district, so they took him into the village and subjected him to several hours of interrogation. He refused to speak. When it became clear that he was not going to reveal Philip's whereabouts he was subjected to the most hideous tortures and eventually shot.(These details Philip only discovered after the war.)

Twenty-four hours later a Japanese patrol found Philip who by then was all but dead. Incredibly he survived to spend the rest of the war in the indescribable conditions of the central gaol in Rangoon. When he was repatriated after the Japanese surrender he wrote a book about his experiences called 'Return via Rangoon". In anticipation of the 50th anniversary the publisher (Leo Cooper) decided to reprint Philip's book and asked him to add any reflections he felt appropriate. I am going to read you one short paragraph.

I cannot put into words what I feel about this man. His utter unselfishness in volunteering to stay behind with me, his devotion in looking after me so well and, finally, his matchless courage in facing torment and death rather than betray me to the enemy - these are things I cannot trust myself to speak of even today. I can never be worthy of the sacrifice he made but, as long as I live, I shall always have the feeling that my life is not my own, and the memory of Maung Tun will inspire me to the end of my days.

Brothers and Sisters, those words could equally well have been written about Jesus Christ, our Saviour, our Good Shepherd, who laid down His life to save us, not from human enemies in time of war, but from something far worse – spiritual death and the fires of hell. So I am going to read that paragraph again slightly adapted, but this time I want you to put yourself in place of Philip and Jesus in place of Maung Tun.

I cannot put into words what I feel about this man, Jesus. His utter unselfishness in volunteering to stay with me,His devotion in looking after me so well and, finally, His matchless courage in facing torment and death rather than abandon me to the enemy – these are things I cannot trust myself to speak of even today. I can never be worthy of the sacrifice He made but, as long as I live, I shall always have the feeling that my life is not my own, and the memory of Jesus Christ will inspire me to the end of my days.

Jesus, my Brother, my Comrade, my Friend, my Saviour, my Good Shepherd, I thank You for Your great love and I weep for Your cruel death on the cross for my sins of which I truly repent. I trust You, I love You, I place my weak heart beside Your Sacred Heart and I will follow You to my very last breath. Amen.

FIFTH SUNDAY AFTER EASTER

FIRST READING - APOCALYPSE 21:1-5

GOSPEL READING - JOHN 13:31-35

The Evangelist John was a visionary. He had met Our Lord as a young man (when probably a late teenager) and he lived to a great age. His writings, chronologically the last works of Sacred Scripture, are the result of a life-time's reflection about the Master he loved so much. He looks behind the actual events he describes to a greater reality he sees beyond.

What is he referring to in today's Second Reading where he talks about "a new heaven and a new earth", "the new Jerusalem coming down out of heaven" and credits Christ the Redeemer with saying "now I am making the whole of creation new"? Surely, you may say, the earth has not altered noticeably since John wrote the Book of Revelation. In what way has God been making the whole creation new?

The answer is to be found in today's gospel which is taken from John's account of the Last Supper. His account is different from those of the other evangelists. He remembers not so much what Jesus did as what He said. It was a unique occasion. The last time Jesus was to have a private conversation with His chosen few before His terrible death. In an atmosphere charged with foreboding and sadness He allowed His apostles the rare intimacy of hearing Him talk to His heavenly Father. At so sacred a moment He gave them His last will and testament. At the heart of it was what He called a new commandment; *"Love one another; just as I loved you, you also must love one another"*. What's so special about that, you may ask? Love must have been around a long time before the Last Supper. What's new about it?

History compresses past time, and often it squeezes out the unpleasant things and leaves us with the nicer things to remember; but nostalgia is a lying jade. When we look upon the ruined buildings or the fascinating artifacts of the Ancient Romans or the Ancient Egyptians we marvel at the level of their technical achievement and domestic sophistication. When we read the writings of the Ancient Greeks we are impressed by their mastery of philosophy and literature. What we tend to forget is that all the ancient civilisations were built on slavery. Slavery has, thank God, not been part of the culture of our country for so long that we have ceased to realise what it once meant. Men and women were bought and sold as we might buy a dog or a cow and were treated with little more consideration than we give to a hoover or a washing machine. If a slave was unsatisfactory you beat him; if he became useless or died you went to the slave market and bought another. Even among the ruling classes there was a great deal of sophisticated cruelty and bestiality. Read Suetonius's 'Lives of the Roman Emperors' on which the film 'I Claudius' was based. In such a world the command to "love one another just as I have loved you", "to love your enemies and do good to those who harm you", was not just new, it was earth-shattering, it was revolutionary.

When we look around us today things in general are not as bad as they were in the ancient world, but we can still see people being cruel to one another. More alarmingly we notice the resurgence in our own country of some of the grosser excesses which we hoped had gone for ever. So what of Jesus's new commandment of love? Certainly for a great many people it is still 'new'.

If, now, when men and women accept the 'new commandment' and, trusting in God, put it into practice, the bitterness and strife within families (separation, divorce) will gradually disappear: the civil unrest caused by the unjust distribution of wealth will subside: the discord and violence between nations and groups within nations (the arms race, Northern Ireland, Nicaragua) will be removed. Between us in the human race we have enough intelligence, we have enough skills, we have sufficient resources to provide more than enough food, clothing and shelter for every living person. It is just not true that wars are inevitable and famines endemic. The 'new commandment' can make a new earth, a new creation. This earth of ours was once a paradise before Satan introduced his poison of lies and deceit, and it can become one again. The earthly Jerusalem through the new commandment of love could become a replica in material form of the heavenly Jerusalem. This is what John saw: "the new Jerusalem coming down from God out of heaven".

Pie in the sky, you say? It's not happened up to now, what makes you think it can happen in the future? But wait! Who was it who gave us that new commandment? Was it not Jesus Christ? He who was not just a good man but true God as well? At the Last Supper He was not just kidding us along with nice phrases: He was not romanticising. He was telling us the truth, and it was that truth which John saw in the Apocalypse.

But we have a part to play. The difference between the religion of the Jews and Christians and that of the pagans was that the pagan gods lived remote from the world and people were at the mercy of blind fate. But, as St John tells us in the Second Reading, our God has made His home among us. His name is Emmanuel, 'God with us'. We are a free people. Our future is in our own hands, not at the mercy of fate. With the living God among us we can change history and bring about the new creation. So how do we begin?

We make a resolution here and now that from this Mass onwards we will stop trying to run other people's lives for them. We will start with the person closest to us - husband, wife, father, mother, fiancee, whoever. We will stop insisting on having our own way, on making sure our point of view prevails, in getting what we want. Instead we will put them first and ourselves last in all things but sin. We will then move outwards and practise 'the new commandment' in the wider family, in our circle of friends and in our work place. And we will not do this in a spirit of martyrdom but we will do it rejoicing with love in our hearts because we have God in our hearts and the fire of His spirit burning within us. And where do we catch the flame from? From our union with Jesus in Holy communion.

Let me leave you with a little piece of advice which I found written in a medieval church in Norfolk:

'Look not at the imperfections of others.
Keep silence
And hold continual converse with God'.

You will be amazed how that will change not only you yourself but the world around you!

THIRTEENTH SUNDAY OF THE YEAR

GOSPEL READING - MATTHEW 10:37-42

"Anyone who does not take up his cross and follow in my footsteps is not worthy of me." This is a hard saying, but it is fundamental to Our Lord's message. So what are we to make of it?

Crosses come in all shapes and sizes. Some are so big and heavy that they are obvious. For example, people who suffer from a long agonizing terminal illness; people who have been involved in an accident which has left them so badly and permanently maimed that they can never again enjoy the things which made life enjoyable for them previously. Such people do indeed have heavy crosses to carry. Thank God not many of us are called upon to carry such heavy loads.

But there are other crosses which to the outsider might seem trivial but to the person involved can seem mountainous. For instance, if we are married perhaps our partner has developed a habit or an interest which drives us up the wall but to object causes arguments and tensions. We feel trapped: nailed to a cross. If we are the parents of teenage children, perhaps one of them has gone off and shacked up with the girl friend, or boy-friend as the case may be, and is living a life-style which we know to be wrong, yet we fear to act the heavy parent in case we lose them altogether and gentle persuasion and understanding has got us nowhere. On the other hand we feel we cannot stand idly by and do nothing, so we worry and agonize and feel helpless.

But may be we are that very teenager over whom our parents are agonizing. If so, we may feel that all our efforts to get our parents to understand us have been fruitless. The adult world just does not seem either to understand or care. Yet deep down inside us we long for some good advice and a guide we feel we can trust. Despite all the gay whirl of student life we feel lonely and uncertain.

But then again we may be adult but single. We long, perhaps, for that companionship and tangible love which others seem to enjoy but which always eludes us. We, too, feel trapped: nailed to a cross.

When faced with a problem, the answer of the modern world is 'get rid of your problem'. If your marriage is in trouble, get a divorce. "You're mad to chain yourself to the dead shell of a marriage", they'll tell you. But if you cannot get rid of your problem, if you feel trapped and depressed and uncertain, then reach for the bottle or get high on drugs or go to your GP and get a repeat prescription for tranquillizers. "Lay down your cross", the world says. Jesus says, "Take up your cross". In this connection I always think of St Thérèse, the 'Little Flower'. She belonged to an enclosed Order and in her day the community had to attend chapel several times a day to sing the Office and pray silently. At one stage the Mother Prioress moved a certain nun into the choir stall immediately behind Thérèse. This nun had an infuriating habit of constantly fidgeting. The noise so distracted Thérèse that she found it impossible to concentrate or to pray. It began to become an obsession with her and brought her near to a nervous breakdown. Chapel became an agony for her and she dreaded the bell calling the community to prayer. She used to break out in a sweat in the effort to control her feelings. Thérèse knew that she could probably solve the problem by turning round and giving the offending nun a withering glance and a piece of her mind, but she was too charitable for that. Then one day it came to her. The nun had been put there by the Mother Prioress who was God's representative in the community. Therefore these distractions were sent by God. She saw that instead of trying to blot out the sounds and pretend the noise was not there, she should listen to it and offer it up as a prayer. Previously her own prayer had been in opposition to the fidgeting: now the fidgeting was her prayer. In no time at all she began to love the sister and to be grateful to her because she was the bearer of a cross which would help Thérèse to get closer to her beloved Lord. Imagine the damage which would have been caused in that community if Thérèse had been resentful, had said unkind things about the nun behind her back or vented her anger to her face! Instead she spread forgiveness, love and joy. No wonder she was such an asset to that Carmelite community at Lisieux! Although she died young in an enclosed convent not long before the First World War she became the inspiration and patroness of the French soldiers who suffered so dreadfully in the trenches and her fame spread rapidly throughout the world. Not long after the war ended the French people erected the huge basilica at Lisieux in her honour which is the focus today of pilgrimages from the four quarters of the globe. Great sanctity is made from the accumulation of daily crosses willingly accepted.

In next week's gospel reading we shall find Our Lord taking us a stage further in the way of the cross. He will explain that "His yoke is sweet and His burden light". But for this week let us spend five minutes each day thinking about what is meant by the cross and asking Jesus to deepen our understanding of what He wants from us in our own personal circumstances.

FIFTEENTH SUNDAY OF THE YEAR

GOSPEL READING - LUKE 10 : 25-37

Of all Jesus's parables that of the Good Samaritan probably needs least explanation: its meaning is so clear. The Jews of the Old Testament considered themselves God's chosen people; and the Jews of Our Lord's day considered Samaritans heretics and half-castes. So the parable means that we should always be ready to go to the help of our neighbour, but especially if that neighbour is neither socially nor ethnically congenial. If we, like the lawyer in the story, ask "Who is my neighbour?" Jesus leaves us to supply our own answer after reading the story. I want to suggest three ways in which our western industrialized society militates against our practising what Jesus teaches in the parable.

Nowadays those people who have a job, have a career, are under intense pressure to cram more and more into the day and bring about a never ending rise in productivity. This applies whether a person is self-employed or working for someone else. Human life is tied to the technological roundabout which rotates with gathering speed. Take the development of the motorcar for example. Modern cars are much faster and more reliable than those of fifty years ago and the main roads much wider. It is possible in one hour to cover distances which would have been unthinkable even forty years ago. Thus the businessman can fit five appointments into his day where his predecessor could only manage two. But if there is a blockage on the motorway his frustration is immediate and the tension in him rises by the minute as he sits stationary in the five mile tailback. When I go to visit my GP I marvel at his ability to keep calm and give me his undivided attention when he is already half-an-hour behind schedule and must be aware that tension and temperatures are rising in the waiting room. Modern life has a kind of momentum of its own. I first became really aware of this exactly twenty years ago. I was a London commuter at the time. I had been ill and my doctor and my family told me I must slow down and take life more leisurely. "Let the others kill themselves with heart attacks; you just let them go by. If you miss one train, get out your book and wait unconcernedly for the next, etc, etc". In the first week of my return to work I remember standing on Holborn Underground station and getting a great kick out of letting a whole trainload dash past me onto the escalator and then proceeding in lordly fashion up an escalator all to myself. "The doctor was right," I said to myself. "They're all crackers in the rat race". Exactly a month later I stood on exactly the same spot on the same station. This time I came to a halt, not to let everyone else go by, but because it suddenly hit me that I was right back in the rat race and hadn't noticed it. Now in these pressurized situations if we come across a road accident or find someone in trouble on the street or in the underground there's a great temptation to pass by and persuade oneself that somebody else will cope, another passer-by, or the ambulance service or the police or whoever. I really cannot afford to miss my next appointment. A lot of money and perhaps my career is riding upon it.

Secondly there is fear. We have all heard stories of crooks setting up fictitious roadside accidents and then when a 'good samaritan' stops they knock him on the head, pinch his wallet and his car and make off. So there is a natural wariness, especially among women, of acting as a good samaritan. Clearly we have to be sensible and listen to advice from those in positions of responsibility, but before we take as gospel the current accepted wisdom of not getting involved, perhaps we should take another look at the parable. Those of you who have been on a pilgrimage to the Holy Land will probably have travelled on the road from Jerusalem to Jericho. Today it is a well metalled motor road but it still passes through desolate inhospitable country. The only people you are likely to see are the occasional bedouin with a flock of goats. Tour operators advise against stopping and getting out of your vehicle. The Samaritan in the parable who stopped to help the man who had been done over by robbers took the risk of being done over himself, but the risk did not stop him and Jesus did not include any advice to be cautious when approaching a victim.

Thirdly there is the effect of original sin. There is in all of us a tendency to put our own interests first and to find a variety of plausible excuses as to why we cannot help our neighbour just at this particular moment. Another time perhaps, but not right now. And of course in the parable Our Lord is not just on about road accidents. The real point of the story is about the willingness to spend time with people who need our help, and this often means giving our time at most inconvenient moments.

To return to my first point, I believe that there are subtle influences at work in today's society which lead us away from the direction Jesus wants us to go. In the more leisurely pace of life in times past people found it more natural to spend time with each other. The more I have read this parable the more I have come to see that its lesson is at the very heart of Jesus's teaching. Some of the nicest, most generous, most open-handed, most kindly, helpful people I have known have been people who might be described as unchurched. They seldom, if ever, went to church and some would not have described themselves as christians, but I believe they are nearer to Jesus's ideal for His followers than the enthusiastic church-goer who is mean and tight-fisted. Ideally we should be both generous good samaritans and enthusiastic church-goers, and I thank God daily that we have many in this parish who are both. Their example and the blessings they gain for our whole community are inestimable. I just think we should be aware that there are influences at work to make us selfish.

EIGHTEENTH SUNDAY OF THE YEAR

GOSPEL READING - LUKE 12: 13-21

There could hardly be a more topical gospel than the one I have just read, and it should make us all think. It is not about wealth as such nor about enjoying ourselves within reason: it is about surplus wealth. The problem for each of us to decide is 'What is the meaning of surplus?'. If we are to bring the parable home to our own circumstances we might replace the words "rich man" by our own name, the word "crops" by income and "barns" by bank, building society or shares.

Now riches or wealth are, of course, comparative terms but they include not just our bank balance but our possessions as a whole, the circumstances in which we live and our ability to get money and support when we need it. I think you will agree that compared to millions of people in the Third World, the thousands of refugees in Europe and many people in the so-called underclass in this country, most of us here in Chichester are pretty well off. As people move up the adult ladder from school to retirement most aim to better themselves, as the Victorians put it, and there's nothing wrong with that. A typical person starts, perhaps, with a bed sit and a push-bike; then they share a flat and buy an old banger; then they marry and buy a two-bedroom house; as their income rises, and probably their spouse's too, and children are born they move to a better three bedroom house and buy their first new car; later they move to a bigger house, own two cars and take more expensive holidays; and so on. Most people in those circumstances live up to their income all along the line. As their wealth increases some former luxuries become current necessities and any serious drop in their standard of living a nightmare. If the bubble bursts, as it did in the early nineties, there are howls of protest and a witch-hunt for scapegoats. Do people, I wonder, ever stop along the way and, admitting they are adequately provided for, decide to give the increasing surplus they have to charitable purposes so that those less fortunate could share in their good fortune? Have we ever made such an assessment? St John says in his First Letter: *"If a man who was rich enough in this world's goods saw that one of his brothers was in need, but closed his heart to him, how could the love of God be living in him?"* How indeed!

But, of course, it is not only to individuals that this gospel applies. What about our corporate record as a people? The European Community is structured on the principle of looking after number one first, i.e. Europe. For example, in order that the Community's farmers may receive a price for their crops which will maintain a high standard of living they are paid substantial sums to take land out of production under the "Set aside" scheme and thus sustain high crop prices. It is ironic that this country is now over-supplied with golf courses and theme parks built on redundant farm land and some are already closing. Today's Western culture is a very selfish one and it encourages selfishness. The huge advertising industry is geared to raising expectations and persuading people that they really must buy more and more of the latest products if life is to be worth living. Not only is there a false and wasteful philosophy behind this sales-speak, but it is a philosophy which is guaranteed to produce greed and envy. It encourages those who are on the 'gravy train' to pull down their existing barns and build bigger ones to accommodate their expanding wealth like the man in the gospel, and it causes those who cannot keep up to envy those who can. In turn the envy, because it cannot be satisfied, leads on to violence. Those left outside looking in eventually break in and take what they cannot buy. A vicious circle develops. Whereabouts on that circle are we?

To people who are like the rich man in the gospel Jesus does not mince His words. " *'Fool'*, He says, *'This very night the demand will be made for your soul; and this hoard of yours, whose will it be then?' So it is when a man stores up treasure for himself in place of making himself rich in the sight of God.'* " If I were to die tonight, am I certain I could face my God with a clear conscience in this matter, or would I wish I had pegged my standard of living some time ago and been more generous? As I said, wealth is comparative. One man's second-hand car is something beyond another's wildest dreams; the price of one family's new washing machine would provide another family (and a bigger one at that) with food for a year. I suggest that all of us, at whatever level we are on the wealth scale, have reason to pray for discernment so that we may see clearly what we ought to do to make ourselves "rich in the sight of God". I have to admit that Jesus's warning in today's gospel makes me very uneasy. *"Watch and be on your guard against avarice of any kind"*, He says, *"for a man's life is not made secure by what he owns, even when he has more than he needs"*. These words echo those of Job: "Naked I was born into this world, and naked shall I leave it". A salutary thought!

TWENTY-FIRST SUNDAY OF THE YEAR

GOSPEL READING - JOHN 6:60-69

The Gospel readings in Cycle B of the Sunday scripture readings are taken from St Mark's gospel, but for five Sundays at this time of the year the readings from St Mark are interrupted and we are given successive readings from chapter 6 of St John's gospel. Unlike the three synoptic evangelists (Matthew, Mark and Luke) John in his account of the Last Supper makes no mention of the Eucharist. He concentrates the whole of his eucharistic theology into chapter 6. It is therefore a chapter of particular importance to us Catholics.

The first eleven chapters of John's gospel compose what is traditionally known as 'The Book of Signs'. John selects seven of Our Lord's miracles which, he tells his followers, are proofs of his Master's divinity. The account of each miracle, or sign, is followed by Our Lord's teaching on the subject. Chapter 6 begins with an account of the Feeding of the Five Thousand and is followed by Our Lord's announcement the following day of the doctrine of the Bread of Life, what we know as the Eucharist. It would seem that historic pronouncement came about half way through the three years of Our Lord's public ministry. His fame and popularity were at their highest. Wherever He went He was besieged by crowds who brought their sick to be cured and who came to listen to His teaching because "unlike the scribes and pharisees He taught with authority". What He told the crowd that day was to mark a crucial turning point in His career as we shall see.

Jesus begins by telling the crowd quite bluntly that the reason they have come is because they want more of the bread which He provided for them so abundantly the day before. But, He says, they ought to be working for the food which *"endures to eternal life; the kind of food the Son of Man is offering you"*. Like the Samaritan woman we heard about on the Third Sunday of Lent, these Galilean people hadn't the faintest idea what He was referring to, but whatever it was they wanted it, so they asked Him what they must do to do the works that God wants. He replies: *"This is working for God: you must believe in the one He has sent". "What sign will you give us to show that we should believe in you? What work will you do?"* they shout. The only other bread they know about was the manna which their forefathers ate in the desert. Jesus reminds them that it was God who provided the manna and that God, who is His Father, will give them the true bread "which comes down from heaven and gives life to the world." *"Sir,"* they say, *"give us that bread always"*. Then Jesus makes the astonishing and historic pronouncement: *"I am the bread of life. He who comes to me will never be hungry; he who believes in me will never thirst."* The crowd is gobsmacked, to coin a phrase, and can hardly believe their ears. In their puzzlement they start to complain. Jesus asks them to believe what He says, and then presses on. *"I am the living bread which has come down from heaven. Anyone who eats this bread will live for ever; and the bread that I shall give is my flesh for the life of the world."* Well, that was even more astonishing! *"How can this man give us His flesh to eat?"* they complain. Has He taken leave of His senses? Is He talking about cannibalism? But Jesus insists: *"I tell you solemnly, if you do not eat the flesh of the Son of Man and drink His blood you will not have life in you. Anyone who does eat my flesh and drink my blood has eternal life and I shall raise him up on the last day. For my flesh is real food and my blood is real drink. He who eats my flesh and drinks my blood lives in me and I live in him."* That was just too much. *"This is intolerable language,"* they cried. *"How could anyone accept it."* The gospel then records that *"after this many of His disciples left Him and stopped going with Him."* Jesus is left standing alone with the Twelve. *"What about you, do you want to go away too?"* He asks them. For me that is one of the most poignant scenes in the whole of the New Testament. Jesus has just announced His greatest gift, but it is rejected because the people, for whom He has done so much, do not believe in Him sufficiently to take His word. "He came to His own and His own received Him not." That day in Galilee marked the beginning of the end of the life on earth of Jesus Christ. His enemies, realizing that the people had lost confidence in Him, began to close in for the kill.

The sign of the Bread of Life, the Eucharist, was a sign of contradiction from the start, and has been ever since. The protestant reformers in this country, for instance, stated in Article twenty eight of the Thirty-nine Articles that "the changing of the substance of bread and wine in the Supper of the Lord cannot be proved by Holy Writ and is repugnant to the plain words of Scripture", and they go on to say of the Mass in Article Thirty One: "Wherefore the sacrifices of masses... were blasphemous fables and dangerous deceits." Personally I do not see how anyone who reads St John chapter 6 can fail to believe that Jesus meant what He said. When the Jews started to complain He did not say: "Don't get upset. I don't want you to take me literally, I am just using a kind of metaphor to introduce a spiritual idea." On the contrary He repeats what He has just said and emphasizes that He does mean exactly what He is saying. Moreover, He says He realizes that many people will misunderstand Him. Nevertheless He insists that *"The words I have spoken to you are spirit and they are life."*

But before we criticize the Jewish crowd for being so thick and disbelieving, let us try to imagine how we would react if the Eucharist did not exist but when we came to church one Sunday morning our parish priest, whom we regarded as a holy and sensible man, stood up in the pulpit and announced that he was the living bread come down from heaven, and told us that unless we ate his flesh and drank his blood we should not have life in us. Would we not think that he had gone mad? Would we not complain that what he had said was 'intolerable language'? Might not we, like the Jews, 'stop going with him' and leave the church? What Jesus announced that day long ago in Galilee was indeed a hard saying and strains peoples' credibility even today despite two thousand years of christian tradition. The truth is that belief in the Eucharist is a matter of faith. If we believe that Jesus is the Son of God and that He is the way, the truth and the life, then we shall accept the truth of what He says, even if our human minds cannot fully comprehend it. It was for faith in His claim to be God that Jesus consistently asked throughout His public ministry. It was because the leaders of the Jews would not accept that claim that He was put to death for blasphemy. It was to convince his christian communities of the divinity of his Master that St John wrote his gospel. Today it is belief in the divinity of Christ that distinguishes christians from non-christians, and it is belief in the real presence of Christ in the Eucharist which distinguishes Roman Catholics from most other christians. Let us today renew our faith in the real presence of Christ under the appearances of bread and wine in our Mass this morning, and demonstrate our belief by our reverence during Mass and when we go into the Blessed Sacrament Chapel. 'Our Father in heaven, help our unbelief and deepen our devotion to your divine Son, Jesus, in the Holy Eucharist. Amen.'

TWENTY-FOURTH SUNDAY OF THE YEAR

GOSPEL READING - MATTHEW 18: 21-35

Harry and Betty had been sweethearts from their school days at the local catholic school. Harry was a fine young man who had begun a promising career at a local engineering firm where he was marked out as a high flyer. He was also a good sportsman and a key member of the local rugby team. Above all he was popular and the life and soul of any party he was invited to. Betty was an attractive vivacious young woman who had passed all her secretarial exams and could look forward to an interesting career of her own, but her greatest ambition was to marry Harry her childhood sweetheart and bear his children. So when their wedding day duly arrived there was great rejoicing in both families and throughout the local community, but one person (and only one) had had a nagging doubt and had sounded a word of warning. That person was Betty's father. He belonged to the same sports club as Harry and had noted the young man's fondness for the bar. Having seen the devastating effects of alcoholism in another branch of the family he could not bear the thought of his daughter, whom he loved as his own soul, becoming a victim. So he had mentioned his concern when Betty told him she wanted to marry Harry and asked for his blessing, but when a person is head-over-heels in love they are not receptive to such warnings and Betty brushed the warning aside. She could find no faults in Harry.

So Harry and Betty set up home in a three bedroom terrace house and to begin with all went well. They were ecstatically happy and went everywhere together. Betty's presence had the effect of defusing Harry's fondness for the bottle, but after about a year Betty fell pregnant and in due course little John arrived. Betty had long ago decided she was going to be the kind of wife and mother now out of fashion: she was going to stay at home until her children were old enough to leave school. So she gave up her job and no longer accompanied Harry on all his sporting and social outings. She was no hermit and went with him when she could, but her baby came first.

Now that Betty's steadying presence was not always there, Harry's intake of alcohol began to rise. In the beginning when he came home from the club having had more than was good for him he would be merry, in fact he was rather fun, and Betty laughed with him. It was all rather a joke. It was after their second child was born that things took a turn for the worse. Alcohol no longer made him merry. He began to have black moods and instead of taking Betty in his arms and kissing her when he got home, he would slump in his chair in the kitchen and glower at her. He began to needle her and try to provoke her into arguments so that he could tell her how stupid she was. His behaviour and his language became more coarse. Often by the morning he was his old self again, but the time of recovery got longer though he always managed to sober up by the time he got to the office. And then one evening Betty tried to reason with him . She begged him to cut back on his drinking and, with great tact and gentleness, she told him what the consequences might be. He listened in silence but with growing fury. When she finished he got up from his chair and gave her such a clout that she fell heavily to the floor, catching her head on the corner of the table as she went down. Next morning Harry was full of remorse when he saw the nasty bruise on Betty's forehead and he promised to reform. For a week or two he kept away from the club, but it didn't last.

By now Betty was desperately worried about their deteriorating finances and feared that Harry might lose his job. Moreover, where once her heart had thrilled at the sound of his footfall on the gravel leading up their front door when he came home, now her heart froze with terror when she heard his steps, then the scratching on the door as he fumbled for the keyhole, followed by the banging of the door as he lumbered into the hall. Finally, one dreadful day he came home earlier than usual and the children were still down stairs. In their innocence they ran to him. He flung them crashing against the furniture with an oath. They got up and ran in terror to their mother. Betty was prepared to put up with any amount of violence to herself but she drew the line at her children. She resolved there and then that she would take the children next day to her parents' house. Her father did not want to add to her anguish so he did not say: "I did warn you but you wouldn't listen". When Harry got home that evening and found her note he was so taken aback that at first he did not know what to do. It had never entered his head that she might leave him. The following morning when he had recovered somewhat he went to her father's house and besought her to return to him, promising over and over again that he would never touch a drop of alcohol again. Disregarding her parents' advice yet again she did return after a few days, but alone. She decided to leave the children with her parents until she had evidence that Harry meant what he said, but she could not contemplate a split family, so eventually the children returned too.

To cut a long story short this sequence of events was repeated many times. Though she tried to keep their problem within the family circle, Harry's increasingly erratic behaviour and the evidence of his cruelty to her which became more and more difficult to hide meant that the unhappy state of affairs gradually became public knowledge. Betty's parents and her close friends begged her to leave Harry, but after a time she always went back and found ways of protecting the children for she was determined to keep her family together; and had she not promised at the altar on her wedding day 'to love and cherish Harry for better or for worse'? When people asked her why she stayed with him, she would reply simply: "I love him, you see." In the end Harry did lose his job and most of his friends, and he became seriously ill.

When it became clear that he was beyond medical help, she had him brought home from the hospital and cared for him herself. When she could see that the end was near she called the parish priest. Harry made a humble almost childlike confession and the priest anointed him. When the priest had gone, Harry turned his head on the pillow and whispered: "I loved you all along, Bet. I don't know why I did it. Please forgive me." She squeezed his hand and laid her head beside his. "I know, Darling", she said, "and I forgave you long ago. I shall love you always." She kissed him, and he was gone. She had forgiven him not seven times but seventy-seven times, as the Lord puts it in to-day's gospel. Nothing Harry had done had broken her love or forgiveness. After his death Betty brought up her children on her own, but, though still an attractive woman, she never re-married. She kept his photograph beside her bed and lived out her forgiveness until she was re-united with him in heaven.

Unconditional love and unending forgiveness beggar description and have no purely human explanation. They are divine and come straight from the Sacred Heart of Jesus. Most of us can only watch the likes of Betty and wonder, yet nothing that Jesus teaches us in the gospels is impossible. He who is 'the Way, the Truth and the Life' cannot teach what is false. He would not be true to Himself if he did. So, no matter how far beyond our personal capability Betty's example might seem to be, we can at least aspire to it in the sure knowledge that God will give us the grace, as He did to her, if we ask for it, should the time come when we need it. In the meantime let us praise and thank Him that our God is a god who loves each of us with unconditional love and always forgives the repentant sinner. Amen.

TWENTY-FIFTH SUNDAY OF THE YEAR

READINGS – AMOS 8: 4-7   LUKE 16 :1-13

Today's Gospel and First Reading from the Prophet Amos concern money, one of the two obsessions of contemporary society, the other being sex; and the two are not unconnected.

The Prophet Amos was much concerned with injustice and he castigated the moneyed class of his day for swindling the needy and grinding down the poor. I wonder what he would have to say were he living today? He would find densely populated countries in Africa, Asia and South America where the vast majority of the people have a very low standard of living and many live in squalor and on the verge of starvation while a small elite of their own compatriots live it up in western style luxury backed up by Swiss bank accounts despite the fact that their countries are in hock to First World banks and multi-national companies. In the West he would find socialism discredited and free market capitalism making a strong comeback, producing a widening gap between rich and poor. But I suspect that what he would find most distasteful in the West would be some of the means employed to make quick and huge profits. He would find ruthless and unscrupulous people preying on the weaknesses of human nature to undermine sexual morality and then titillating and inflaming sexual passion by a stream of ever more crude pornography, and by prying into the private life of anyone whose birth or career might provide a salacious and eye-catching headline if some sexual misdemeanour can be unearthed. In recent times the Church has become a prime target. This is devilish work. Under the plausible but false argument that the public has a right to know, the characters of otherwise good people are assassinated and the public appetite for scandal fed and aggravated. We all recall the Gospel story of the woman taken in adultery, of how Jesus dealt with that situation and of how the elders slunk away one by one beginning with the eldest. In many cases the media moguls, editors and hacks who perpetrate the kind of thing I am talking about are in no position to throw stones, if they had any honesty or decency. Moreover, now that this country has caught the American disease of litigation, anyone who bears a grudge against someone or some institution resulting from some action, no matter how long ago it occurred, knows that there may be big money in a successful resort to law, so they are queuing up to have a go, especially if they can negotiate legal aid.

When people have been abused or harmed by anyone, be they priest, religious or lay-person, certainly prompt and effective action should be taken and the victims cared for, but for propagating scandal solely for money there can be no excuse. In the traditional prayers for the Stations of the Cross, at the fourteenth station "Jesus is stripped of His garments", the script reads: 'He was exposed to the vulgar gaze of the rude and scoffing multitude'. I cannot myself conceive of a greater psychological crucifixion than to have one's private life thus exposed. Even if one was innocent it would be bad enough, but suppose one was guilty...? There are effective but sensitive and compassionate ways of dealing with such matters, and I am sure that we as fellow Catholics will not allow ourselves to be scandalized by, nor join in scandal-mongering about, the priests whose sins have recently been revealed in the national press, but perhaps their fate should make us ponder over the means of acquiring money and the uses to which it is put. Could it possibly be that inadvertently, without realizing it, we have in some small way been helping to perpetuate the injustices in the Third World or the demolition of christian morality in the First? At the end of today's Gospel Jesus says: "You cannot be the slave of both God and money". We have to choose.

TWENTY-SIXTH SUNDAY OF THE YEAR

GOSPEL READING - MARK 9:38-43, 45, 47-48

At first sight the last part of today's gospel sounds pretty gruesome, but I think there are two things to be said about it. In the first place I do not suppose the language would have sounded so way-out in the more blood-thirsty period in which Jesus lived; and in the second I think Jesus clearly intended to use fairly lurid language to make his hearers sit up and take notice because He was dealing with a fundamental point of His teaching.

I think I have pointed out before that we humans find great difficulty in maintaining a proper balance in our affairs, and that this applies as much to spiritual matters as to secular. The pendulum continually swings from one side to the other. The 16th century Protestant Reformers laid great emphasis on personal morality and were not overly concerned with social justice. Thus during the Industrial Revolution you could find wealthy industrialists who were sticklers for attending church on Sundays and not infrequently built churches and chapels at their own expense and applied all sorts of pressure on their work forces to attend. Yet these same people saw nothing incongruous between their passion for church attendance and their perpetrating, or at least countenancing, outrageous injustices in their factories and workshops. It has to be added that Catholics were not immune to this kind of moral blindness. Even today there are Christians who maintain that the Churches have no place in politics and business: those things are the province of the laity. The job of the clergy is to thunder away at personal morality from the pulpits and to keep their noses out of secular affairs.

In the 60s and 70s the pendulum swung violently in the opposite direction. Christianity was thought by some to be synonymous with social justice. Personal morality was a private affair to which christianity was irrelevant. Hence you could have people calling themselves christians who campaigned and marched for numerous causes of social justice and might be willing to suffer hardships and privation to help the Third World but who could see nothing incongruous between that and having sexual relationships outside marriage, in milking the welfare state for all it was worth and sometimes being outrageously rude and hurtful to their parents and those nearest to them. That kind of person sees the Church as a kind of religious welfare organisation.

To get the right balance we have, as always, to go to the gospels. Yes, Jesus had quite a lot to say about social justice in the context of how we are to treat our neighbours, but He always stressed that our first obligation is to God. Although the Second Commandment is linked closely to the First, it does come second. His

Apostles and the early Fathers of the Church continued to emphasise this point. St John in his First Letter says: *"We can be sure that we know God only by keeping His commandments. Anyone who says: 'I know him' and does not keep His commandments is a liar, refusing to admit the truth"*. Was it not Jesus Himself who said: *"If you love Me, keep my commandments"*? Faith is a gift, but it requires an act of will on our part to accept it if it is to bear fruit. We cannot opt out of moral responsibility. Without this, free will has no meaning and human dignity goes down the drain with the bath water. We are each responsible for our own salvation, and the rest of God's creation, including our neighbour, is there to help us. But we are free to misuse God's creatures. I can, for instance, use other people for my own sexual gratification. I can use food, drink and material possessions for my own enjoyment without a thought for other people. In today's Gospel Jesus says, in effect, that it would be better never to have had a sexual partner than through sexual immorality to spend eternity regretting one's folly: it would be better to be a teetotaller than to suffer spiritual death through unrestrained alcohol abuse: it would be better to live one's life as a poverty-stricken peasant in some Third World backwater than to live a life of selfish luxury in a First World jet set and find oneself in hell for living off the backs of poor people through economic blackmail. "If", says Jesus, "on reflection you find yourself in danger of such a fate through misuse of God's creation, then cut that abuse out of your life, even if it leaves you maimed in some way".

Christian socialism was inspired by the Gospels, and the welfare state to which it gave birth had many admirable features, but, like most things, it can and has been abused, and the abuse tends to produce a mentality which assumes that there will always be someone around who will pick up the pieces no matter how big a mess we make of things. It tends to diminish a sense of personal responsibility. The aftermath of communism in Eastern Europe should be a kind of mirror which reveals the causes of some of the ills in our own society. We shall not redress the balance by swinging back to 19th century laissez-faire, but I believe the Churches must re-emphasise the fundamental principle of personal morality without this time ceasing to emphasise the parallel obligation of social justice.

I will end by reminding you of the well-known analogy of the carpet-makers. In the East where they still make carpets on hand looms, several people sit on a long bench and each weaves a specific part of the pattern on the reverse side of the canvas. Provided they each do their share of the work properly a perfect pattern will result, although they cannot see it while they work. But if one of them is more concerned about someone else's pattern and goes off to help them instead of attending to their own the overall pattern will be ruined. God has a specific role for each of us in his plan for our generation. If we devote our attention and energies to correcting other people's morality instead of first attending to our own, God's plan will be frustrated. If we can do both – fine, but God comes first.

TWENTY-NINTH SUNDAY OF THE YEAR

GOSPEL READING - MARK 10:35-45

In the 60s and 70s 'leadership' became a pejorative word in some quarters because it was thought to have autocratic and military overtones, and in the 60s it was fashionable to be anti the military. Selection also became a dirty word. If everyone is equal then everyone should not only have the same chances but be given the same treatment. In the Catholic Church the pejorative term was 'triumphalism'. In fact, anything which might be construed as 'elitist' was definitely out. In case these ideas are still around and accepted uncritically it might, perhaps, be a good idea to re-examine today's gospel, because it is as significant for what Jesus did not say as for what He did. Let's look at the background.

From all the hundreds of people Jesus must have met and known He selected just twelve. He did not ask for applications; He called those twelve men individually and specifically. So He was not against selection. Then during the three years of His public ministry He devoted most of His time to giving special training to the twelve, training which He did not give to others. We know this, for instance, from the parables. After He had spoken to the crowds He explained the parables privately to the Apostles. Once they asked Him why He did this. *"Because"* He replied, *"the mysteries of the Kingdom of Heaven are revealed to you but not to them... the reason I talk to them in parables is that they look without seeing and listen without hearing or understanding"*. St Matthew adds: *"He would never speak to them except in parables"*. What could be more elitist than to be given private tuition by the Son of God!

The aim of this selection and special training was to provide leaders for His Church, so He approved of leadership. And then from the twelve He appointed one as head, or commander if you like. Peter was not chosen by democratic vote. Jesus decided on his appointment off His own bat, and we learn from the Acts of the Apostles that the others accepted Peter's primacy. So the Church Jesus founded was hierarchical from the start.

But now comes the point of today's gospel, which should be read in conjunction with St Matthew, Chapter 20, verses 20-28.

The mother of the sons of Zebedee had ambitions for her boys. She wanted to see them powerful and prosperous in the kingdom Jesus was always talking about. Now there's nothing wrong with ambition, in fact it is a natural human instinct without which the human race would never have progressed, but its justification depends upon the object of one's ambition – and this is the point Jesus makes. There is nothing wrong in having an ambition to be holy, in trying to be as like Jesus Christ as we are capable of being. Jesus said Himself; *"You must be perfect as your heavenly Father is perfect"*. There's nothing wrong if your ambition is to devote your life to helping the sick, the elderly and the poor. It's a good thing to want to do your work to the very best of your ability, and to become competent in your profession and hobbies. Hopefully, for example, all doctors and nurses, priests, engineers, administrators, teachers want to become good doctors, nurses, priests, engineers, administrators and teachers. But, says Jesus, ambition can be misconceived and misdirected. The world sees privilege, talent and education as a means of advancement to power and wealth. Jesus says this is not to happen to His followers. He was not giving special training to His disciples so that they could become ruthless autocrats like the despots who surrounded them in the pagan world. No, His leaders must approach their tasks as the servants of the communities they were to lead. It is significant that for St John, the apostle closest to Jesus, the event at the last supper which most stuck in his mind was not the institution of the Eucharist but the washing of the feet.

Good doctors and nurses are those whose patients have first call on their time. Only when they have attended to their needs do they think of putting their feet up. The good service officer is the one whose first concern is the safety and care of his men. Only when they have been attended to does he think about himself. The good parish priest is the one who puts the needs and care of his parishioners before his own interests and comfort. He must provide a lead for his parish, that is one reason why he is a PP, but not as an autocrat. An absence of leadership is a recipe for chaos: autocratic leadership is a recipe for tyranny. As always there is a right balance somewhere in between: a balance not always easy to strike.

If we are honest I guess we would all have to admit that we get a bit of a kick out of one-upmanship, of seeing our ideas triumph over the opposition's – and this is true whether we are operating as individuals or as members of a group. Victory is sweet! Alas, unrestrained ambition to get the better of the opposition can rear its ugly head within the family circle and within the parish community. It is not a purely commercial or political phenomenon. This is why Jesus warned His disciples. If you don't watch yourselves, He told them, you could very easily use your position to feather your own nests and become like the pagans. And lest we think all this applies only to people in positions of authority, let's recall that by comparison with more than half the world's population all of us here this morning are privileged by virtue of our education, our standard of living and above all by the gift of faith we have received. Let's see if we cannot use what talents we have for the benefit of the communities which we live in, to be of service to them, including, I say again, our families. Public service used to be an occupation much respected. Too often nowadays it has become public manipulation.

THIRTIETH SUNDAY OF THE YEAR

GOSPEL READING - LUKE 18:9-14

When a friend of mine became headmaster of a well-known school I happened to be one of the first visitors to his official residence. It so happened that he was on the telephone when I arrived and his secretary asked me if I would mind waiting in his drawing-room, so I had a chance to look round before he came in to greet me. There were a number of interesting pictures on the walls, but one in particular immediately attracted my notice. Unlike some of the others it was only a print, but the subject so obsessed me that I was determined to find the original, which eventually I ran to earth in the Episcopal Cathedral in Edinburgh's West End. The title of the picture is "The Presence" and it was painted by A E Borthwick, an Edwardian artist, in 1910. In the picture the artist places you, the viewer, at the back of a large gothic church. At the far end is the high altar where a mass is taking place. The priest is elevating the host above his head and the congregation, who occupy the front benches in the nave, have their eyes fixed on it. The front part of the church is bathed in brilliant light. There are no lights at the back; what light there is is reflected from the front. There is just enough light, however, to discover behind the rearmost column on the left the figure of a beggar crouching on the floor. He is obviously feeling so out of place and so unworthy that he can barely bring himself to look at the altar, and he is holding his right hand to his forehead to shade his eyes from the light. Just behind him, in a kind of ghostly halo, is the figure of Christ who has his arm outstretched and is just about to place his hand on the beggar's shoulder. I can never now read the story of the Pharisee and the Publican without seeing Borthwick's picture in my mind's eye. It has brought home to me, as nothing else has, the relevance of Jesus's story to our contemporary world.

Jesus had some pretty hard things to say about the Jewish hierarchy of His day, and in particular the Pharisees. He called them hypocrites, whited sepulchres and a brood of vipers. In fact the Pharisees had their good points, but what Jesus disliked most about people in authority, whoever they were, was insistence on the external ritual of religion while failing to practise its real meaning, and exacting the penalties of the law from others while not observing it themselves. Worst of all he abhorred the snobbishness and pride by which they thought of themselves as superior to the lower classes and to foreigners. *"I thank you, God, that I am not grasping, unjust, adulterous like the rest of mankind, and particularly that I am not like this tax collector here. I fast twice a week; I pay tithes on all I get,"* says the Pharisee in the story. Yes, he may have kept the rules, but he despised the Publican because he was an employee of the hated Romans for whom he collected taxes. The Jews thought of themselves as God's chosen people and on that account a cut above the pagans by whom they were surrounded; just as the Romans, who were pagans, thought of themselves as the master race and a cut above all foreigners including the Jews. If we are honest, I think we have to admit that similar tendencies can be found at times among both Roman Catholics and the British; less today, perhaps, than a couple of generations ago but there just the same.

Jesus was a Jew born into the royal house of David, yet he went out of His way to make friends of people who belonged to what we should nowadays call the working class and to those on the margins of society – prostitutes, tax gatherers, lepers and others. Moreover, we know that He did not restrict His miracles to the Jews for there are instances in the gospels of His healing Romans and other foreigners. We know that He had followers and friends among the better off – Nicodemus, Joseph of Arimathea, and probably Lazarus, for example – but we find Him mostly among the poor. No one who came to Him in trouble seeking help, no one who came to listen to His teaching with a genuine desire to follow Him, did He ever cast out, no matter who they were or where they came from – and neither should we. If Catholics are true followers of Jesus and worthy of the claim their Church makes of being the only repository of the whole of revealed truth, then they should welcome everyone: snobbishness and pharisaism should not be so much as known among them.

The Roman Catholic Church puts much time and energy into its liturgy to make it reverent, relevant and an inspiration to those who attend: it even goes so far as to make attendance at Sunday mass obligatory. But if those who preside at and those who take part in the liturgical ceremonies do not in their daily lives try to conform to the precepts Jesus sets out in the gospels then they are in danger of the very things He criticized in the Pharisees. It seems to me very significant that in His description of the Last Judgement (which is recorded in St Matthew, chapter 25) Jesus does not mention anything remotely connected with liturgy; His sole criterion for salvation or damnation is how a person has treated his neighbour. This does not mean that liturgy is unimportant, but it does indicate, surely, that care of our neighbour is more important. St Paul hammers home the same point in his First Letter to the Corinthians (chapter 13): *"If I have all the eloquence of men and of angels, but speak without love, I am simply a gong booming or a cymbal clashing. If I have The gift of prophecy, understanding all the mysteries there are, and knowing everything, and if I have faith in all its fullness, to move mountains, but without love, then I am nothing at all. If I give away all I possess, piece by piece, and if I even let them take my body to burn it, but am without love, it will do me no good whatever."* St John uses different words but expresses the same idea in his First Letter: *"In this way we distinguish the children of God from the children of the devil: anybody not living a holy life and not loving his brother is no child of God's. This is the message as you heard it from the beginning: that we are to love one another...His commandments are these: that we believe in the name of his Son Jesus Christ and that we love one another".* When one of the Pharisees asked Jesus which was the greatest commandment of the Law, He replied: *"You must love the Lord your God with all your heart, with all your soul, and with all your mind. This is the greatest and the first commandment. The second resembles it: You must love your neighbour as yourself. On these two commandments hang the whole Law and the Prophets also."*

To try to emulate Jesus involves accepting the cross. *"Unless you are willing to take up your cross daily you cannot be my disciple,"* He said. If we stand up for justice for the poor and the unpopular, if we stand up for christian principles of morality and refuse to be seduced by false prophets, if we let it be seen that we do not follow the way of the world, then sooner or later we shall incur the hostility of the world and its leaders. Archbishop Warlock and Bishop Sheppard of Liverpool, who have defended the rights of the poor and fearlessly criticised government actions which they considered unjust, have regularly been the target of criticism by the Establishment. Irina Ratushinskaya, the physicist and poet, who spent several years in a Soviet gulag for her outspoken christian views, was once asked what shocked her most when, after her release, she came to the West. "Half-hearted christians," she replied. "It has become possible in the West to be all things to all men and to deny you are a christian. In my country there is no point in pretending to be a christian because it might cost you your life."

We catholic christians should be known for our welcoming love, for our lack of discrimination in our care for others, for the absence of snobbery in our communities, for our humility and generosity, for the genuine sincerity of our liturgy, so that we may each in our own way be a little light to lead people out of darkness into the light of faith in our Lord and Saviour, Jesus Christ. May the God of light and of power and might be with you all. Amen.

THE FEAST OF CHRIST THE KING

THE LAST SUNDAY OF THE LITURGICAL YEAR
GOSPEL READING - JOHN 18:33-37

If someone were to ask me: "Are you a Catholic?", if I was to be strictly honest, I think I should have to reply: "I don't know", because, you see, I am not absolutely certain what 'being a Catholic' means. Does it mean someone who regularly attends Sunday Mass? Is it someone who acknowledges the Pope? Is it someone whose name is written in the baptismal register of a catholic church somewhere? Are there degrees of being a Catholic? Can I say that Mrs X sitting in the front row is a better Catholic than Mr Y who sits one row behind? If I can, then by what criteria do I decide?

Our Lord gave us some tests by which we could tell whether we might consider ourselves His followers. *"If you love me, keep my commandments"*, He said. *"Love your neighbour as yourself"*, He said. He also said, *"Love your enemies"*: *"Forgive and you will be forgiven"*. So what about my friend down the road who is not a Catholic but who keeps the commandments better than I do; who is more charitable than I am; who is more generous and forgiving than I am? Are we to say that because he is not a Catholic his chances of getting to heaven are pretty slim, whereas because I am a Catholic mine are pretty good? Surely that can't be right. But if it isn't, why is it important for me to be a Catholic? In other words, what is catholicism? Does it consist of a minimum level of knowledge about God which a person must have before they can call themselves a Catholic — a sort of catechism test? Or is it a kind of religious package which if I possess I am in, if I don't I am out? The picture which follows is intended to help us answer some of these questions:

A word about the picture. You can see a road meandering across a landscape. There are lots of people walking along it, but there are others who have wandered off the road into the countryside round about. In fact there are some so far from the road they probably don't know that it even exists. In the middle of the picture there is a fork in the road. Some people have gone off to the right. If they go far enough along it they will find it comes to a dead end. (Perhaps you have taken some dead end turnings in your life and have had to retrace your steps. I certainly have.) At the back of the picture are some mountains and beyond them the Eternal City, the heavenly Jerusalem. Those people who continue along the right road will eventually reach it.

Every man and woman starts the journey of life at birth. Once started there is no turning back. Time takes us ever forward. Running through life is a road of faith laid down by God who made the world and created life. We are at liberty to walk along that road or to walk across the untamed country to either side. As they make their way forward everyone is searching for something which will enable them to make sense of life, to give it meaning and purpose. Many people never find God's road, but owing to His goodness we have. Moreover he has given us a map for our journey which we call the Bible. But others besides Catholics have the Bible and, let's face it, many non-Catholics know a good deal more about it than some of us. What we have, but nobody else has, are guides specially commissioned by Christ Himself. If any of you have stood in the middle of Dartmoor in the driving rain with a map but with no points of reference visible and not the foggiest idea where you are, you will remember that your map was pretty useless. What you wanted desperately was a good guide who could either lead you to your destination or at least explain to you where you were and point you in the right direction. We have just such guides on our journey in faith. We believe that through the laying on of hands down the centuries our Pope and bishops are the successors of St Peter and the apostles to whom Christ gave the keys of the Kingdom. We know that in the essential items of faith and morals they will not lead us astray but show us the right turnings to take. This is why it is important to be a Catholic. This is why we should value very much the gift of faith we have been given. But let's be clear. Faith is a gift from God freely given. *"You did not choose me: I chose you"*, He said. Why He should have chosen us we don't know, but that He has should make us extremely humble and never smug. We are just as prone to wander off the road into the bush as anyone else if we don't stick with our guides.

But a journey, of necessity, involves change. As you move along you pass through different types of countryside, some smooth and pleasant, others rough and forbidding. And we change too. Physically and mentally none of us is the same person we were this time last year, nor are our circumstances the same. So it is with our faith. If my understanding of my faith and my knowledge of God has not grown then there is something wrong. This is why it is such a serious mistake to think of our faith as a package of some kind. To possess a package implies completion; there is no room for expansion. Some people's faith seems to have become frozen, as it were, in childhood and has never grown since, even though they may now be quite old. In the same way, if we are always looking to the Church of the past as some kind of golden age, we are like people walking along the road backwards, not looking where we are going. Our mind is elsewhere and we are oblivious of the countryside around. There is no way we can recreate the past.

The old Tridentine Church which some of us loved so much came to an end in 1965 when the Second Vatican Council finished. We can no more bring it back than we can our own youth. The world of 1995 is a very different world from that of 1935, and the Church must adapt itself to the new circumstances of the times. What is always the same is God's truth, which is the same yesterday, today and the same for ever. But because it is a living truth it has to be re-interpreted and made relevant to each successive age.

But our faith has not been given to us for ourselves alone. Our Lord told his followers that they are to be "the light of the world". *"You do not light a candle,"* He said, *"and place it under a barrel but on a candlestick so that it may light up the room." "A city built on a mountain top cannot be hidden"*, He said. So He wants us to spread the light of our faith to those around us, and He showed us how to do it. In that wonderful episode on the road to Emmaus he came quietly alongside the two disconsolate disciples, as one wayfarer coming upon another, and just listened to their troubles. He did not make them feel spare by criticising them or, as we might say, by ramming religion down their throats. He let them finish their story and then offered an explanation. By making them feel at home in His presence He restored their confidence and became their friend. So much so that when the day began to draw in they tried to persuade Him to spend the night with them. To listen, to understand, to be able to restore confidence and offer a meaning to life, is how we too can help the people we come into contact with on our own journey of faith. This is what the Rite of Christian Initiation of Adults is about.

So as we join together as pilgrims along God's road of faith, it is our privilege to share in the evangelistic mission of the Church, by faithfully and joyfully helping other pilgrims we meet to find the Way, the Truth and the Life. This is our destiny. It was for this that we were baptized. It was for this that we were confirmed. It was for this that the Son of God humbled Himself and was born of a woman so that He could be with us in all things, except Sin, even temptation. He Himself has trodden this very same road and has experienced the rough and the smooth. Having given the last drop of His blood for us He did not leave this world as we do when we die. He rose from the dead. He came back. He is alive. He is with us on our journey. This is the great, the unique, christian message; the good news. And as if that was not enough, to reassure us of His presence and strengthen our faith He is sacramentally present whenever and wherever the words of consecration are said, as they will be very shortly at this altar. Our religion is not a book religion. It is not something static like a building or a package. It centres on a person; a real, live, loving, person: Jesus Christ.

He is also our king in the old understanding of that word. The way politics have developed we tend to think only in terms of dictatorship or democracy, but originally a king was a law-giver and judge, yes, but also the father of his people. The one who warded off danger from them, who saw they had food, and clothing and shelter, who was approachable and who set their wrongs to rights. Jesus is our king but also our humble companion. "Behold your king comes to you, humble and riding on a donkey", as the prophet foretold.

To those of you whose lives at the moment seem perhaps to be drab and dreary; perhaps filled with unhappiness, or apparent failure, even despair, I would say with the Psalmist: “Lift up your eyes to the hills whence comes our salvation”. Though from where you are now (like those two people at the bottom right-hand corner of the picture) the Heavenly City may be obscured by the trees and the undergrowth around you, or by the mountains in the distance, if you keep your hand in the hand of your King, your Companion, your Divine Guide, He will lead you through the thickets and over the boulders and bring you soon to those “fresh and green pastures, and those restful waters”, mentioned in the responsorial psalm, and thence to His heavenly kingdom where one day we all hope to be. Amen.

A SELECTION

of

HOMILIES AND TALKS

for

SPECIAL OCCASIONS

A HOMILY FOR MIDNIGHT MASS

CHRISTMAS 1984

One of the wickedest things done by the godless world we live in is to deprive children of their innocence. It is done in the name of something called 'realism', which means that if something exists or happens the knowledge of it should be freely available, irrespective of the age, mental capacity or the ability of the person to cope. Censorship in any form is shouted down. So things that, as recently as my youth, were in the main known only to adults are known about in all their earthy details by quite small children. A recent survey estimated that four out of ten children over the age of six see sadistic sex and sickening violence, mostly portrayed on home videos. Is it any wonder that many teenagers and young adults complain of being bored! "How boring everything is", they say. One reason is that they have already seen, and perhaps experienced many of life's mysteries, so there is little else to wonder at, no new heights of human experience to scale.

I am sure you will have noticed in media coverage of our Holy Father, Pope John Paul, how he makes a beeline for the little children whenever he plunges into a crowd come to see him. He is, of course, only following the example of our Divine Lord who, we know from the Gospels, also had a predilection for little children. In fact, He said that unless we become like them we shall not enter the Kingdom of Heaven.

You see, there is something very special about innocence and purity. Only the pure of heart shall see God, Jesus said. Our sins and our worldly wisdom block the channels of grace between us and God, but the minds of the innocent are open to His graces. This is why He said that the mysteries of faith are hidden from the clever and learned and revealed to little children.

Because Our Lord values innocence so highly He was withering in His condemnation of those who scandalize children. If you allow the bud of a beautiful flower to open in its own good time, it will develop naturally and show you the beauty of creation in all its glory. If you prize open the bud and try to pull out the petals before they are ready, the flower will grow up dog-eared and deformed. So too, if you subject small children to all the ugliness and trauma of adult life, they too will grow up with their minds and souls scarred and unbalanced. Remember Our Lord's words for those who destroy the innocence of children: *"They would be better drowned in the depth of the sea with a great millstone round their necks".*

On this Christmas Night I appeal to the parents of young children, to all who teach in primary schools, and also to teenagers and young adults who have younger brothers or sisters, to protect the innocence of your little ones. I know the tide is running strongly against us, but we must do all we can. Let us never forget that there is an 'off' switch on the TV, that we are entitled to censor the literature coming into our houses, and that we do have rights as parents in the schools our children attend.

So at Christmas time let the little ones have their fantasies; let them continue to "see the world in a grain of sand: a heaven in a wild flower". Above all, take them to the crib. Explain to them who the Child is lying in the straw. Talk to them about angels, shepherds and kings. Those things were not beneath the dignity of the Lord of creation, so they should be very real to us. Perhaps for the adults who have been through God's grinding mill in the world, this is the time to become once again 'like little children' alongside our own little ones and to contemplate in the silence of the night the simplicity of Bethlehem, the things which God loves but the world scorns: innocence, purity, utter dependence on the God who loves us, and the joy of security in the arms of Mary, Virgin and Mother.

Know you what it is to be a child?
It is to be something very different
from the man of today.
It is to have a spirit still streaming
from the waters of baptism, it is to
believe in love, to believe in loveliness,
to believe in belief.

It is to be so little that the elves can
whisper in your ear; it is to turn pump-
kins into coaches,mice into horses,
lowliness into loftiness,and nothing into
everything, for each child has his fairy
godmother in his own soul.

It is to live in a nutshell and consider
yourself the king of infinite space.

It is:–
'To see the world in a grain of sand,
And a heaven in a wild flower,
To hold infinity in the palm of your hand
And eternity in an hour.'

Lines from Francis Thompson
Verse by William Blake

SPIRITUAL COLLOQUY WITH A PARISH SMALL GROUP

'WHAT DID YOU GO OUT INTO THE DESERT TO SEE?' (Matt 11:7)

At last week's 'Opening Doors' several people expressed their problems and doubts about being conscious of God in the midst of the hustle and bustle of the ordinary working day, and about the feasibility of making one's work (whether paid employment or family duties) into a prayer. I thought a few ideas on the subject might be a help.

We live in a world which is full of noise. It is scarcely possible to find a place where you cannot hear the sound of an aeroplane, or the hum of traffic pounding along a main road, or the blaring of canned music, or some other man-made noise. I sometimes have wondered what has happened to the bird-song I used to hear as a child. If I stop and listen hard enough it is still there but overlaid by lots of other noises.

We also live in a world in which the media bombard us with news, supposed news, scares, disasters, opinions, rumours, forecasts: things which are constantly pulling our minds this way and that. The Catholic Church has not been exempt from this turmoil.

A growing number of spiritual writers have been drawing attention to the lessons to be learnt from the example of the early desert fathers, who in the midst of the controversies and heresies of the first Christian centuries retired to the solitude of the desert in search of God. A similar thing happened several centuries later when civilisation in the West disintegrated with the collapse of the Roman Empire. St Benedict led the way into remote places where small groups of people lived together in monasteries where the regime consisted of alternate prayer and work with periods of silence built in.

God is not to be found in turmoil, frenetic activity and constant noise. Jesus told us that He will come and live in us: He in us and we in Him, but we cannot find Him within us or hear His voice if our minds and heart are full of all sorts of other things. In the physical world it is impossible to hear properly what someone is saying and concentrate on their words if there is a cacophony of competing sounds blaring in our ears. If we would find God within us and develop a constant awareness of His presence we have to create within us a spiritual desert to which we can retreat. It takes time and practice, but the further into the desert we can take our hermitage the less we shall be troubled by the noises and the siren voices of the busy world, which will become progressively less distracting and important to us. We can then fly to our desert for five minutes, two minutes, twenty minutes, however much time we can spare, and sit quietly at the feet of our beloved Master who will always be there waiting for our visits, to calm, to comfort, to instruct, to love.

Let me give you a few short quotes from a book I have been reading:

> *'We have indeed to fashion our own desert where we can withdraw each day and dwell in the gentle healing presence of Our Lord.'*

> *'The Word of God is born out of the eternal silence of God, and it is to this Word out of silence we want to be witnesses. Silence is the home of the Word. Words (about God) are meant to disclose the mystery of the silence from which they come.'*

> *'The desert fathers did not think of solitude as being alone, but as being alone with God. They did not think of silence as not speaking, but as listening to God. Solitude and silence are the context within which prayer is practised.'*

One way to carry prayer with us into the working day is to take a short phrase, such as 'The Lord is my shepherd' and repeat it often, rather as we might whistle a catchy tune or sing a line from the latest hit song as we go about our work.

> *'This way of simple prayer, when we are faithful to it, and practise it at regular times, leads us slowly to an experience of rest and opens us to God's active presence. When, for instance, we have spent ten minutes or so in the early morning sitting in the presence of God with the words 'The Lord is my shepherd' they may slowly build a little nest for themselves in our heart and stay there for the rest of the day. Even while we are talking, studying, gardening, or building, the prayer can continue in our heart and keep us aware of God's ever-present guidance. The discipline is not directed toward coming to a deeper insight into what it means that God is called our Shepherd, but toward coming to the inner experience of God's shepherding action in whatever we think, do, or say.'*

As our desert hermitage becomes more firmly established we shall find ourselves slipping back there more and more often, even in the midst of the most hectic day, because our awareness that He whom we love is there will draw us there every moment we can spare. We shall, in fact, have fallen in love with God and want to spend any spare moment with Him.

When we return from our desert to the hurly burly of city or home we take our Loved One with us and thus are able to sanctify all our actions so that our work becomes a prayer in itself. We are working in His creation with His creatures. As the bread and wine are offered at Mass for sacrifice, so our work is offered for sacrifice too.

In this way we shall gradually become pools of peace in a turbulent society. Last week we were discussing how to attract the young to the Church.

> *'It is that restful heart that will attract those who are groping to find their way through life.'*

> *'May mind and tongue made strong in love,*
> *Your praise throughout the world proclaim,*
> *And may that love within our hearts*
> *Set fire to others with its flame.'*

You may think at first sight that what I have said sounds like advising withdrawal from reality to live in a fantasy world of make-believe. In fact God is the true reality. When we find Him and begin to live our lives with Him and in Him we shall become more balanced and restful people who are able to put the happenings around us into perspective, the proper perspective of eternal values. Moreover, as love of God and love of neighbour are intertwined we shall find it much easier to love those with whom we live our lives, and they will find us much easier to live with.

> *'Prayer is the deep personal meeting with our Lord which must have repercussions in our daily meetings with others. Do not be satisfied with a 'time for prayer' but keep that fresh and 'seeking' attitude towards the God of your heart'.*

If you want a daily phrase to take with you while you work, may I suggest you try the First Letter of St John, phrase by phrase?

If this makes any sense at all I strongly recommend two little books by Carlo Carretto from which the quotations are taken: 'The Desert in the City' and 'Letters from the Desert'

MAUNDY THURSDAY 1985

A HOMILY ON CHRIST'S AGONY IN THE GARDEN

The mental agony which Jesus Christ suffered in the Garden of Gethsemeni the night before His death on the cross has, I believe, a special relevance to, a special message for, the Western World of the 1980s. There cannot have been a time when so many people have suffered from depression, neuroses and mental illnesses of different kinds. Doctors' surgeries and psychiatric hospitals are full of people suffering from such problems; and let's not make the mistake of thinking that a lot of them are weak-minded malingerers. Modern life imposes stresses and strains unknown to former generations. Severe depression can be a form of hell. It can be caused by many things. It may be bereavement; it may be the inability to cope with financial matters or the demands of the workplace; it may be the break-up of a relationship; it may be a weakness of character which leaves us open to addiction to alcohol or sex or drugs; but whatever the cause the victim gets caught up into a vicious spiral which drags him or her down and down. In such a condition a person feels increasingly helpless, that life has got out of control. Beyond a certain stage the soul finds itself outside the range of help provided by well-meaning people – relatives, friends, doctors. The soul sinks deeper and deeper into a kind of black, bottomless pit, eventually finding itself forced into a corner from which there is seemingly no escape. All about is darkness. This is, I suggest, a real form of hell, akin to that permanent hell reserved for those who die unrepentant. In this extreme condition the soul comes face to face with despair, that final refuge of broken humanity – and one of the deadly sins, because once a soul has gone over the edge into total despair even God Himself cannot rescue it.

But strangely enough it has been when on the very edge of despair that some souls have found their God for the very first time. He appears first as a tiny dot of light in the darkness. In my despair I make one last groping effort to move towards the light. Eventually I sense that someone has me by the hand. As Gerontius says in Cardinal Newman's wonderful poem:

Another marvel: someone has me fast within his ample palm.
A uniform and gentle pressure tells me that I am not self-moving
But borne forward on my way.

It is God who has taken my hand. I begin to feel the warmth of His grace seeping back into my soul which had been chilled to the point of death. And then, as we say every morning in the 'Benedictus' in the Divine Office:

He will give light to those in darkness.
Those who dwell in the shadow of death.
And guide us into the way of peace.

or as the Psalmist puts it:

He conceals me with His pinions
And under His wings I find refuge.

It is then that I know, that I know beyond the possibility of doubt, that it is God who has saved me, that my God is really and truly alive: that "Our God reigns".

He can save us and restore our health of mind and body because He is God, but He can comfort us and win our love because He has been down into that dreadful pit before us. That night in the Garden He got as near to despair as it was possible for Him who was both man and God to get.

St Luke tells us that "His sweat fell to the ground as great drops of blood". That is not a flight of poetic licence; it is, I have been told, a condition known to medical science. Admittedly it is very rare and occurs only under the most extreme conditions of mental torture, great fear, profound emotion and physical debility – but it happens. Not only was Jesus terrified at the prospect of the physical torture which He knew was now only a matter of hours away, but He was conscious of the terrible insult to His heavenly Father which the sin of mankind represents. Moreover, it seemed at that moment as if His whole life and ministry had been a total failure and waste of time. On top of all that was the crushing let-down of being abandoned by those He had taken into His intimate friendship and trained to carry on His work. He felt crushed, flattened, and in His agony and terror He cried out to His Father: *"Take this cup from me"*. He felt He couldn't go on: He had reached the end of His tether. Yet even in that extremity He somehow dredged up enough courage to add: *"But let Your will be done, not mine"*.

My Brothers and Sisters in Christ, there is no human condition so hopeless, so appalling, so terrifying, so humiliating, so degrading, that He does not understand, that He cannot cure, that He cannot surround and consume with His fantastic love. By His mental agony, His physical sufferings and His death on the cross we are healed. Sin pulls us apart: His love restores unity within us and puts our life back into balance so that we become whole and at peace within ourselves and also at peace with the world around us. We can echo the words in Psalm 17:

He snatched me from my powerful foe,
From my enemies whose strength I could not match.

By His stripes we are healed: in His death is our victory.

This is the good news: Our God lives; Christ has risen; Jesus saves; He brings back the lost sheep into the fold; He rescues the lost soul from the depths of hell on earth; but above all, He loves us. Indeed He loves us so much that before He left the upper room for Gethsemeni He said the very first Mass and left His body and blood to us for all time so that we could always go to Him in a visible form to draw strength and healing. If we really believe this, how can we keep it to ourselves? Must we not go out from here and tell the whole world, that world outside which needs Him so badly but which does not know what we have been given? As Andrew said to Peter the morning after He had first met Jesus: "We have found the Messiah".

THE HOSPITAL SERMON

FEAST OF ST LUKE – SUNDAY 20TH OCTOBER 1985

CHURCH OF ST PAUL & ST PETER THE GREAT, CHICHESTER

Scripture Reading: Genesis Chapter 3

"You will be like gods, knowing good and evil"

To read some of the things which have been written, and to listen to some of the things which are said, one might be forgiven for thinking that christianity and medicine were of their very nature antipathetic and antagonistic. On the one hand there are churchmen who belay the medical profession as though it was hell-bent on perverting public morals: on the other there are medical scientists and doctors who are so puffed up with pride in their achievements that they will admit in the sphere of medicine no judges but themselves, believing that they alone are qualified to judge in their own cause. They regard God as an irrelevance, of no more scientific interest than Hans Anderson's fairy tales.

In fact, there is every reason why christianity and medical science can, and should, work together earnestly and in harmony for the greater good of humanity, as Archbishop William Temple reminded us when he founded the Churches' Council for Health and Healing some forty years ago. Even the most cursory reading of the gospels reveals that Christ spent much of His public ministry healing people of both physical and mental illnesses. When He sent out His disciples on their missions He enjoined them to heal the sick. The care of the sick has been a central activity of Christianity ever since. In medieval times it was the Church which in Europe built and ran the first hospitals. Even in more recent times, prior to the establishment of State medical provision, many of the hospitals in this country relied a good deal upon the Churches to raise funds for them and provide all sorts of voluntary assistance. To "visit the sick" is one of the corporal works of mercy.

At this point I want to pay my personal tribute to the medical profession. It is easy to criticize doctors, many of whom are overworked, but when I am in pain or seriously worried about my health I am jolly glad to see my doctor and I find it difficult to imagine what I should feel like if there was no doctor to come to me. I also want to bang the drum for nurses. I have been in many hospitals, both as patient and visitor, and I have yet to find a lazy unpleasant nurse. They seem to me to be angels of mercy (since we don't know whether the heavenly angels are sexual beings I include male nurses in what I am saying) who do most unpleasant things for us with a smile and good humour, who work long hours and who don't go on strike when offered a miserable pay award. I cannot think of any profession we should miss more if it was not there. I personally do not want to go back to the days of Trafalgar when they gave you a couple of tots of rum and then proceeded to cut your leg off with a hack saw. Come to think of it, I don't even want to go back to times as recent as those of my boyhood. I still have nightmarish recollections of a fearsome man named Mr Pimley, a dentist, who bored away mercilessly at my tooth while pounding away on a foot treadle. He maintained that injections were warranted only for extractions, but even then his practice was not as good as his theory. On one occasion he made such a mess of an extraction that my parents had to take me back to his surgery late at night because my mother was afraid that if the haemorrhage was not stopped I might not be around to say good morning to her next day. No, I am thankful for modern medicine.

So why is there sometimes conflict between religion and medicine? I suggest the answer is pride. Pride was the first sin, that of Lucifer and his rebel angels, and it has been at the root of most sins ever since. Churchmen (and I speak as a member of the clergy) are inclined to think that they alone have been given the gift of wisdom and that their pronouncements on matters involving moral judgements must be accepted as though they had just descended from Mount Sinai. When medical scientists develop some new technique the Church is wise, in my opinion, if She takes time to assess this new phenomenon. To rush in with instant theology can lead to red faces later on. We do well to remember the case of Galileo. Churchmen should have the humility to listen carefully to the explanations and advice of reputable doctors, and to pray earnestly with an open mind, a mind attentive to the voice of the Holy Spirit. The full implications of something new are not always evident in the first instance. On the other hand, there are some matters about which the Church long ago made up its mind. Abortion, for example, has been around for a long time, as far back as the generation of Cain and Abel, I would guess. Modern developments have done no more than refine the techniques and remove the physical, though not, I think, the mental dangers. The Church is clear about its condemnation of abortion, though there should always be compassion for the victims, both the living and the dead.

But humility is needed as much by the medical profession as by the Church. We live in an age of fantastic scientific and technological achievement, the speed of which is gathering pace all the time. There is a very real danger that modern man may be so eaten up with pride in his achievements that he will come to think he can manage the universe: to kid himself that, given a little more time to perfect the computer, he will be able so to organize things that he will bring about that fabled millennium of happiness and prosperity for all. As the reading from the

Book of Genesis which we have just listened to has reminded us, it was falling for temptation of 'know all' which destroyed the first paradise, and it will certainly not usher in a second. *"Then the Serpent said to the woman: 'No. You will not die. God knows in fact that on the day you eat the fruit your eyes will be opened and you will be like gods, knowing good and evil ".* To be like gods has been the ambition of proud men all down the ages, but the living God will brook no rival, and the anger of God is terrible, as the Scriptures warn us. To find out what this kind of overweening pride might lead the human race to we have only to look at the frightful engines of war which this same modern science has produced; and I am not just thinking of nuclear weapons which have grabbed the headlines, but of chemical and biological weapons and the terrifying power of the latest so-called conventional weapons as well. Ours is the first generation in the whole history of mankind to know how the world could be destroyed. Until now people could only speculate. If medical scientists persist in forging ahead with experiments on the human body and its reproductive system without any regard to a moral imperative, without reference to the Creator, without engaging in serious dialogue with men and women of prayer and responsible people at all levels of society, then I believe there is a very real danger that evil things will be set in train which it may not be possible to control or halt.

In Old Testament times God did not save a wicked and adulterous generation from the consequences of its own folly, when it refused to listen to those whom He sent to warn it, so why should we think He will save this generation if it persists in ignoring His precepts and refusing to read the writing which is very clearly on the wall? All of us – doctors, priests, lay people – need to go on our knees before the God who made us, to humble ourselves, admit that we don't know all the answers and beg Him to guide us with the wisdom which only He possesses. Let us ask Him to take away our pride, so that we may indeed continue to discover the wonders and riches of His creation, but in a way which will be for the real benefit of human kind and not that which leads to its destruction. In all the controversy surrounding the contraceptive pill there are two things, often connected with it, and in particular where girls under the age of consent are concerned, which are seldom mentioned, often, surprisingly, even by christian disputants and commentators. These two things are fornication and adultery, both of which are condemned in both the Old and New Testaments. The modern world may choose to disregard Scripture, indeed it may choose to disregard God as our Creator and Lord, it may even deny His existence, but it does so at its peril, and that means our peril too because we all live in the same world. God forbid that we should ever hear those words addressed to us: *"You have been weighed in the balance and found wanting"*. What a terrible indictment!

THE BRITISH CHRISTIAN OUTDOOR CENTRES CONFERENCE

MEDINA VALLEY CENTRE, ISLE OF WIGHT

TALK GIVEN ON 7TH NOVEMBER 1985

I have a feeling that I am not going to say what you have presumed I would be saying. I am assuming that the function of a visiting speaker is to stimulate, even at times to provoke. I come in a spirit of fraternal and sisterly charity, hopefully to help, so if at times what I say sounds critical I hope you will be able to see it in its setting. Occasionally we all need to make a re-assessment of our position and a conference like this provides just such an opportunity.

As far as I am concerned I am here because I am a Christian. My current professional appointment has provided me with the opportunity to get a bird's eye view of the youth scene in Britain, right across the social spectrum from the most expensive public schools on the one hand to the most deprived areas in Northern Ireland on the other where are to be found all the effects of industrial decline and degradation familiar on the mainland but where there is the added complication of sectarianism.

Of one thing I am certain: the problem of human degradation, the poverty, both material and spiritual, but especially spiritual, the despair which produces uncontrolled violence, the problems of drug and alcohol abuse, of promiscuity and the diseases which result from it, none of these things will be solved by money alone, and where the spiritual is concerned not by money at all. As a matter of fact many of these problems had their modern origins at a time when Britain had 'never had it so good', when there was virtually full employment, when jobs were easy to get, when the explosion of consumer goods occurred, when the era of the continental package holiday dawned, when the contraceptive pill destroyed the last natural barrier to sex on demand and lured adolescents into believing that if they didn't have a sexual relationship almost as soon as they were physically capable of it there must be something wrong with them. It was the period when the old type of shop with its counters and shop assistants gave way to the supermarket with its serve-yourself shelves, which in turn spawned the shop lifting bonanza now costing high street firms millions of pounds each year. It was the period when people working in offices and shops came to regard it as their right to use the company telephone for their personal calls and the company photocopier to run off copies for themselves and the leisure groups they belonged to. Yes, all this happened before the coming of the current wave of mass unemployment. The effect was to raise the general levels of expectation. The present teenagers grew up accepting all these things as normal. What unemployment has done is to frustrate those expectations, which are being perpetuated and constantly reinforced by commercial television, by advertising in the press and by the soap operas, all of which bang out the same message day after day: 'this is the good life; these are the things you simply must have; this is the road to happiness.' More, more, more.

Those who have work get caught up into the mad whirl of the wage spiral. Every year they witness the annual scramble as one group fights another to grab from the national pile a bigger share for its members. No trade union leader is likely to keep his job if he cannot produce a salary increase year after year. At the wealthy end of the spectrum materialism is equally rampant. There it is dog eat dog. Company executives drive themselves into coronaries and become alcoholics in a desperate attempt to impress the bosses and keep up with the pace set by the workaholics of iron constitution. It is a continual round of dashing hither and thither, trying to think out how to overtake the competitors, make important decisions, dictate letters and papers, wrestle with the computer, and all this while getting from one meeting to the next by plane or in a car which goes faster with each new model but which is continually being slowed down by the ever-increasing volume of traffic on the roads. In between there is the game of squash to be fitted in during the lunch hour, the game of golf at weekends, interminable parties, sleeping pills for rapid sleep and stimulants for rapid waking. And in the background a wife who is getting to the point where she cannot cope any longer with being left on her own, having her meals constantly ruined by the uncertain hours her husband keeps, having to bring up the kids with very little help from their father, and then when she is thoroughly fed up and worn out being expected to appear at short notice at yet another firm's party where she knows her role is to charm those who have the power to advance her husband's career. By this time she is near to keeling over from fatigue as she holds her glass and balances her plate having stood on her two feet for the past couple of hours. The whole thing is mad. The whole economic machine, which in the West is now harnessed inextricably to a technology which is becoming more efficient and more fast-moving every year, is being urged on to produce more and more goods so that the consumer will demand more and more possessions which must be changed more and more frequently. The cry is ever for more. And as we see, the human machine cannot take it. The politicians and their gurus cannot control it all. One idea after another proves ineffective; the physical and moral failures which have undermined previous civilisations are proving just as resistant to the modern sticks and carrots as they did to the old ones. The computer will no more solve the problems of mankind than did the abacus.

What is wrong is that the world in its mad rush for prosperity and pleasure passes by the only source of wisdom which can provide the right answers. There is only one source of wisdom, from which human wisdom takes its rise: God the creator of the world and the Father of mankind. So long as the world neglects Him and the truths He has revealed to us, so long will the madness continue and the problems remain intractable. Neither Mrs Thatcher, nor Neil Kinnoch, nor David Owen nor David Steel, nor all of them together, will solve our problems in the long term and produce the millennium, not unless they humble themselves before God and can inspire the nation to do the same. The human race has become too clever to be let loose without wisdom. This is where we, as Christians, come in.

If one studies the life of Christ or any of the saints and outstanding Christians down the ages we find that they did the exact opposite to what the world does. Because Christ was God, when He took flesh at the incarnation he could have chosen to be as rich as Croesus and as powerful as Caesar; He could have chosen to be born into one of the great families with a silver spoon in His mouth and with the levers of power readily to hand. We know from St Matthew's account of the temptations in the desert that Satan offered Christ just those very things but He resolutely turned His back on them and gave Satan the quick heave-ho. Instead He chose to be born into the family of an artisan in a country town in a backwater of empire which the Romans despised, and during the last three years of His life, when He set out to found the kingdom, He tells us Himself that he had nowhere on which to lay His head. When the rich young man came to Him to ask what he must do to become His follower, Christ first quizzed him about his life and went through the commandments. Finding that he had kept them all from his youth, we are told Jesus looked on him and loved him. Keeping the commandments is the first step in following Christ, but only the first. The real essence of Christianity is exercising the free choice, which we all have, between things which in themselves are perfectly good. All God's creation is good, so possessions in themselves are not wrong or sinful. But Christ says, if you really want to follow me, go and get rid of your possessions and then come, follow me. *"None of you can be my disciples unless he gives up all his possessions."* (Luke 14) All the great Christians have divested themselves of their riches as far as they could within the bounds of charity to their relatives and those who depended on them. Throughout Scripture there are repeated warnings to the rich and repeated warnings about the seduction of riches. Moreover, no-one, surely, who reads the Scriptures with an open mind can doubt that God has a special care and predilection for the poor.

What has all this to do with outdoor centres? Just this. If the voluntary youth movement tries to compete with commercial entertainment and to provide for commercial aspirations, it is on a hiding to nowhere. In no way can it do so, and in no way, in my opinion, ought it to do so; not, that is, if we are talking about christian youth organisations. And there is a danger of it attempting to do so.

Most of the voluntary youth organizations in this country, including many outdoor centres, were founded by people of christian vision with the aim of helping the children of poor families and those struggling to keep afloat financially in times of economic difficulty. As well as providing useful and stimulating activities the leaders sought to inspire their charges by the call of Christ in the gospels. In furtherance of their aims the founders appealed personally to the wealthy for funds to acquire the premises and equipment they needed. In the early years of this century those requirements were modest by today's standards, but the response from young people, certainly in terms of numbers, was much greater than it is now. Changing circumstances demand changing responses, and in recent times the older youth organizations have been trying to modernize their image and provide new activities which they hope will appeal to the youth of today.

In the sixties and seventies the local authorities entered the field and established a statutory youth service which had the benefit of funding from the public purse. To keep pace the voluntary sector sought funding from commerce and industry which were beginning to be interested in outdoor activities as a feature of executive training. But there was a price to pay for commercial sponsorship. If firms were going to patronize outdoor centres they wanted accommodation and facilities suitable for people of managerial status. The competition of the market place entered a world whose modest aims had hitherto been supported largely by volunteers and charitable donations. Facilities were indeed improved; to attract the better qualified staff, full-time professionals on professional salaries were employed; national directors, suited and carrying briefcases de rigueur, began to appear. Fees began to climb. In those early heady days the theory was put about that the organizations would continue to fulfil their founders' aim of helping the poor by operating a 'Robin Hood' policy: the profits from commercial clients would be used to subsidize the fees for young people who would benefit from the improved facilities. Nothing wrong with that, you may say. But the god of mammon has a crafty way of edging out the God of the Israelites and the incarnate God of the gospels who chose to live among the poor. In many cases the Christian content of courses was increasingly diluted until in some instances it disappeared altogether. Ironically this is happening at a time when poverty is on the increase and beggars are once again appearing on our streets.

The Christian Church has always been at its most effective when it has followed Christ away from wealth and status. It began with a few frightened men and women who were fired by the Holy Spirit at the first Pentecost. 'What can we do, the problems are too vast?' we often say. People are overcome by the vast scale of national and international problems. But nothing could be more daunting than trying to start a worldwide church with a couple of hundred people; but with God amongst them it happened. When the Church became wealthy and powerful in the Middle Ages it ceased to lead men to God; it became corrupt and collapsed from within. The Reformation was an attempt to get back to the simplicity of the early days. The Church is strongest now in countries where it is persecuted or down-trodden.

Britain is no longer a Christian country. Conversion has to begin all over again. When Patrick, Aidan and Augustine took the faith into Europe at the end of the so-called 'dark ages', they had to go amongst fierce pagan tribesmen who would as soon have roasted them alive as look at them. Yet they went, not with bags of gold, not with armies and weapons to outdo the pagans at their own game, but with a cross and the gospels, because that was what Christ wanted. Actually He told His disciples not even to take a script. From such unlikely beginnings sprang the establishment of Christendom, when for a time the whole of Europe recognised the lordship of Christ. If we want to roll back the tide of neo-paganism and convert the young tribal hooligans in our inner cities then we have to do the same. We have to get in there and take the message of the gospel onto the streets and into the pubs and the entertainment arcades. This was how the tide of corruption was turned back in the early Middle Ages by the friars: this was how the abuses and despair among the workers in the first industrial revolution were transformed. The Church of England did this country a great service when it refused to let John Wesley preach in its churches. It turned him away from the churches and drove him into the fields and the streets where his great missionary work was done. The success of the Salvation Army was due to its policy of taking the gospel onto the streets and into the pubs. What we need today is a new campaign of that sort, updated to suit the conditions and psychology of the age, instead of trying to breathe new life into structures which are perhaps obsolete.

Outdoor pursuit centres provide a good opportunity for Christian instructors to talk to young people about spiritual things in pleasant surroundings, away from the hassle, threats and worries of the cities. There is much that can be done there, but in my opinion outdoor centres can too easily become peripheral to the heart of the problem and the real need. They can help, but only if they are integrated with a system which is based in, and whose main work is in, the cities, for that is where the bulk of the youngsters at risk are. At the moment most of the adults who work in youth organisations, either voluntary or statutory, or who work in the social services, are effectively commuters. They may work long hours in the city but at the end of the day they return to their homes which, in the vast majority of cases, are situated in areas which are pleasanter, less deprived and removed from the squalor and dangers. Most of the people who live in the areas of greatest deprivation, particularly the criminal element, regard churches and religion as irrelevant. Visit almost any inner city church, of whatever denomination, and you will see what I mean. In order to establish the gospel and found His church Christ came and lived amongst us; He did not visit us by daily commuting from heaven, and retire to safer pastures when the going got tough. He lived among those he came to save (wine bibbers, prostitutes, tax-gatherers) and had to cope with the hostility of the Establishment; He allowed Himself to be put to death as a criminal. But by His death on the cross He overcame the world and His blood was the seed from which sprang the worldwide church. The reason why the communists and other revolutionaries get such a hold in areas of deprivation is because they are prepared to go and live in the areas where they want to get a foothold. People there can identify with them because they see them sharing their lives. Before the growing army of the deprived and the frustrated will listen to the gospel message they must develop confidence in those who preach it, and they will not develop that confidence unless they see that they are willing to share their lives.

Those are the people, if there are any, who should be taking parties of young people into the countryside and using the environment to open their minds to the wonders of God's creation. But if young people are sent from the inner cities to centres run by people who live there but not in the cities, the experience may be a pleasant interlude but its effect will soon be lost once they return home if there is no one there to support and guide them and daily to reinforce the vision they saw on the hillside. Of course, qualified instructors are needed if outdoor pursuits are to be properly conducted within the law, but there is a danger of those who work in outdoor centres developing an ivory-tower mentality, perhaps without realizing it, and of outdoor pursuits becoming an entity and objective in themselves. Ideally, in my opinion, all wardens and instructors in outdoor centres should spend a month each year working at clubs and centres in inner cities or periurban estates and living in tower blocks or condensed housing while those who normally live and work there have a working holiday at an outdoor centre. This principle is much neglected in the modern world. Hence architects design houses and offices which no-one wants to live or work in. Academic scientists work in a rarefied atmosphere far removed from the realities faced by industrialists to whom they presume to lecture; managers and salesman often never work on the shop floor. Too often do politicians, sociologists and administrators gather in five star hotels to discuss poverty and deprivation.

In this context it is amazing what a single individual can do. During the 19th century there was a series of people who almost single-handed, and inspired by

Christian ideals, brought about major social reforms or started movements which spread widely. I refer to such people as William Wilberforce, Elizabeth Fry, Baden Powell, William Smith and George Williams. But there were many other people who started individual boys' clubs, schools, orphanages and other institutions. It was an age of philanthropy. Philanthropy is now a dirty word; it is considered a sign of condescension. But different words can be coined for the same or similar thing. It is surprising how people will happily take a medicine which has a different colour or flavour which previously they refused. There is a great need in today's world for charity, for caring for others, for love. Hostility, suspicion, disinterestedness can often be dispelled by the sympathetic approach of the person trying to help. Sympathy is not the same as condescension or the sloppy syrup of all-things-to-all-men. The young especially like straight answers to straight questions.

The solutions of one age do not necessarily suit another. The structures of the family and society which made church-going or club-going the norm for many young people around the turn of the century are no longer there in many cases. The churches are emptying or emptied, as are many clubs. The situation is much more akin to that of the early centuries of the Christian era when Christians gathered in small groups within a hostile world. It was the fervour and example of the people in these small groups which caused the gospel to spread. The apostles and the early bishops, presbyters and deacons went to where the people were, they did not wait in their churches for the people to come to them. There were very few churches anyway. Unless those who would spread the gospel today, the modern descendants of the apostles, do the same, the traditional Christianity in the West will continue to decline. The increasing multiplication of house churches and fellowships seem to me to give an indication of which way the wind of the Spirit is blowing. The reason why the Church in South America (mainly the Roman Catholic Church there) has had such a spectacular renaissance is that the priests and nuns have left their churches and convents and gone to live among the people they minister to. They share the poverty, the squalor, the discomfort and often the disease. The Church is also growing behind the iron curtain where it is persecuted. It is only in the West that Christianity is in decline.

If the subjects which you have selected for the five main sessions of your conference are anything to go by, its main purpose concerns the practical problems of running outdoor centres and the means which might be adopted to improve marketing, fund-raising, and all the things in fact which might be found on the agenda of a conference for a commercial or publicly-funded organisation with no connection with Christianity. There was a 'Thought for the Night' yesterday and a 'Thought for the Day' this morning, and there is 'The Lord's Supper' this evening, but in the list of subjects for discussion in the main sessions there are only two items which look specifically religious. May I be bold enough to suggest that, as this year's conference has been devoted mainly to practical matters, if you hold another conference next year it should be devoted principally to the implications of the Christian dimension of your work which, in my opinion, should go far beyond the boundaries of centres, otherwise you may end up as purely commercial organisations and lose your credibility as Christians. You might even end up like the Churches with fine buildings and equipment but no congregations.

ONE MAN'S SEARCH FOR PEACE

CHICHESTER PEACE FORUM, 6TH DECEMBER, 1985

I spent my childhood in the shadow of the First World War. Like most other families in the land members of my family had served in the Armed Forces and also like most other families we had our war dead. My father came from a family of thirteen children and the youngest boy, the favourite of the family, had been killed in the trenches on the Western Front. One of his elder brothers had been studying for the priesthood before the war started and he was ordained in 1916. Almost immediately he was sent to the front as a Roman Catholic chaplain and spent the next two years ministering to the dying and the wounded in the trenches and the field hospitals. After the war some of my relatives made the Army their permanent careers. The profession of arms was considered in my family to be an honourable career provided arms were taken up in defence of one's country and were not used for aggression. Like most boys at the time I had toy soldiers and books with pictures in them of scenes from the war which I found very exciting. No one ever told me there was anything wrong about all this. Later in my life for a time my path ran alongside that of my Uncle Joe, the priest, and I got to know him well. He was a gentle, kind, humble man, the last person one could have described as belligerent or war-mongering. I truly believe he was a holy man and he died an edifying, peaceful death. To his dying day he had no doubts that he and his brothers had acted honourably in rallying to their country's call and he had no doubt that wearing the uniform of an officer, which chaplains do to this day, had been a great help in giving him access to the men he served so devotedly.

You will not be surprised, therefore, to learn that when in my turn I joined the Armed Forces, in my case the Royal Air Force, I took the whole thing for granted. It never occurred to me that I might be aiding and abetting something wrong, something sinful, even though by then the atomic bomb had been invented and the RAF operated the delivery systems. I accepted things as I found them and I enjoyed my service career. It was only when retirement was within sight that I had my first doubts and began to question my position. By then I was a senior officer and found myself posted to the Officers and Aircrew Selection Centre at Biggin Hill. We were put through a high pressure course to learn the professional art of personnel selection. I then became a member of one of the boards whose job it was to select young men and women for flying duties or ground commissions. We saw a fascinating array of young people from all manner of backgrounds. The procedure lasted two-and-a-half days, a key element of which was an in-depth interview conducted by two officers. One of the mandatory questions was: 'If you were the pilot of a front-line aircraft and Britain became involved in a major war you might be ordered to fly your aircraft over enemy territory to drop a nuclear weapon on it. You would be aware that by dropping that weapon you would almost certainly kill thousands of people. Could you press the release button?' For non-aircrew the question was differently phrased but had the same implication. To some extent, of course, that type of question is unrealistic because we none of us know precisely how we would react in a given situation until we have actually been in it. Nevertheless the negative side of that question was important to the Air Force. Whatever talents a candidate might have he would be of no use if he, or she, was in fundamental disagreement with the accepted policy of the Service.

For the first time in my service career I began to ask myself what I would answer if the roles were reversed and I was the candidate. This led me to start questioning the whole ethical implication of nuclear war, indeed the ethical basis of war itself.

At this point I think I should make it clear that, although it is nuclear weapons which have grabbed the headlines and received most of the publicity, there are other weapons in the modern armoury equally terrible. For instance, the viruses of certain kinds of plague could be put into the water supply and decimate a major city very quickly. Research into lethal gases proceeded during World War II but fortunately they were never used. Subsequent research has produced even more effective gases since. There are types of nerve gas of which a drop no bigger than a pin-head can kill a person in seconds. When we recall what a toothache is like the suffering experienced in those dying seconds hardly bears imagining. We saw something of the horrors of chemical warfare in Vietnam. Just to rub in the point, I think we should not forget the carnage and devastation caused by what are now known as conventional bombs during the last war in such operations as the destruction of Dresden. Conventional weapons are now many times more powerful and effective than they were then. When considering this question of war and peace I think it is a mistake to concentrate solely on nuclear weapons, terrible as those are.

So in my dilemma I looked around for someone whose integrity I thought I could trust, who would know from experience the military point of view, but who had demonstrated that he followed the teachings of Christ. I did not have far to look because someone who seemed to fulfil all these requirements was a well-known public figure. I refer to Leonard Cheshire. His story is too well known to need repetition here but just let me say that I believe he is among the outstanding Christians of our age. As you know, it is his view that the dropping of the two bombs on Japan was justified because they saved even more lives than they destroyed. My wife's brother fought throughout the Burma campaign and I have known other men who served in the Far East. They were lined up to take part in the assault against the Japanese mainland. If that assault had taken place and been fought with conventional weapons I have no doubt in my mind that the loss of life which had taken place in all the other theatres of World War II put together, including the Russian Front, would have paled into insignificance. The Japanese would have contested every inch of ground. I have yet to meet a man who was destined for that hell who does not think that the bombing of Nagasaki and Hiroshima was justified. Nevertheless one is up against the moral problem of the end justifying the means. Is one entitled to take one life in order that several may be saved? Or even one other saved? Are doctors justified in taking the life of the baby about to be born in order that the mother's life may be saved?

In the whole of the peace movement which has developed since World War II I think it relevant to mention something which I find intriguing. I think it is not unreasonable to wonder whether the people who might have been expected to be most prominent in the peace movement would be those who had been most affected by war, namely the men and women who had faced its full horrors; those who had fought in actual combat, those who suffered permanent damage to their health, the wives who have been bereaved, the doctors and nurses who have had to deal with the wounded. Yet in general this has not been so in the Western World, at any rate until the Vietnam War. Those most vocal in the peace movement are mainly people who have never personally seen a shot fired in anger, have never been bombed, have never served in the Armed Forces, never in fact had anything to do with war at first hand. I would suggest that it is easier to be a pacifist when there is no danger of being attacked than it is when the chips are actually down. Not a great many of those who had been against war in the 1930's stuck to their principles as conscientious objectors when war actually happened. And this brings me to my own present personal dilemma, a dilemma I had plenty of time to contemplate. On leaving Biggin Hill I was sent unaccompanied to Gan, a coral island in the middle of the Indian ocean where the RAF had a staging post at that time.

If one is a Christian then it seems to me that the only logical position to hold is that held by the Society of Friends. If I am correct they believe that to kill a human being is wrong in any circumstances and that therefore all violence is wrong. 'Thou shalt not kill' is absolute. I respect my Quaker friends for their view and wish I could accept it as wholeheartedly as they do. Perhaps I shall eventually arrive at that point, but as yet I have not. And I have not because as I see things at the moment I believe I would be a hypocrite to hold a view which I knew that in practice it would be very unlikely that I could give effect to. If anyone who preached had to be as white as the driven snow before attempting to do so, no sermon would ever have been preached, but I think there is a difference between hoping that with God's help there is a reasonable chance that you might not fall into the errors you preach about and being pretty certain that you will fall. It seems to me that the position of the true pacifist must be absolute. Once you admit that there are circumstances in which violence or killing are allowable, even one circumstance, then I would suggest there is no end to the argument and the door is wide open. It becomes a matter of debate and personal opinion as to what the exceptions are.

Suppose I had to cross London late at night and I am below ground in one of the many passages linking underground stations. I come round a corner and find an elderly couple about to be attacked by a gang of skinheads. The elderly couple, the skinheads and I are alone at this point. I am faced with three alternatives. I can run like hell and hope the skinheads don't come after me and I can get away: I can interpose myself between the elderly couple and the skinheads and try to protect them with my body but remain physically passive while trying to persuade the attackers to desist: I can go into the attack hoping to frighten them off at best, at worst to go down fighting. I am only too well aware that I might easily chicken out and run but I hope I might find the courage to defend the weak and resist those of evil intent.

Suppose there is a knock on the door of my house one night. I go to answer it. Two men burst in and push past me before I have time to realise what is happening. One of them starts attacking my wife, the other one is about to silence my child with a hefty blow before turning to knock me out of action. Again I hope I would find the courage to go into the attack so as to get them out of my house as quickly as possible.

In either of those circumstances, if I am honest I know that partly out of terror, partly from the adrenaline running high, I should not be very careful about my choice of method or my choice of weapon. I should seize the first thing to hand and I should not worry too much if I maimed or even killed. Considering such a possibility in the abstract and the comfort of my armchair I could probably think of all sorts of ways of passive resistance and of defence short of killing, and in the cool light of day after such an event I might bitterly regret having gone over the top and used more force than a cool subsequent appraisal showed was necessary, but in my experience there are very few people indeed who in such circumstances can remain so cool, calm and collected that they can keep a detached view throughout and either allow themselves to be mown down without putting up any resistance or who are able to apply just the right degree of force to get rid of the attackers with the minimum of hurt all round. The vast majority of people are just not like that. If it is a case of the attacker's life or mine, most people instinctively choose their own. The same is true of communities. When a community or a nation is attacked it resists. I would say that there is something basic in human nature which prompts people to defend their lives and property. Therefore I think that total uncompromising pacifism, however desirable it may be, is just not realistic. It is something we have continually to strive towards.

How does all this fit into my Christian commitment?

I believe in what is commonly known as The Fall, in the flawed nature of our humanity. I believe that Satan is a reality and not a figure of fun, and so I believe there is an active force of evil in the world. I do not believe there will ever be a perfect world: I think we have to wait until we get to heaven for that. I believe, therefore, there are always likely to be men and women of evil intent who will have to be resisted by force, if nothing else will stop them, in order that the innocent may be protected, that freedom, which is what distinguishes human beings from the animals, may be sustained; that men and women may be able freely to worship God by Whom and for Whom they were made in the way that seems most appropriate to them.

Having said that, I believe that Jesus Christ came to preach a gospel of peace; that He wants His followers to be peace-makers; that God's original intention was that the world should be peopled by peace-loving human beings who would love Him and love each other. Because He wanted human beings to love Him with real love He made them free, and that decision of His necessarily included the possibility that they might reject Him. This happened. He calls us to follow Him and showed us how we must live if we want to make a better world. I therefore believe that our first job as Christians is to love our fellow human beings, to forgive them if they do us wrong, to help those in distress, to try to mend divisions where they exist and heal the wounds of society; to be, in other words, men and women of peace. I believe it is my duty to do everything in my power to bring Christians together and thence to reach out to all men. I think governments, all governments, should dismantle their armouries as far as possible by mutual agreement, which involves their being willing to meet and discuss their differences in a civilised manner, but I think the basis for this should be not a kind of business deal on the lines of deals struck between multinational companies, but because the arms industry represents a denial of Christ's injunction to share with each other the riches of the wonderful world He has given us. Among men and women today there is enough expertise to bring about a situation, and very quickly if there was international agreement, where no one need starve and no one be without a home. As it is, the armaments industry is using up vast quantities of the earth's finite resources, and the refusal of people to forgive each other prevents the just distribution of the wealth which is generated. I do not decry those who feel it is their mission to put their energies into campaigning for unilateral disarmament, but for myself I think it is a more urgent priority to try to remove the causes of war by preaching the gospel of charity to one's neighbour, by trying as best one can to demonstrate one's beliefs by the example of one's life, by trying to live the beatitudes. The world desperately needs forgiveness, the burying of hatchets. It needs people to offer each other the hand of friendship. To some extent I think too great an obsession with world causes can distract us from what we can all do every day in the circumstances in which we find ourselves. In some ways it is easier to attend a demonstration in Trafalgar Square than it is to treat with generosity and fraternal charity those irritating next-door neighbours or even to live unselfishly with one's own family. Some of the worst and meanest sins are committed against people with whom the perpetrator is closely related – wives, husbands, children, brothers, sisters, uncles, aunts, cousins. Truly, charity often really does begin at home. If we can heal the divisions within our immediate circle, love and peace will radiate outwards to the world around. This is how Christianity spread in the early days; this is how the world will be converted now. This should be our first priority.

So I am not a unilateralist (not yet, at any rate) but a multilateralist. I think on balance that the British nuclear deterrent is a nonsense when viewed beside the enormously greater nuclear arsenals of the super powers, but I think there is such a thing as deterrence and there are historical examples, the most relevant being the experience of poisoned gas in World War I which deterred even an international maniac like Hitler from using it in World War II. I think there is a very slow but nevertheless perceptible realisation that somehow the peoples who live on the earth have got to work out some kind of ratio vivendi because the alternative is annihilation. I am not without hope, and I think governments are wise to proceed with caution rather than by making dramatic gestures. We must trust in God and the power of prayer. He is our sure hope. He has assured us He will listen if we have faith in Him. So for us Christians I say again, I think our first priority must be to put our own lives in order so that the world may see that we are people of peace who know how to live peacefully together. By this shall all men know that we are His disciples. Then they will copy us. Then there is a real chance that the arsenals will be dismantled.

HOMILY FOR THE TELEVISED MASS FROM ST RICHARD'S CHURCH, CHICHESTER

FEAST OF THE PRESENTATION, 2ND FEBRUARY, 1986.

Not so long ago I was in an aircraft flying northwards over the west coast of central Africa. Down below it was still pitch dark, but in the east there were the first signs of dawn, and in the tropics the sun comes up quickly. We were flying at maximum altitude, over 40,000 feet. From that height it is possible to discern the curvature of the earth, and you can get a feeling of detachment as if you were looking at the earth from another planet. It was a magical moment as the sun rose above the horizon. I watched the light roll back the shadow of darkness across the face of the earth, bringing daylight and warmth, and revealing the landscape below. The early morning air is often very clear and so it was on that morning. I could see for hundreds of miles across the coastlands and the savannahs to the great Congo forests beyond. In the sea beneath I could just pick out a ship by the whiteness of its bow wave. It must have been a large vessel but from my lofty perch it looked minute.

I watched entranced as the world beneath me came to life, and I reflected that, high as I might seem, I was in fact quite near the earth, but even so men and women were too small to be visible with the naked eye, and yet there were millions of them on the planet at which I was looking.In a few hours I should be down there amongst them. Then it was that the mind blowing realisation hit me. Amongst all those millions God knew me. Not only did He know me now but He had known of my existence from all eternity, aeons and aeons before time began. More incredible still He loved me, and to prove that love came Himself onto the earth to show me how I should live so that I could eventually share His life with Him in heaven for ever. For what seemed like a long time, but was in fact probably only a minute or two, I seemed to be looking at the earth through the eyes of someone suspended in space outside the busy beat of time. The vastness of God's creation was all about me, galaxy upon galaxy as the astronomers tell us; all the heavenly bodies perfectly balanced. And this God of power and might knows me and holds me fast within His ample palm, as Cardinal Newman put it. Must not He who created the universe and holds the stars on their courses also have the affairs of men under control on this small planet? Surely I could trust Him with my own little life? Surely I could believe His word? We can only see the individual threads as they are woven, but He can see the completed tapestry of life across the whole span of history.

Today's feast of the Presentation is a festival of light. Our candles proclaim Christ the light of the world. Just as the sun brought light and warmth to the African landscape in that dawn I have tried to describe, so Christ brings the life-giving light and warmth of His presence into our lives, rolling back the darkness of evil and sin. Many people today often feel crushed by the enormous and seemingly intractable problems with which our world is faced. They feel that as individuals they are powerless to alter things for the better; their voice is too small to be heard. Even in our private lives things sometimes get on top of us, and then somehow nobody seems quite to understand or be able to help. Then is the time to lift up our eyes to the hills whence comes our salvation, as the Psalmist says. For there is someone who cares; there is someone who knows our inmost needs; someone who has called us individually by our names into His loving embrace. That someone is none other than the Creator God who, as today's feast reminds us, took our flesh and was born of a woman, and so knows our human condition from personal experience. Surely this is the most fantastic revelation of all history!

Yet He will not force us to follow Him because He has given us free will so that we might return Him real love, freely given. The essence of Christianity is this personal relationship, freely given and accepted, between Jesus Christ and you, Jesus Christ and me; Jesus who is full of mercy and compassion; the Good Shepherd who cares for His sheep.

> *"The Lord is my light and my salvation, whom shall I fear?"*
>
> *"If I should stand in the valley of darkness, no evil would I fear,*
> *because You, my Lord, are there."*

So, yes, we can trust Him because He has first loved us. 'The Lord is at my side: I shall not fear.'

I want to end by quoting Cardinal Newman again. I am sure you will all know this lovely poem because we sometimes sing it as a hymn.

> *Lead, kindly Light, amid the encircling gloom,*
> *Lead Thou me on;*
> *The night is dark, and I am far from home,*
> *Lead Thou me on.*
> *Keep Thou my feet; I do not ask to see*
> *The distant scene; one step enough for me.*

I was not ever thus, nor prayed that Thou
Shouldst lead me on;
I loved to choose and see my path; but now
Lead Thou me on.
I loved the garish day, and, spite of fears,
Pride ruled my will: remember not past years.

So long Thy power hath blest me, sure it still
Will lead me on
O'er moor and fen, O'er crag and torrent, till
The night is gone,
And with the morn those angel faces smile,
Which I have loved long since, and lost awhile.

May Jesus Christ, the light of the world, on this Sunday which is dedicated to Peace, bring peace to your homes and lead you gently but surely towards that heavenly home where we all one day hope to be. And may He bless all of us here in Chichester, and you who are watching on television wherever you may be, now and always. Amen.

THE FEAST OF THE ASSUMPTION OF OUR LADY

ST RICHARD'S, CHICHESTER, 16 AUGUST 1987

Down the years some Catholics in their enthusiasm to show devotion to Our Lady have embellished their mariology to the extent that they have given the impression that Mary was more than a normal human being; that she is on a plane of her own somewhere between God and us; that her life was so pre-planned by God that she could do no wrong; in fact, that she is not really one of us. I have no doubt such people were sincere but I also think that such exaggeration diminishes Mary's real greatness and does a disservice to both her and the Catholic Church. Let's be clear: Catholics do not worship Mary. They honour her as the Mother of God in His humanity; worship and adoration are reserved for God alone.

Mary was as human as you or I, with free will and thus as capable of accepting or rejecting God as we are. Were this not so the choice she made to accept God's proposal at the Annunciation would not have been a real one. She would have been no more than a puppet doing what God had programmed her to do. Had that been so the whole theology of the Incarnation would be phoney.

It seems to me that the principal Marian doctrines of the Annunciation, the Immaculate Conception and the Assumption are inextricably interwoven in a single unified tapestry, and, therefore, when considering Mary's Assumption, as we do today, we must consider the Annunciation and the Immaculate Conception as well.

[The reader should here refer to the homily for the Fourth Sunday of Advent on page 35]

We must remember that we have grown up knowing about Jesus, about His revelation of the Trinity, about the Redemption and the subsequent history of christianity. Mary knew none of this. It had not happened when God put His proposal to her that day at Nazareth. That Mary believed what the heavenly messenger told her and was willing to face a very uncertain future required a colossal act of faith.

Such considerations should help us to get some idea of the pivotal role which Mary played in God's plan for the redemption of the human race, and therefore of her greatness. And I must re-emphasize that she was free to accept or reject God's proposal. The doctrine of the Immaculate Conception does not mean that Mary had no choice. This doctrine, which has caused so much difficulty for non-catholic christians, is the result of the Church looking back and meditating on the whole of Mary's life and its immense consequences and meaning. Yes, of course, she was sinless, and, of course, God had seen this from all eternity, but if for a moment we turn history on its head and assume the Church had been in existence before the Annunciation, then there would have been no need for a definition of the immaculate conception: it would have been obvious. Because Mary had free will things could have gone wrong at the Annunciation. In fact they did not. It is only with hindsight that it is possible to recognise the wonderful way God's providence works through His creatures.

So Mary was the very first person to make an act of faith in the Incarnation, in Jesus Christ as God made man, Son of God and son of man. I think we sometimes can get the impression that St Peter was the first when he answered Our Lord's question, "Whom do men say that I am?" Mary had answered that question more than thirty years before.

Our Lord's resurrection and ascension were confirmation and proof of His whole life's work and teaching. As St Paul said: "If Christ be not risen our whole faith is in vain". The Jews had only the vaguest idea of what happened to people after death. It was Jesus who told us plainly about the four last things – death, judgment, hell and heaven. He told His apostles that He was going to prepare a place for them and that in His Father's house there are many mansions. The Church has always taught that entrance to heaven depended on the redemption brought about by Jesus on the cross. That means that, looking at it from our time-bound earth, those who died before Jesus and who had merited a place in heaven had to wait until the redemption had been accomplished on calvary. For God, of course, there is no such thing as time so I am sure the real explanation is much simpler. At all events the whole of human kind would have been debarred from eternal happiness had the redemption not taken place. It took place because of what happened at Nazareth when Mary agreed to God's seemingly preposterous suggestion. It was her act of faith on that occasion which was to result in the opening of heaven to all men and women of good will down the ages. Implicit in that act of faith was belief in the resurrection of her Son, in His victory over death, in His ascension into heaven. What do we say at the end of the creed? "I believe in the communion of saints, the forgiveness of sins, the resurrection of the body and life everlasting". Through Mary's act of faith all those blessings came about. Jesus's victory over death was demonstrated by His resurrection and by the ascension of His incorruptible body into heaven, as will happen to our corporeal bodies at the end of time (that's what we mean by "the resurrection of the body" in the creed). He merely anticipated in time what will happen to us all. The ascension of His body uncorrupted was the necessary completion of His earthly life, implicit in His victory over death by His resurrection. Mary was the co-author of that life and an integral part of her Son's redemptive work. So the assumption of her body, also uncorrupted, was implicit in her act of faith at the annunciation and therefore inevitable and a necessary consequence. Her assumption was not, as some writers have implied, a kind of reward for services rendered but an integral part of the redemption of the world. This has been the belief of christians from apostolic times and was not something thought up by Pius XII in 1950, as some critics of the definition have implied. The Marian doctrines are an integral and essential part of our faith. This is why we rejoice and celebrate this feast with such solemnity, because it foreshadows our own destiny and is the hope by which we live.

So the lesson of this great feast is the virtue of faith. If we have real faith we shall, if God asks us, be willing to step out into the unknown with no-one to rely upon but only God, as Mary did by her act of faith at the Annunciation. Faith means learning from Jesus and Mary as they accompany us through life. Let us ask Our Lady on her feast day to lead us into an ever more intimate knowledge and love of her divine Son and obtain for us the gift of real deep faith, if we do not yet have it, and to strengthen it if we have. "Holy Mary, mother of God, pray for us sinners now and at the hour of our death. Amen".

SERMON FOR THE FEAST OF ST PHILIP HOWARD

ST RICHARD'S CHURCH, CHICHESTER, 1987

I want to begin with a bit of family history. The Victorians, especially Victorian men, tended to marry later in life than is customary today. At all events the men in the two generations ahead of me in our family did. My father and grandfather were nearly forty when they married. My father was born in the 1870s, over a hundred years ago, and my grandfather in the late 1830s. In 1845 anti-catholic feeling was still pretty strong in parts of this country and an anti-papist mob got out of control in Birmingham and burnt down a catholic chapel. The priest was forced to flee for his life. My family's home was in Worcester, barely thirty miles away, and my grandfather as a child could remember this alarming news being brought to the house. The history of the catholic church in Worcester is similar to that of many catholic churches which were built early in the 19th century not long after the Catholic Relief Acts were passed. One of the effects of those Acts was that it ceased to be a criminal offence for Mass to be said in public. The land was bought by a catholic layman supposedly for his own use, because no-one would have sold land in the City if they had known it was to be used for building a Catholic place of worship. To avoid causing a rumpus the church was designed to look like a non-conformist chapel. The stone frontal you see today was put up later. My grandfather used to recall how Catholics would go to church in ones and twos to avoid attracting attention, and that gathering outside the church on a Sunday after Mass was unthinkable. In the next generation my father was only the second Catholic mayor of Worcester since the Reformation. To make sure he did not compromise his faith and to let everyone know that he was a Catholic he insisted that the official church service on Mayor's Sunday should be held at the Catholic church and he sent his deputy to the cathedral with the retinue of officials who refused to attend a catholic service. That was in 1926. In those days to stand up and be counted took great courage.

So it was that I grew up very aware that the faith which was being handed down to me had been kept alive throughout the penal times at great cost. The sacrifice of Catholics like St Philip Howard was still very real to us. I was aware that Catholics were not popular among my own contemporaries. In order that my brother and sisters and I could receive a Catholic education we had to be sent away to boarding school. The day I had to say goodbye to my mother when I was not yet six years old is still etched on my memory.

Thank God, during my lifetime the climate of opinion in England has changed enormously. In Chichester, as indeed in Worcester, relations between the various Christian Churches are today very good and I am myself much involved in the ecumenical movement, as I think you know. I rejoice in this, and I hope that I may be privileged before I die to see the separated parts of Christ's Church reunited. But I do not forget the debt I, and all of us here, owe to St Philip Howard and those who refused to compromise where their faith was concerned and who kept it alive when they were only a tiny minority. At the back of this church, in the porch, you will find a small metal plaque which refers to the Countess of Newburgh. It was the Newburgh family who kept the faith alive in this part of Sussex. They owned the Slindon estate where they harboured priests and ran the risks of allowing Mass to be said in their house. After the Catholic Relief Act the first post-reformation catholic church around here was built at Slindon and is still in use. Occasionally a priest would come to say Mass in the building at Southgate which is now the Bedford Hotel, but mostly Catholics from Chichester had to go to Slindon to hear Mass until the old St Richard's was built in Theatre Lane where Rumbelows now stands. That was in 1856, I think.

When I lived in Africa I used sometimes to stay on one of the mission stations. At a weekend people would start arriving at the mission on Friday evening. All through Saturday others came, and by Sunday morning when Mass began the church, which was a large one, would be full. The people I am talking about were what at that time we over here might have called primitive Africans. Their only form of transport was their feet. Many of them had walked through the bush from as far afield as fifty miles away, some of them walking through the night. Most of them were first generation christians, or at most second. The first missionaries had only arrived in the country about fifty years before and most of the missions were more recently established than that. Many people in the congregation might not have been able to read, they might not have been able to explain one theological truth or one liturgical custom, but their faith was as firm as a rock and their expression of it put to shame the formalism which sometimes characterised the liturgy in the European churches. Africans have a natural way of harmonising and they sing all day long. When they got going at Mass they lifted, literally, the mind and heart to God. It was not possible to be a part of one of those Masses and not feel the presence of God.

Now where does all this leave us?

Compared with penal times, being a Catholic today is pretty easy in the England of 1986. There are parts of the world where it certainly is not, so we are very fortunate. In this parish alone we have a choice of nine Masses every weekend and there is at least one Mass every weekday. Our priests are always available to help us, to visit us when we are sick, to advise us when we are in trouble, to administer the sacraments. Most of us have cars or can arrange some form of transport to get us to Church. So:

How many of us, I wonder, even if we were capable of it, would be willing to walk twenty miles, ten miles, five miles, even two miles, just to go to Mass if we had no transport?

How many Catholics, if they wanted to spend the day on the golf course, or on a boat, or if they wanted to go away to see friends or relatives, or had a late party the night before might decide to give Mass a miss?

How many Catholics have given up going to Mass for no stronger reason than that they found the sermons boring or the liturgy dull? National statistics indicate that only about one third of baptised Catholics practise their faith as adults.

How many Catholics, even though Catholic schools are available without fees, have decided not to send their children to Catholic schools because a non-Catholic school was more conveniently located or they thought gave a better academic education? In an ideal world Catholic schools would give a good religious grounding as well, but if, as parents, we were faced with having to choose, which would be our first priority, our children's faith or their earthly careers? Which are we prepared to take a chance on? If we say we'll choose a non-Catholic school because we think it gives the best education and we'll take care of our children's religious grounding in the home, are we really doing it? How much time are we setting aside regularly each week for teaching them specifically about God?

Are we ready to stand up and be counted as Catholics, or indeed as christians, in non-Christian company when to reveal our beliefs might lose us popularity or make life positively unpleasant?

These are just some of the questions we ought to ask ourselves today on the feast of the Co-Principal Patron of our Diocese. The Church only canonizes people, declares them to be saints, because they have set an example which the Church wants us to follow. That is not to say that there are not a lot of other people who were equally holy, but the Church wants us to take note of the saints and try to emulate them. Our saint, Philip Howard, was willing to pay the supreme price of life itself rather than compromise his faith. Please God we shall not be called on to face so daunting a decision but, as he looks down upon us from heaven on this his feast day, do you think he is proud of our record as catholic christians? Do I think my own record is something he can be proud of?

SERMON PREACHED IN THE CHAPEL OF LORETTO SCHOOL, EDINBURGH

AT MORNING SERVICE ON SUNDAY 15TH NOVEMBER 1987

If the total world population is taken into account then we, here this morning, are numbered among the wealthiest five per cent. So the New Testament reading which we have just heard about the rich young man ought to have something to say to us. Let's have a look at it:

If the rich young man was a Lorettonian, when his parents came to visit him at a weekend they might well turn up in an E registered 2-litre estate car. There would also probably be at least one other car at home, a runabout for Mum. We are told that the young man himself kept all the commandments. (Let's call him Hamish. His name wasn't Hamish because he was a Jew, but it might have been if he had been a Scotsman). So Hamish would certainly have been head of his house, if not Head of School, and would have been the apple of his house-master's eye, because he was reliable and kept the rules. He might easily have been in the 1st XV and would certainly have worked hard at his A levels. So he would have done well at university and then entered his Dad's business with good career prospects ahead of him. He didn't play fast and loose with the girls, he loved his Mum and Dad and tried to please them, and he was truthful and just to those in his care. In other words he was a thoroughly good chap, the sort of young man anyone would be glad to have on their staff and who would have no difficulty in being accepted for membership of the New Club in Edinburgh. The Gospel tells us he was very rich so it may not be too fanciful to assume that for his twenty first birthday his Dad had given him a Porsche.

But we also find that Hamish had a conscience and was attracted by this new teacher, Jesus of Nazareth, whom he must have listened to on several occasions, keeping his distance at the edge of the crowd, I would guess, because the majority of the people who crowded round Jesus were pretty rough working class types. A rich young man would not want to be too conspicuous. He couldn't get Jesus out of his mind. At last he couldn't restrain himself any longer, so when this particular meeting was over and the crowds were dispersing he edged his way towards Jesus and knelt at his feet. "What must I do to receive eternal life?" he said. Jesus questions him about the commandments. He has kept them all, as we have already seen. St Mark tells us: *"Jesus looked straight at him and loved him"*. How marvellous to be loved by Jesus Christ! What in effect that look of

Jesus's was saying was: "Well done, Hamish, you're a good lad. I know you've done your best and I'm proud of you. You are just the sort of young man I need to help me found my kingdom. You've got all the right qualities. You are good and honest; you are well educated; you could be a fine leader. But you've come to ask me what you must do if you want to follow me and receive eternal life. Well, look at us. I am just a wandering rabbi with no fixed abode. The foxes have holes, the birds of the air have nests, but I have nowhere to lay my head. And these are my companions, mostly uneducated working men, with the odd tax-gatherer and prostitute among them. I'm afraid they are not the sort of people you are used to associating with. So if you really want to be one of us, then you must go home, sell the Porsche, ask your Dad to give you your share of the family inheritance and make your brother the heir, and then sell everything you own and give the proceeds to the poor. When thus you yourself are poor, come back and in time you will become a great apostle. But you won't fit in to my little group, you won't fit into my kingdom, so long as you hang on to your wealth. You cannot serve both God and riches."

Mark tells us that when Hamish heard this "gloom spread over his face and he went away sad, because he was very rich". At this point it is important to notice that Jesus did not call him back. As he saw him walking sadly away He didn't call after him: "Son, come here, come back. I was a bit hard, wasn't I? But I was just trying you out. Now look, let's work out a compromise. You sell the Porsche and make do with an old banger instead. I quite see that you can't give up a promising career, so come and join us at weekends instead of going off to sail your Dad's yacht. I am sure we can fit our life-styles together." No, Jesus lets him go and we never hear of the rich young man again. On the contrary, when the apostles expressed their astonishment at the hard line Jesus had taken with him, Jesus rubs the lesson in. *"It is much harder"* He said *"for a rich person to enter heaven than for a camel to pass through the eye of a needle."* Elsewhere He said that anyone who was not prepared to leave father, mother, brother, sister, children, yes, even his own life, was not worthy to be His disciple. If we are to follow Christ and live the Gospel our commitment has to be total.

Why do you think it is that Mother Theresa of Calcutta is not only idolised by the poor and defenceless but sought after and consulted by kings, princes, presidents, prime ministers, popes, bishops and all manner of important people? Why is it that girls, many from well off families, flock to join her Missionaries of Charity? I'll tell you why. It is because Mother Theresa is an authentic witness to the life of the Gospel. She not only lives among the poor but she shares their poverty with them. She has consistently disregarded the advice of well-meaning people to put her Congregation on what they would regard as a sound financial footing. She refuses to appeal for funds. When addressing a large gathering of Franciscans in the United States she began with these words: "Don't let them take your poverty from you. Don't let them rob you of the freedom your poverty gives you. Be true to the poverty of your founder Francis".

Mother Theresa's life has been in two halves. She left her home in Albania to join the religious order called, interestingly enough, the Sisters of Loretto who sent her to India to teach at their school in Calcutta. It was an independent convent school for the education of young ladies from upper-class Indian families, the Calcutta equivalent of St George's in Edinburgh. In time she became headmistress and was very popular and successful. That was before her second conversion, which resulted from her reaction to the appalling slaughter which occurred in Bengal in the run-up to independence in 1947 and the even worse slaughter after it. Poverty, already widespread, engulfed the city, services collapsed and disease rocketed. Mother Theresa got permission to leave her Order. She took off her Loretto habit and put on the plain white sari worn by the poorest of Indian women. She left her convent with nothing but the clothes she stood up in. On her first day outside she knocked at the door of a house to ask for food and was sent round to the back to the servants' quarters.

Why is it that some of our bishops, moderators and high ranking churchmen are not listened to and are considered by some to be irrelevant anachronisms? Why is it that congregations have dwindled and many churches been closed? Why are a lot of young people turned off by the Christian religion? (Perhaps this is true of you). I am afraid one has to say that at least one reason is because some of the Church leaders as well as some of us in the pews do not live the Gospel life. True, the salaries of bishops are poor in comparison with what they might earn in commerce or industry, but they live with some of the trappings of wealth. Some bishops live in palaces and castles and big houses. Some have chauffeur-driven cars when they go on official visits. A career in the ministry of the Church has over the years become a profession on a par with the law, or the Armed Services, or medicine or accountancy. It is part of the Establishment, a respectable occupation. When young men or women come to the Church and say they would like to devote their lives to the ministry, what does the Church do with them? It sends them to university or theological college to study theology and scripture. When they have been awarded their degree or certificate the Church considers them qualified to preach the Gospel; just as a doctor, or surveyor, or architect must acquire a certain body of knowledge before being let loose on the public.

It is interesting to note how this contrasts with how Christ dealt with His disciples. He didn't say to Peter: "Now look, old chap, I think you'll make an excellent leader of my kingdom in time, but you must admit you are a bit short on education. So first of all I want you to go to night school and get two or three good A levels. Then we'll get you into the university at Jerusalem. When the Temple authorities pass you out with a degree then we'll see about making you the rock on which I want to build my church". No. When He sent out His apostles on their missionary journeys and gave them their instructions there is no mention of what they are to say or how they are to say it. His instructions are all concerned with how they are to conduct themselves. *"Don't take anything with you on your journey except a stick – no bread, no beggar's bag, no money. Wear sandals and don't carry an extra shirt".* Christ's teaching in the Gospels is almost always about practical ways of altering a person's life so as to imitate the way the Son of God lived and behaved. It is not about theological niceties and intellectual discussion. Yet today Christians are divided by just such things, particularly in the affluent West. By contrast Christ's gospel is flourishing in the poor countries where people are up against the basics of life. Christianity will continue to decline in the West until Christians start to live the gospel life which demands the rejection of riches and worldly honours. It might be more appropriate, perhaps, if the Church, instead of sending its potential ordinands to university for three years, sent them instead to spend a couple of years living at the level of a social security income in somewhere like Niddrie or Muirhouse and there learn how to make the Gospels relevant to people who live at the bottom of the social pile. Then perhaps a final year spent in reflection, prayer and study might have more point to it.

In the psalm which we sung a short while ago the psalmist reminded us of the futility of chasing after wealth. No matter how great our wealth we can take none of it with us when we die. And in the reading from Isaiah the Lord said: *"These people claim to worship me, but their words are meaningless, and their hearts are somewhere else. Their religion is nothing but human rules and traditions."* If we are here in this chapel this morning because the school timetable says we must be, or if we come because we like to listen to nice music, or if we are here because to go to chapel is part of our traditional background, then I have a feeling Jesus Christ would not be very comfortable in our midst. If we have been coming to chapel for two years, or three years, or four years, or even for twenty years, or thirty years, or forty years, and if we have not changed, if our life-style has remained unaltered, then I suggest we have not heard what Christ has been trying to tell us. We may have listened to the scriptures but we cannot have understood the message. Christianity is not a matter of ritual, even of tearing our garments in remorse, but it is allowing our hearts to be broken. Being prepared to meet Jesus Christ in person, like the rich young man, and to face His challenge, but, unlike the rich young man, to accept the challenge and follow where Jesus leads. Shall we, like the guests invited to the wedding feast say to Jesus: "Yes,

Lord, I think your ideas are marvellous and I do admire you and will pray for the success of your mission, but I'm just on the threshold of a promising career and I'm sure you wouldn't want me to give it up; or, I've just bought a farm and must now go and look after it; or, I've married a wife so I'm sure you will understand that I can't come now. Later, perhaps. So please hold me excused. But not now, Lord." Later, later, always later.

This is the challenge you and I are faced with this morning. Can we accept it? Can we alter our lives? Clearly our personal circumstances differ widely, from you young Lorettonians who have yet to make up your minds what you are going to do with your lives to those of us who are married with families, so it is for each one of us to decide how we ought to respond, but respond we must if we are not to duck out and, like Hamish, go sadly away. Do we, or do we not, respond positively like the apostles and follow Jesus? Well, that is what we have to pray about. When the apostles asked: *"Who then can be saved?"* Jesus looked straight at them and answered: *"This is impossible for man, but not for God; everything is possible for God"*. Of this I am sure: if Lorettonians can accept the challenge of Christ, if they can come to chapel and allow Jesus to mould them like a potter moulds his clay, then this chapel can become the beating heart of a missionary movement so strong that it would change the face not just of Musselburgh but of Scotland too.

HOMILY FOR A SERVICE OF RECONCILIATION

ST RICHARD'S CHURCH, CHICHESTER, HOLY WEEK, 1988

On my travels a fortnight ago I had occasion to visit a relative and was somewhat shattered to discover that the marriage of his wife's daughter had come to grief after twenty-three years. For the sake of anonymity we will call the couple Janet and John. They seemed to have everything going for them. They have two good sons, a nice house and both have reasonable jobs. Even their relatives and close friends thought they had a normal sound marriage and were unaware that anything was amiss. However, one day John walked out and is now living alone in a two-roomed flat. Janet remains in the matrimonial home and keeps house for the two sons, aged nineteen and twenty-one. There seems to be no third party involved. Janet says the front door is open if John wants to return, but she's not going to run after him, and if he comes back he will have to eat humble pie and admit he was in the wrong before she will even consider such things as conjugal rights. John says he is willing to go back but he is not going to take the initiative. If she wants him Janet must come to him and admit she was in the wrong. Clearly, so long as they remain in that frame of mind there is no possibility of a reconciliation. Neither will make the first move. In the meantime you have two people who are lonely, unhappy and embittered, and two sons who are fed up with all the argument and are likely to leave home, also unhappy and embittered.

All of us are here this evening to ask God for forgiveness. *"Forgive us our trespasses"*. But there is a second part to that appeal: *"as we forgive those who trespass against us"*. When we have a row with someone, yes, we may be right in what we say; yes, we may be right in the opinion we hold. But are we also self-righteous? Did we put our point of view with gentleness and sensitivity? Did we listen to what the other person was trying to tell us – not necessarily by the words they spoke, for perhaps their very abrasiveness was a silent cry for help and love. Jesus was right in what He said: He was right in what He did. His enemies were definitely in the wrong. Never in the whole of human history was there a clearer case of right and wrong, yet on the cross Jesus begged His Father to forgive them. It was the one Who was wronged, not the wrong-doers, whom we find asking for forgiveness.

For most of us, it is not a question of having to forgive real enemies, as Jesus did, more often it is husbands or wives or children or parents, or friends or relatives or people at work. These are the people we are most likely to have rows with, rows which, as in the case of Janet and John, can lead to serious rifts, and even permanent breaks in our relationships. The father of the prodigal son did not wait for his son to reach home and then force him to confess his sins and rub his nose in the dirt. As soon as he saw his son, still a long way off, he ran to meet him. He asked no questions but flung his arms around him. And how many times did Jesus tell us we must be prepared to do this? Peter asked that very question. *"Not seven"*, said Jesus, *"but seventy times seven"*.

My Brothers and Sisters, look around you. I hardly dare mention Northern Ireland, but it is, alas, a seemingly permanent warning of what can happen when forgiveness is refused and anger and bitterness are allowed to become entrenched. Jews and Arabs, Iranians and Iraquis, black and white, north and south. The world is riven by people who insist on their righteousness and refuse forgiveness and reconciliation, who prefer the gun and the bomb. But look nearer home. One in three marriages ends in divorce, and the proportion is going higher. How often have you seen a person interviewed on television about some tragedy in their life say: "Yes, I'm bitter. Very bitter. I want him hanged." What, by contrast, started the conversion of the angry young people of the Red Brigade in Italy who murdered Aldo Moro? It was the picture on television of his sons at his funeral saying they forgave his murderers and asking for forgiveness for the whole sorry mess. You cannot drive out anger by more anger; personal relationships cannot be healed if the persons sit firmly on their high chairs waiting for the other person to grovel. *"Calm your anger and forget your rage"*, says the Psalmist. *"Do not fret, it only leads to evil. For those who do evil shall perish; the patient shall inherit the land"*.

Jesus says that before He can accept our offering at the altar we must go and be reconciled with our brother or sister if there is anything between us. So we must here and now examine our consciences to see if there is any unsatisfactory relationship in our lives; if there is anyone we have not forgiven; if there is anyone we are avoiding because they irritate or annoy us. If there is, then we must not only confess this but, when we leave the church, we must take the first opportunity to go to that person and offer our love and forgiveness. If you have stolen £100 it is no good confessing it to a priest if you continue to hang onto the money. The sin will not be forgiven until the money is restored to its rightful owner. So, too, the effects of our anger, our jealousy, our snobbishness, our sheer lack of charity cannot be properly repaired unless we are willing to go to our brother or sister and seek reconciliation.

And as for all our other sins, the sins we perhaps think of as our private sins known only to God and ourselves, let's not kid ourselves that other people are unaffected. In his latest encyclical Pope John Paul has made it clear that the evil structures in society are the collective result of individual sins. By our individual sinfulness we add to the sum total of evil in the world. In contrast the sum total of anger and violence in the world is lessened each time you and I ask pardon from those we have wronged and forgive those who have wronged us. The level of dishonesty and fraud is lessened each time you and I turn down an opportunity to better ourselves and get what we want by dishonest means. The level of sexual permissiveness and immorality is lessened each time you and I resist temptation and turn away from an occasion of sin. The cause of truth and justice is strengthened each time you and I refrain from dissembling or telling a lie when to do so might make things easier for us or perhaps increase our popularity.

If you are like me and have been coming to confession for the past half century and find yourself confessing the same sins as you did ten, twenty, thirty, forty years ago, take heart: there is an answer. It means we have not yet learnt to open ourselves truly to God and let Him have His way with us. We shall never overcome our faults and failings by our own efforts; but with God all things are possible. Like the prodigal son we have only to take the first step towards our heavenly Father and He will come running towards us and clasp us in His loving arms. No sin is too hideous for Him to forgive; no sinful tendency, no matter how entrenched, is beyond His love to purge and heal. But we have to trust Him. No one ever learnt to swim by hanging on to the side of the swimming bath. First you have to learn to trust your instructor and then you discover that the water will hold you up after all. Learn first to trust the advice of your priest confessor, then you will find that God can change you after all. Don't hide anything from Him: don't try to kid yourself. He opened His arms to you on the cross: open yourself to Him and let His love consume you.

During the quiet time of the Service you might like to reflect on the following passages from the Gospels of Luke and Matthew which are relevant to what I have just said:

While he was still a long way off, his father saw him and was moved with pity. He ran to the boy, clasped him in his arms and kissed him tenderly. Then his son said, "Father, I have sinned against heaven and against you. I no longer deserve to be called your son." But the father said to his servants, "Quick! Bring out the best robe and put it on him; put a ring on his finger and sandals on his feet. Bring the calf we have been fattening, and kill it; we are going to have a feast, a celebration, because this son of mine was dead and has come back to life; he was lost and is found."

Luke 15 20-24

When they reached the place called the skull, they crucified him there and the two criminals also, one on the right, the other on the left. Jesus said, "Father, forgive them; they do not know what they are doing".

Luke 23 33-34

So then, if you are bringing your offering to the altar and there remember that your brother has something against you, leave your offering there before the altar, go and be reconciled with your brother first, and then come back and present your offering.

Matthew 5 23-24

Then Peter went up to him and said, "Lord, how often must I forgive my brother? As often as seven times?" Jesus answered, "Not seven, I tell you, but seventy-seven times."

Matthew 18 21-22

THE REMEMBRANCE SUNDAY SERMON

THE CHAPEL, GORDONSTOUN SCHOOL, SCOTLAND

SUNDAY, 12TH NOVEMBER, 1989

When it became clear that the Allies were going to win the Second World War we British began to turn our minds to the future. A future we would not have had but for the thousands of our comrades who gave their lives that we might triumph over the evil forces against which we were fighting: the men whose planes did not recover from an uncontrolled dive, whose submarine never surfaced, who were felled on the field of battle by the merciless whip of automatic fire. These men we remember and salute today. War is an evil thing, but strangely enough it can have beneficial side effects. It tends, among other things, to break down social barriers. Aerial bombardment is no respecter of persons: bombs fall on rich and poor alike. In the aftermath of a raid everyone rallies round to help the injured, the bereaved and the dispossessed. On the battlefield men, and sometimes women, from all social backgrounds have to learn to work as a team, often in the most uncomfortable of circumstances. And if someone saves your life it doesn't matter a damn whether he is a prince or a dustman, he is your friend for life. So when we thought about the future we wanted a new world in which there would be fair shares for all. We wanted an end to the terrible injustices of the past when too often the medical care a person received depended on his/her bank balance, and when unless you were bright and could get a scholarship, or your dad was well off, you could not be educated beyond the age of twelve. Socialism seemed to encapsulate what we wanted and it was the Service vote which swept Labour to power at the War's end. Yes, we appreciated what Churchill and others had done for Britain, but the Conservative Party to which he belonged didn't offer the radical change we felt was needed. We had a dream of a fairer, more just society.

But it was not many years before things started to go wrong. It was not the dream which was wrong; what happened was that the faults and weaknesses which have dogged human progress down the centuries began to rear their ugly heads again. These faults you and I know only too well – selfishness, jealousy, laziness, arrogance, infidelity, and lying and cheating to boot.

Once the war was over directors in their boardrooms went back to putting the balance sheet and the interests of their shareholders as their prime objectives and neglected their workforce. Salesmen adopted a take-it-or-leave-it attitude to potential customers: Britain had won the War so the world owed us a living. The trades unions, once they discovered they had the bosses on the run, pushed their demands higher and higher until they ruined, or nearly ruined, many of the firms for whom their members worked. The Welfare State which we had embraced so enthusiastically became increasingly inefficient as its employees became increasingly lazy.

What I am describing was not unique to the 1950s and '60s. Selfishness and greed have frequently prevented human beings from realising ideals which were within their grasp, as Mrs Thatcher has discovered. "For years when I was young and in politics with all the hopes and dreams and ambitions, it seemed to me that if we got an age where we had good housing, good education, a reasonable standard of living, then everything would be set and we should have a fair and much easier life. We now know that that isn't so. We're up against the real problems of human nature. Why, when you have got everything, do some people turn to those fundamental things which undermine the whole of civilization?"

Science can tell us a lot about ourselves and our world, technology and engineering can produce many things which make life easier, but neither science nor technology can help us to avoid the mistakes which have ruined so much of human history. The solutions to the problems of human relationships, the inspiration to reach out to a better world, the empowerment of the spiritual in human nature are not to be found in the science laboratory or the computerised Stock Exchange (pace the Head of Science and the Head of Business Studies). The wisdom which can save the world and liberate humankind to enable us to harvest its immense potential is to be found in this book (the Bible), because this book contains not just the distilled wisdom of men but the wisdom of God Himself. A quarter of an hour spent reflecting on the life of Christ in the New Testament or on the teachings of the prophets in the Old will do more to teach you happiness, contentment, serenity and peace, those priceless gifts the world cannot give, than many hours of concentrated work in a laboratory or department of business studies. My contemporaries who died in the Second World War gave their lives that we (and they, had they lived) might continue to enjoy the freedoms which we in Britain have never surrendered, among them the freedom to worship God and to read His word. But, alas, the victory was only partial. We rid Europe of the evil of Nazism but there was another evil force lurking in the wings. Before the war was even over the communist barons got their iron claws round Eastern Europe and with each succeeding year tightened their grip. They swept every Bible from their countries, closed the churches and declared that God was dead. During that period of repression friends of mine took their lives in their hands to smuggle Bibles to Christians behind the Iron Curtain, but the number of Bibles they could cram into a suitcase was very small. As Mr Gorbechov and the other people leading the reform movement in Eastern Europe are discovering, despite four decades of persecution Christianity in their countries is alive and very vigorous. Now that the ban has been lifted there is an insatiable demand for Bibles and all manner of religious literature. The Bible Society here in this country cannot get new editions printed fast enough to satisfy all the orders. So, learn from the misfortunes of others, cherish the freedoms which have been won for you, learn the wisdom which is freely available to you. Then, indeed, you will be blessed and, as lights in the darkness, will help to lead your generation along safe paths to a better world. So, yes, the chapel has a purpose, and a very important one. It's up to you, in concert with your Chaplain, to make sure that the meetings within it are anything but boring.

ADVENT SERMON 1990

PREACHED AT THE CHURCH OF ST PAUL & ST PETER THE GREAT, CHICHESTER

God has been very good to me. I have never been without a home. My parents provided me with a stable loving home to which I always longed to return when I was away from it; and for over forty years a faithful and loving wife has kept the homes fires burning for me. I, therefore, find it very difficult to think myself into the psychological state of a person who has no home and may never have had a home to which they wanted to return, rather, on the contrary, wanted to get away from. That such people exist, and in our country, and in larger numbers than you may imagine, I have no doubt. Throughout the Eighties I travelled the length and breadth of Britain for an organization, my branch of which was concerned with young people. I met young people from right across the social spectrum; from those enjoying the privilege of a public school education to those living on the margins of society in some of our inner cities or, what are sometimes worse, the post war peri-urban estates.

'Why should anyone be homeless in the Welfare State? If anyone is homeless or down-and-out, is it not their own fault? Why should we be expected to cough up for charitable schemes to prop up their profligacy and inadequacy?' It is interesting that whenever I have heard people utter those or similar sentiments they have always been themselves well housed and comfortably placed. True, they may have worked hard to establish themselves but I cannot recall one who had ever been without a home. Certainly there are among the homeless the lazy and the feckless, but there are very few indeed who have chosen to be homeless.

Let me cite just one case history. Kathy was born to a promiscuous and inadequate mother in one of the concrete jungles on the outskirts of Liverpool. She never knew a father, indeed her mother was not sure which of her succession of boy friends was her father. Her mother had no more children, though she had several abortions, so Kathy had no brothers or sisters. Kathy was a nuisance from the day of her birth. Her mother was more interested in her male companions than in her daughter, and the men found a child in the house an embarrassment and a bind. So from a very early age Kathy would be sent out of the house with nowhere to go but the street. She was subjected to physical abuse and, on a number of occasions, sexual abuse. Not surprisingly when she went to school she was disruptive: she never did her homework: she was often scruffy and dirty. The social workers who were called in to deal with her could make no progress with her and her teachers eventually gave up. But despite all this, like any other human being, Kathy longed for love and affection. When she began to develop in her very early teens she grew to be physically very attractive, so you will not be surprised to learn that she became the focus of attention for the local boys. Lacking any kind of affection at home, she thought she might get it from her admirers. Having witnessed some of her mother's sexual exploits, she had no moral sense and assumed that that was how adults behaved normally, and thought that somehow love could be got through sex. So her first love affair filled her with hope and expectancy. She soon discovered, however, that the boys were not really interested in her as a person, only in her body. She suffered crushing disillusionment which only made her even more aggressive and difficult to cope with. So first she played truant and then, when she was about fifteen, she left school and home and went on the streets. But all the time she longed for a home and someone to love her. She discovered that as a single person over sixteen the Local Authority had no obligation to house her, but that if she had a child it did. It also occurred to her that if she had a child she would, for the first time, have someone who would be really hers, whom she could love and be loved by. Thus she deliberately set out to get herself pregnant. She had despaired of male love but at least a man could help her to achieve what by now had become a burning ambition. In due course she had her child. While in the maternity ward at the hospital she learnt from another girl in a similar situation that life was much better in the countryside than in the town, and that there were a number of young Liverpudlians living rough around some of the seaside towns in North Wales. Kathy had never been to the country but decided to give it a try. Once out of hospital with her baby she got a series of lifts from lorry drivers and turned up in North Wales. Not knowing how to go about getting accommodation she took it into her head to seek advice at a local youth club. Fortunately for her the leader of that club was a wise and caring man who had helped numerous young people in trouble. He first took her home where he and his wife looked after her, and he then got her a room in a Council hostel. It was at the youth club that I first met Kathy. On several annual visits I had long talks with both Kathy and the club leader, and I learnt a good deal from them both. With a baby to love and at last someone who took a genuine interest in her, Kathy began to learn the meaning of responsibility and to drop some of the defensive barriers she had built around her. I have lost touch now but often wonder what has happened to her. I also wonder what would have happened to me if I had grown up in Kathy's circumstances.

Do we as Christians have any responsibility towards the Kathys of this world? Broken homes, feckless parents, cruel relatives, an inability to cope with the speed and complexities of modern life, mental breakdowns, alcohol and drug abuse – a whole range of things can cause a person to sink through the web of normal society and become rootless and homeless. If there are such people in our neighbourhood, do we assume they are the responsibility of the Statutory Authorities and no concern of ours, or do we see some connection between them, ourselves and the Gospel? Should we, as the Victorians did, try to sort them into categories – the 'deserving' and the 'undeserving' poor? Is that what Christ did?

One of the criticisms levelled against Him by His enemies was that He consorted with tax-gatherers and sinners and that He ate with wine-bibbers. You may remember that on one occasion, when the Pharisees tackled His disciples on the subject, His reply was pretty caustic: *While He was at dinner in the house it happened that a number of tax-collectors and sinners came to sit at the table with Jesus and His disciples. When the Pharisees saw this, they said to His disciples: "Why does your Master eat with tax-collectors and sinners?" When He heard this He replied: "It is not the healthy who need the doctor, but the sick. Go and learn the meaning of the words 'What I want is mercy not sacrifice', and indeed I did not come to call the virtuous but sinners".* Lepers in those days were expelled from the towns and condemned to eke out a precarious existence on the fringes of society. Jesus deliberately went among them. The passage from St Luke which was read as our gospel this morning indicates pretty clearly that Jesus does not discriminate between the worthy and the unworthy where compassion and generosity are concerned. Moreover, in His account of the Last Judgment in St Matthew He tells us that He will take our response to need among our fellow men and women as our attitude to Him. He teaches us not to judge. He tells us to visit the imprisoned who by definition have broken the law; not to wag our fingers at them, just to visit them. He even gives us advice about choosing our guests: *Then He said to His host: "When you give a lunch or a dinner do not ask your friends, brothers, relations or rich neighbours, for fear they repay your courtesy by inviting you in return. No, when you have a party invite the poor, the crippled, the lame, the blind. That they cannot repay you back means that you are fortunate, because repayment will be made to you when the virtuous rise again".* And He says that He and His heavenly Father are more concerned about the fate of the one sheep that has gone astray than the ninety-nine who are all right. Is that true of us?

He also had much to say about the corrupting effects of wealth, and told several parables about what happens to people who cling to their riches. Of course wealth is comparative. When we look at people like the Duke of Westminster or the Marquis of Charlmonderly with his £118 million and two large estates, we may think we are pretty badly off, but half the world's population who live on the breadline, and some of our fellow citizens who have to manage on Income

Support, might think most of us pretty well off. You will recall what Jesus had to say about the man who pulled down his barns in order to build bigger ones; But God said to him: *"Fool. This very night the demand will be made for your soul. And this hoard of yours, whose will it be then? So it is when a man stores up treasure for himself in place of making himself rich in the sight of God."*

So, if God required my soul of me tonight, which would I rather be able to tell Him: "Lord, I have been very responsible with my money; I have kept my house nice, the furniture polished and the carpets swept. I have been quiet and sober and kept up the respectability of the neighbourhood", or, "Lord, remember that I several times gave the the spare bedroom to people I had heard were without accommodation, I helped with the parish day centre and the night refuge, and I joined the list of visitors to Ford Prison"? At the outbreak of the Second World War my father was a member of a city council and had the task of finding accommodation for the evacuees from the East End of London. I remember his telling my mother that he and his colleagues never had any trouble in getting working class families to take one or two extra into the family, but the greatest difficulty in getting anyone in the better-off part of the town to take an evacuee. They were afraid they would muck up the furniture and drop their food on the carpet, and generally not know how to behave in a civilized manner. The more and the better the possessions a person has, the more they are terrified of their being spoilt. When a person has next to nothing, and what they do have is worth little, they have little to lose. Have we taken on board what the Scriptures say about offering hospitality to strangers? Am I, this Christmas, going to do anything about the lonely people living around me, even if they are not on my normal visiting list? Am I going to help with the project in the Church Hall across the road, or am I going to join the ranks of the objectors? For, be sure, anything of that kind will rouse opposition. Nor should we be surprised if it does. *Remember the words I said to you: "A servant is not greater than his master. If they persecuted me they will persecute you".* Your Vicar has set us a fine example. Of the people we asked to help us with accommodation he was the only one who without hesitation said 'yes', knowing full well that his decision might land him and us in hot water. In fact, where similar projects have been set up in other towns the fears of local residents proved to be largely illusory. They imagined that the whole district would be swamped with winos, thieves and vagabonds. There are only a few such round here and our project is not only for them, but also for anyone who is lonely and who wants a little fellowship and warmth at this time of the year. Most people applaud efforts to help the homeless and distressed so long as they are not personally involved or affected in any way.

Jesus came not to found an individualistic religion in which people's spiritual life is kept separate from the rest of their lives, but to.found a community, a Church. It is easier and more comfortable to keep God inside the church and to deal with the rest of life in a good old-fashioned, no nonsense, businesslike manner where people are kept in their places and efficiency is rated higher than compassion. Jesus came to reveal His Father to us, and what He made clear was that God loves us with an everlasting unconditional love. He does not say;"I will love you if you are good", no, "I love you without limit and will come and search for you if you go astray. All I ask in return is that you love one another". And love is not the soft option it is sometimes made out to be. Once we give our love we are vulnerable and the going may get tough, but can we really doubt that this is what God wants? Remember, Jesus Himself knew homelessness from personal experience. Bethlehem had no room for Him. Had His parents been told to register in the London of 1990, instead of Bethlehem in AD 4, He might have been born in the so-called 'cardboard city' at Waterloo. I think He is sympathetic to the homeless, and I have a feeling that if He were physically present in Chichester this Christmas we should find Him lending a hand in your Hall across the road.

HOMILY FOR THE FEAST OF THE EXALTATION OF THE TRUE CROSS

THE CARMELITE CONVENT, CHICHESTER, 1990

GOSPEL READING - JOHN 3:13-17

I feel personally connected with today's feast on two accounts. Firstly, the true cross was, as you know, discovered by St Helen, the mother of the Emperor Constantine in 326AD. My wife Helen is named after her and she's had a big cross to carry through life in the shape of her husband! But the true cross was subsequently stolen by the Persians and we are celebrating today its triumphant return to Jerusalem in 629A.D. Secondly, a fragment of that cross has been in the possession of my family for so many generations that we are uncertain how this came to be, but one of my earliest memories is of my father bringing out the relic from the place where he kept it with great devotion and solemnity each Good Friday and taking it down to our parish church for veneration by the faithful at the Mass of the Presanctified. The relic has been passed through the eldest son of each generation and is now in my brother's possession.

Because the cross has been from the very beginning of the Church the symbol of Christianity it was inevitable that it should fire the imagination of artists and craftsmen down the ages. There are many wonderful paintings of the Crucifixion and many magnificent crucifixes. There is nothing wrong with works of art but these have had the unfortunate effect, I think, of often diverting our minds from the real significance of a cross and perhaps more importantly from the real meaning of Christ's sacrifice and what He meant by the need for us to take up our own crosses. So I want to dwell for a few minutes of the word 'True' in the title of today's feast.

The cross in the time of Our Lord was nothing more than an executioner's gibbet devised by the Romans. Over the centuries men have thought up many dreadful ways of torturing each other, and, I fear, are still doing so, now using the sophisticated instruments of modern technology. Even so, doctors of our own generation have asserted that nothing has yet surpassed the cross in its ability to cause agony to every part of the body and at the same time to prolong that agony over several hours, or sometimes days. So horrific was the effect of crucifixion on its victims that the Romans did not allow it to be used on their own citizens. It was reserved for slaves and foreigners for whom the Romans had utter contempt. There was nothing artistic about the true cross; it was just two pieces of rough wood, tough enough to hold up the weight of a grown man. It was dreaded. No wonder Our Lord was so frightened in the garden of Gethsemeni that He sweated blood. Anyone else would have run away in the hope of escape. Not he. He faced up to the horrific prospect and waited like a lamb to be taken – for us. For you and me. He was tortured for our sins. My stomach turned over the other day when I heard that our Father Laurence had shut his finger in the door of the safe. The pain of shutting one's finger in any kind of door is excruciating, but a door can be opened and the finger released. Imagine a large rough nail being driven through the middle of your hand or wrist – and staying there. Then the other hand. Then each foot. Then the cross being lifted up vertically and the whole weight of your body tearing at those four tender wounds.

Today's gospel is about the meaning of the cross for us. It is worth recalling the context. Jesus was talking to Nicodemus who had come to Him at night. Nicodemus was, as you know, as Pharisee, a member of the wealthy upper class. The Romans had clipped much of the Pharisees' political power but they still had a great deal of influence among the Jews. This incident took place quite early on in our Lord's public career. Nicodemus had been impressed by Our Lord and by His teaching and wanted to find out more, but he knew that if his fellow Pharisees found out that he had been in Our Lord's company he would have risked being ostracised. So he came under cover of darkness. Even then the shadow of the cross lay across the life of Jesus Christ.

Throughout His teaching Jesus tried to get his hearers to understand that there was a spiritual dimension to all He did; that there was another life beyond this one, from which He came and to which He would return; that His kingdom was not of this world. To be able to understand this a person had to be reborn. At the beginning of the passage from which the gospel reading is taken Jesus tells Nicodemus that *"Unless a man is born from above he cannot see the Kingdom of God."* Nicodemus found this very puzzling, and the majority of those who listened to Jesus couldn't get the hang of it at all. Before Pentecost even the apostles still thought that Jesus had come to found an earthly Kingdom. So it is today. Unless we are given the gift of faith by the Holy Spirit the teaching of Jesus and the significance of His Church are meaningless. "To the world a scandal," as St Paul put it. Without the gift of faith the Mass, for instance, is just a kind of ritual play-acting. So also with the cross. Without the gift of faith it remains an executioner's gibbet or a work of art.

The first reading tells us of the Jews who complained about the hardships they were faced with in the desert. "Why did you bring us into this?" they shouted at

Moses. That cry is echoed today by those who cry out: "Why must this happen to me? If God is a god of love, if He is meant to be compassionate, why does He allow this to happen to me? Why does He allow suffering in the world?" It is not for us to know the mind of God but Jesus has shown us how to cope with suffering and that it has a purpose. He has shown us that suffering is an inevitable part of life and that to accept it for His sake is necessary for salvation. *"Anyone who does not take up his, or her, cross cannot be my disciple"*, He says. The world sees suffering and death as disasters. To those who have faith Calvary leads to the resurrection: suffering is the prelude to heaven. Even from a purely human standpoint, if we want to live in reasonable contentment and happiness we have to come to terms with life's difficulties. If you want proof, you need only visit two places. A psychiatric hospital is full of unhappy people who for one reason or another have been unable to cope with their problems. Visit a hospice for the terminally ill and you may well be surprised how happy people are. If we cannot learn to cope with our present circumstances the chances are we shall do no better if the circumstances are changed.

Whether we are married and live in a family or whether we live in a religious community, we have to live at close quarters with other people. Because we are all human, all individuals with our own ideas and our separate wills, living with other people, even if we love them dearly, has its inescapable problems. In most religious communities there is usually at least one person who is difficult to live with, who is a thorn in everyone's side. The friction which this causes can become a terrible cross. Thérèse of Liseiux showed us in her life how to use these frictions as a means of sanctification. Through accepting her small crosses for love of Jesus she became a great saint.

If we get rid of our crosses we usually find that, after a brief period of relief, we have stepped out of the frying pan into the fire. Many married people who have decided they cannot stick their partner any longer, who have walked out and got a divorce and then married someone else who, they thought, was going to make life so happy and sweet, have discovered that their second marriage turned out to be just as difficult as the first. On top of that, they have come bitterly to regret breaking up their first family with all the unhappiness and trauma this caused their children and their first partner.

Many priests who have given up their priesthood, and many religious who have left their Orders, have discovered that the crosses they chose for themselves in so doing turned out to be much crueller than the ones Jesus had asked them to hang from; that the yokes they have stuck their heads into and from which they cannot now extricate themselves cause more painful sores than the yokes He laid on them with so much sweetness; the burdens they have chosen for themselves are much heavier than the ones His Sacred Heart laid on them with so much love.

In the desert Moses was told to lift up the brazen serpent so that the Jews might look on it and be cured of their poisonous adder bites. Today the Church tells us to exalt, to lift up, the cross that we may pour out our love and praise on Him who redeemed us by His suffering and death and come to understand what the true cross is all about and how we need it in our lives so that we may be true followers of our Saviour. Let us learn to thank Him for the suffering He sends us and pray that, by accepting our own personal calvarys, we may one day rejoice with Him and the whole company of heaven for ever. 'This is the wood of the cross on which hung the saviour of the world – come, let us worship.'

HOMILY ON MARRIAGE AND FAMILY LIFE

CHURCH OF OUR LADY OF THE ASSUMPTION, BOSHAM, 1991

The great destroyer of marriages, the great destroyer of family life, is selfishness: not just the desire to have what we want but the determination to have our own way irrespective of the consequences to other people. It is impossible for a really selfish person to live in harmony with others for any length of time. Such people create confrontations wherever they go.

Whether at table or in bed, at work or at play, a successful personal relationship requires that we first consider the needs and happiness of the other person before imposing our own. The Scriptures, especially the New Testament, continually teach us to seek the lowest place and to rejoice in other people's success. Our Lord praises the lowly, the humble and the childlike, as in today's gospel reading. His mother says in her 'Magnificat' that He puts down the proud, the selfish, the clever and the insincere.

But being human we frequently fail to live up to this ideal. Often it is more from thoughtlessness than anything else, but thoughtlessness can be very hurtful. For instance, if after work the boys at the office decide to go round to the pub for a quick one and I join them, perhaps a pint becomes two pints, and then three, and before I realize, a couple of hours has passed. In that time my wife has to watch her cooking spoil and then begins to worry when it becomes obvious that I was not on my usual train nor on the next one either. It would not have cost much for me to have gone to the nearest phone and tell her that I would be late. The repetition of such minor episodes can lead to many arguments and the generation of much unnecessary anger.

Because of our human frailty, the two great saviours of marriage, the two great saviours of family life, are repentance and forgiveness. Our Lord had a lot to say about forgiveness, amongst other things telling us that there must be no limit to the number of times we forgive a person. A golden rule for all families, which ought to be framed and hung in a prominent position so that every member of the family sees it every day, is: *"Never let the sun go down on your anger"*. If we can say we are sorry and if we can forgive by the time we go to sleep, we shall not go far wrong.

But to some extent these things are negative. The great dynamic of marriage and family life is love, not Hollywood, TV, love, but real love, and no one has given a better description of what true love is than St Paul in that marvellous passage from his First Letter to the Corinthians, chapter 13, verses 1-13, which we have just heard read to us. If we were wise we would all read it thoughtfully at least once a week.

As for children, in my experience if they know they are loved and wanted, really loved and really wanted, they can take almost anything in their stride. Although it is no longer politically correct, the occasional clip of an ear can do a power of good and cause no resentment. Even if Mum sometimes loses her rag and throws the proverbial rolling-pin around and Dad is known on occasions to blow his top and kick everyone out of his workshop, it can all be a bit of a giggle if after the storm everyone makes it up and has a good laugh. It is when children sense that Mum and Dad don't love each other any more, that there's something phoney about their relationship (and children are very sensitive) that things begin to go wrong: and as we all know, things can go horribly wrong.

Finally, the indispensable oil of family life is a sense of humour. It is usually easy enough to laugh at other people, but we have to be able to laugh at ourselves as well. There are few tricky situations which will not yield to the tactful injection of a bit of humour at the right moment. May God bless us all with this most useful but underrated gift of His.

SERMON FOR THE ANNUAL SERVICE OF THANKSGIVING & REMEMBRANCE FOR ST WILFRID'S HOSPICE, CHICHESTER

OCTOBER 1993

Before I come to the theme of my address I want to take this opportunity to pay my personal public tribute to the doctors and nurses, the support workers and the many volunteers, who together have made St. Wilfrid's Hospice an oasis of peace, hope, compassion and spiritual healing in what for many people is a turbulent and frightening world. It is your professional skill and your dedicated humanity which has eased the pain and removed the fear from numerous terminally ill people in our community. But your compassionate ministry and your support extend beyond the hospice itself into the homes of your potential patients before they need to enter the hospice proper, and after their deaths to their bereaved relatives and friends. Yours is a truly christian work and you will be greatly rewarded by Him who said that for those who are compassionate *"there will be gifts for you: a full measure, pressed down, shaken together, and running over will be poured into your lap: because the amount you measure out is the amount you will be given back."* (Luke 6 38.) So in the name of all those you have helped, and of our whole Chichester community, may I say a big "Thank you"?

You who work at the threshold where life meets death know more than most of us about the last few yards of the path which leads to that threshold, but what happens at the moment of death when the door above the threshold opens, and what lies beyond, remains one of the two great mysteries of human existence: the other being the start of life. We know all about eggs and sperm, but human beings for all their cleverness cannot create life; neither can they control the moment when it ceases. Through the advances of medical science and technology doctors can now keep the functions of the body going after the brain has died, but that elusive thing the spirit, the human soul, which is the spark of life itself, remains mysterious. So what do you think happens at death? When with all your care and skill you have helped your patients to die painlessly and peacefully, and the undertakers have come and wheeled the body away, is that the end for those people? Is that finality?

If we knew pragmatically and beyond doubt that there was life after death, and what that life consisted of, there would be no room for faith and hope. Human beings would no longer be free to choose how they lived their lives because the knowledge would be so overwhelming as to remove free will. Christians believe that God is the creator of the universe and the source of all life within it. We reaffirm this belief every time we say the creed: "We believe in one God, the Father, the Almighty, Creator of heaven and earth, of all that is, seen and unseen" Christians also believe that God created men and women with free will so that they could respond to, and return, the great love with which He loves them, and by loving each other praise and worship Him, the author of life and love. Now you cannot get love out of a computer. You cannot force people to love you. Love must be spontaneous or it is nothing. Automatons are the antithesis of freedom. So in order that we may be free certain things have to remain mysterious. A mystery is not something which is untrue but something the explanation of which remains unknown. A mystery is solved by discovering the explanation. So in forming our conclusions about death and its sequel we must piece together such evidence as we can find - and there is quite a bit.

There have been numerous examples, both in our own day and in past generations, of people who have come so close to death that those about them thought they had actually died, though subsequently it turned out that they had survived. I refer, for example, to cases of people who have been involved in road accidents, or left for dead on a battlefield, or whose vital bodily functions stopped on the operating table. Some such people (and they are too numerous to disregard) have subsequently testified that, while they were thought to be dead, they experienced a consciousness outside the body: that they found themselves in an environment of suffused light, being drawn towards the ever-increasing brilliance of the source of that light. Common to all their experiences is their insistence that they experienced a sense of great peace and a total absence of fear. Most record that eventually they heard a voice (usually that of a loved one) calling them back, and how disappointed they were that they could not continue their ethereal journey. I should add that by no means all of these people were what we might call 'religious'. Some had previously had no belief in either an afterlife or a god.

Now this type of testimony dovetails very well with what the Evangelists tell us in the gospels about Jesus, particularly in the chapters dealing with what happened after the resurrection, but we should not overlook the account of Jesus walking on the Sea of Galilee and that of His transfiguration on Mount Tabor. In both those accounts Jesus was surrounded by an aura of light. The disciples who were present were at first terrified, but once Jesus spoke they experienced calm and peace. After the resurrection a new strange element enters the accounts of those who saw Him. At first they failed to recognise Him. How could that be? If you had been in someone's company almost daily for three years, would you fail to recognise them after a gap of only three days? Surely not. The disciples, like everyone else in Jerusalem, were convinced that Jesus had died and been buried; yet here He was. The Evangelists specifically mention that it was not a ghost they saw, a disembodied spirit, and emphasize this by recording that in the upper room, at Emmaus and by the lakeside in Galilee Jesus joined His disciples in eating a meal. So why that initial failure to recognise Him? I suggest the explanation is that after death when, in due course, we are reunited with our bodies, they will not be the poor bodies distorted by disease or age which the undertakers wheeled away, but new bodies designed for the new spiritual environment in which we are to spend eternity in "our Father's house", as Jesus so beautifully put it; bodies no longer bound by time or space. A seed is functional and a necessary step in the life cycle of a plant, but the seed cannot be compared in beauty to the flower which develops from it; nor the acorn in grandeur to the oak tree. Both seed and acorn must disintegrate before the beauty or grandeur of its ultimate purpose can be revealed.

So, too, the grub bears no comparison with the magnificence of the butterfly or the moth to which it gives rise. Why should we be any different? We are spiritual beings made for a spiritual home. So is it not understandable that the body in which we begin our existence should disintegrate, as does the seed or the grub, in order that we may evolve into a new and more elevated form? The human being is body and soul inextricably fused into a single unitary person. The soul, or spirit, is not a kind of implant but an essential element. Therefore in life after death we shall still be that same person, hence the christian belief in the resurrection of the body, also enshrined in the creed: "we believe in the resurrection of the body and life everlasting." But the process by which we transfer from earth to eternity is often painful and distressing, a condition it is your vocation to alleviate, though you cannot prevent it. If you have ever watched a butterfly emerging from its chrysalis, or a chicken fighting its way out of an egg, I think you will readily understand the comparison with a person on their deathbed.

Now let's return to the gospel reading (John 20 11-16). Mary Magdalene loved Jesus with all her being and she was first on the scene that Easter morning. Discovering that the tomb was empty, she was desperate to find the body of her Beloved. When people have something all-absorbing on their minds they frequently miss the obvious. Mary was not looking for a living person but a dead body, so, when unexpectedly confronted by this man, she assumed he must be some kind of functionary; the man whose job it was to look after the graves perhaps. Notice how Jesus plays with her at first, as lovers often do, teasing her. But then He says her name: "Mary!" Immediately she recognises Him. "Rabuni, (Master)", she replies. In those two words, "Mary", "Rabuni", is a whole world of love. When true lovers meet, a single word can convey a volume of meaning.

Whenever I read that passage from John's gospel I always recall the occasion when I have been separated from my wife for several months by military service and had gone to the airport where we were due to meet. I was desperately looking for her among the crowd coming through the arrival passage, but she had spotted me first. I heard her voice call my name – and that was it! No more words were necessary. And that, I think, is how it will be when we pass from life in this world along that corridor suffused with light that some people have experienced, as I mentioned earlier. But instead of hearing a voice calling us back to earth we shall hear His voice calling our name, as He once called Mary Magdalene's beside the tomb. I just long to hear Him call my name: "Hilary". "Rabuni", I shall reply; and then I shall know I am really on the way home to my Father's house in which He has a room set aside for me, as we learn in Chapter 14 of John's gospel.

However, we do not have to wait for that moment beyond the grave to enjoy His friendship and grow in His love. As the angels said to the other women who went to the empty tomb: "Why seek the living among the dead?" Christianity is not based on the life of an historical figure who died and was buried like other people, but on one who, having died, rose again. As Paul says, "If Christ is not risen, our faith is vain". In that same Chapter 14 of John's gospel we read that the night before He suffered Jesus made this promise to His disciples:

I will not leave you orphans; I will come back to you.
In a short time the world will no longer see me,
but you will see me, because I live and you will live.
On that day you will understand that I am in the Father
and you in me and I in you.
If anyone loves me he will keep my word,
and my Father will love him,
and we shall come to him and make our home with him.

So we can enjoy the presence of Jesus here and now, and the closer we come to Him the easier will be our passage from this material world to our Father's house. Occasionally over the centuries since that first Easter, very occasionally, our risen Lord has shown Himself in His resurrected humanity to certain chosen souls to reassure the rest of us that our faith is indeed not in vain. I want to end by reading you a short poem by Maud Sumner. I think it unlikely that you have heard of her. She was a South African artist and poet, well known in her own country, who divided her time between her parents' home near Johannesburg, Paris where she had a studio, and her aunts' house in Warwickshire. She was a deeply religious person and produced some outstanding religious art. She died, never having married, in 1985. In 1966 she was on her way from England to South Africa on one of her regular home visits. At that time, because of the anti-apartheid feeling in Black Africa, South African Airways had to route their aircraft round the western bulge of Africa, and this necessitated a refuelling stop at Las Palmas, which belongs to Spain, then ruled by Franco. On this occasion her plane landed at night, appropriately in a thunder storm. For some reason she was last out, and instead of following the rest of the passengers into the airport building while the refuelling took place, she took it into her head to go for a stroll at the side of the airfield. I will leave her to tell you the rest of the story which is recorded in her poem entitled "Las Palmas 1966".

Sheer down the runway, brakes shrieking,
the Boeing sped,
Shoving up, shuddering, came to a
standstill.
Dozens of tourists disembowelled, drove to
the pavilion.
But I was late, limping down the ladder,
and the trolley gone,
So wandered down the tarmac alone in the
night of stars.
Clouds on the horizon, lit by lightning,
showed the hill lines of the
Las Palmas landscape as I walked and
lingered,
Smelling the night air, heaving with fumes as
the great bird refuelled.
Then suddenly, feeling a presence, someone
behind me,
I stopped and turned, and there He stood,
some paces from me
Unseen in the darkness, a compelling power
More intense than all seen things.
Enveloping, embracing, He drew me like a
magnet and
Waited as I slowly walked to meet Him there.
"You here?"I asked. "Yes, here and
everywhere", He replied.
He smiled as we sauntered up and down
Hearing the crunch of pebbles, avoiding
petrol puddles.
Seen as it lightened again and again
The whole vast universe receded into
nothingness,
Unreal in the face of this reality, this All in
all.

Time stopped till I heard a call from the
Boeing
"Hi, come back. Don't go so far alone."
"Alone!" No one was ever less so. But it was
once
The earthy voice had called, broken the
thread, and I returned – alone.

(Maud Sumner, Painter and Poet
by Frieda Harmson
published by J.L. van Schaick)

SERMON FOR CHRISTIAN AID

GIVEN AT THE CHURCH OF ST PAUL & ST PETER THE GREAT, CHICHESTER, ON FRIDAY 13TH MAY 1994

Theologians identify four types of justice:

Commutative Justice: how we as individuals relate to and treat our individual fellow human beings.

Legal Justice: The principle that everyone, male/female, rich/poor, high/low, white/black should be treated equally and fairly under the law of the land.

Social Justice: This relates to the social and governmental structures by which daily life is regulated.

Distributive Justice: The just sharing of the resources available to the community and the complementary sharing of the community's burdens and responsibilities.

I suggest that it is mainly with distributive justice that Christian Aid, Oxfam, Cafod and other aid agencies are chiefly concerned. So let us spend a few minutes looking at distributive justice in our world.

Everything necessary to sustain life on this planet of ours has been provided by the Creator, by God. The earth's proximity to the sun ensures the necessary heat and light: the earth's atmosphere ensures a sufficiency of air and moisture – rain, springs, rivers, seas: the earth's rocks contain all the minerals we need and the soil all the chemicals necessary for plant life. The seeds from which plants grow, the animals, the birds and the fish provide food and materials for clothing. All these things have been provided. Over the generations of human existence men and women have learned to understand the composition of the earth's resources and to develop them to a highly sophisticated degree – but they have created nothing. All that grows and lives on the earth, and the very earth itself, belongs to God who created them. Human beings are his collaborators, but not his equals. Moreover, God has provided all these things at no cost to us. If everyone worked without salary or wage all the world's resources would be available free. The only cost is self-imposed by Man himself who insists on being paid for his work. So how did the present state of things come about?

In the beginning when human life was at a primitive stage families gathered food from wild plants and wild animals. They clothed themselves with animal skins and the wool and hair taken from them. They built their shelters from what materials they could collect. They led a nomadic life, moving on when they had exhausted the food freely available about their camps. In time they learnt to grow crops and domesticate animals, and later still to make use of minerals in the ground. But they did not all produce the same things, so they learnt to exchange products by bartering. As life became more sophisticated, and communication between one district and another became possible, money was invented as a convenient and practical means of exchange. But money also put power into the hands of those who had it. Together with land acquisition it enabled individuals and countries to amass huge resources and to lord it over those who had them not. Those who got control of resources and the goods made from them charged those who did not have them but wanted them, and they made sure that they profited hugely from the transacton. The workers who developed the resources and made the goods also demanded payment. This is, of course, a very simplistic account of how certain groups of people came to control the distribution of the resources provided by God for all, but it sets the scene.

There is, of course, another element in the equation – evil. Human nature is flawed, as the Book of Genesis tells us, and people are by nature selfish. Observe a nursery class of 3 year-olds and you will be left in no doubt about the acquisitive instincts a child inherits with its genes. If this selfish part of our nature is not acknowledged and controlled it leads to greed, conflict, xenophobia and the ruthless exploitation of people and resources. Look at our world today and you will see evidence of this on every hand, even in our own country. Tribal conflict in Africa, the Middle East, the Balkans, Northern Ireland and elsewhere; the ruthless exploitation of natural resources by huge multi-national companies; the 'haves' jealously guarding their standard of living while the 'have-nots' receive sympathy and aid which is little more than crumbs from the rich man's table. But the root causes of most of the trouble remain unaddressed. If the huge resources devoted to the arms industry, both by those who manufacture armaments and those who buy them, were transferred to civil engineering and land reclamation, the deserts could be made productive and enough electric power generated to supply those areas where at present there is none. Even though the total world population has increased enormously in the past 200 years there are adequate resources to provide everyone with a standard of living sufficient to enable people to raise families and live with dignity. But only a handful of people who have plenty are willing to make a substantial reduction in their standard of living so that the very poor might have theirs raised. Even within our own country this is evident. We have got ourselves locked into the expectation of such a high level of prosperity as if by right that many couples in this part of the world consider it necessary for both of them to work in order that a high mortgage can be sustained, that two cars can be kept on the road, that the household gadgets nowadays considered essential can be bought and maintained and that the children's expectations of clothes, toys, leisure pursuits and holidays can be met. On top of this it is assumed that the State can and will provide ever more sophisticated health and social services free at the point of delivery. As galloping technology obliterates more and more jobs the blight of unemployment has settled upon the country like a mediaeval plague. Those in work make sympathetic noises about the plight of the unemployed but show no sign of work-sharing. The fact is that if we had stable families, if we were prepared to reduce our standard of living and be satisfied once again with one wage earner per family, and if the huge sums milked dishonestly every year by both rich and poor from the national purse were devoted to better training and re-training, there would be enough work to go round. As it is, the gap between those in work and those out of work widens inexorably. If not checked, this imbalance will destabilize society. And the same thing is happening on a global scale. The wealthy industrialized countries which control most of the world's resources produce so much food that, for instance, one supermarket in this country contains enough food to feed whole villages for months in the Third World. While they starve we go on slimming diets to control obesity and pay our farmers to take land out of production. The United Nations, which in effect means the G7 because most of the other members seldom pay their dues, cannot be roused to effective action in trouble spots unless someone threatens their commercial interests, and then no cost is too high. Unless the major powers, both their leaders and their people, come to their senses and realize the inescapable necessity of distributive justice there will be increasing international as well as national instability, and we shall reap the harvest of the dragons' teeth we have sown. All very well, you may say, but what am I, little me in Chichester, to do about all this? I suggest we can all do two things:

In order to prepare Himself for His public ministry, Jesus made what nowadays we should call a retreat. He went into the desert for 40 days where He fasted and prayed to His Father. He was also visited by Satan who proposed three spectacular ways by which Jesus might achieve His aim of founding a kingdom and bringing all peoples under His sway. You remember what they were: to manufacture food miraculously, to announce His arrival as a deus ex machina, stunning people by a spectacular appearance, and by the assumption of political power. Jesus rejected all three. Instead He returned to His home district of Galilee and set about His Father's work as an ordinary Galilean. As far as his compatriots were concerned he was the son of Joseph the carpenter. I think this has an important lesson for us.

Bob Geldof's television spectacular raised huge sums for famine relief in Ethiopia, but, good thing though it was, it left unaffected the root problems of civil war, personal greed and global maldistribution. The TV religious channels in the USA have made fortunes for the televangelists but done little to arrest the national moral decline. The kingdom of God comes to reality not by media hype but by hidden incubation in the hearts and minds of individual people, and is enlarged by the personal holiness and example of His followers. Holiness begins to drive out evil when enough people live the life of the Gospel which Jesus came to preach and to demonstrate. We may think that a few people in Chichester can in no way influence massive Third World problems, but consider! When you make a cake a single grain of sugar is not enough to sweeten the whole mixture, but several spoonfuls made up of individual grains will. In God's mixing bowl our few Chichester grains when added to those from other places are vital for His work. So the first thing we can do is to keep trying to make ourselves ever more Christlike. Secondly, like Dorothy Peacock whom we laid to rest on Monday, we can help to raise funds locally for Christian Aid by being generous ourselves and by giving time and effort in helping to organise local events. Every little helps. The tiny grain of sand grows into the pearl of great price.

During the last 24 hours tributes to the life and work of John Smith, Leader of the Labour Party, have come from across the nation. Among his virtues two have been universally remarked upon: his honesty and integrity rooted in his Christian faith, and secondly his passion for justice. He saw in his own constituency and during his tours around Britain the widening gap between rich and poor and the devastating effects of unemployment. Had he come to power he was determined to arrest the imbalance and bring about full employment. It was this passionate crusade which drove him forward, eventually, as we now know, to his death. Perhaps we need a bit more of that passion ourselves – the passion for justice.

So, as Jesus said: *"Be of good heart. I have overcome the world"*. Small though our contribution may be, if we stick with Him we shall be there at His triumph. The recent triumph of another passionate crusader for justice, Nelson Mandela, should give fresh hope and renewed energy to us all.

SERMON PREACHED AT THE OPENING OF THE PETWORTH FESTIVAL

AT ST MARY'S PARISH CHURCH, ON SUNDAY, 3RD JULY, 1994

My cultural home, and in one sense my spiritual home, is the Royal Festival Hall on the South Bank in London. It has been my good fortune to spend many happy, and some inspirational, evenings there. It is with the account of one such experience that I am going to begin. It happened one evening some years ago about this time of the year, when during the interval you can go out onto the balcony and look across the Thames to the beating heart of London in the mellow light of the late evening. The programme played by the BBC Welsh Symphony Orchestra under James Loughran included Prokofiev's Third Piano Concerto with Peter Donoghoe as soloist. It was one of those evenings when there is magic in the air.

As I listened to the Concerto I fell to marvelling at Peter Donoghoe's memory which could contain all the hundreds of notes, not just of the piece I was hearing, but of many other works besides. I marvelled at his brain and nervous system which could convert the notes in his memory into impulses which activated the muscles of his fingers and made the grand music I was enjoying. But then, I thought, how much more marvellous the mind of Prokofiev who had conceived and written this great work. Before a composer writes a single note of the manuscript he has heard the work in his mind. Imagine what it must be like for a composer when he attends the very first orchestral rehearsal of a new work. His creation becomes a reality of sound and is heard by other people for the first time. There must have been a point in time when God's creation took form before him. We are told He saw that it was very good. You see, God created the talent not just of a Peter Donoghoe but the talents of every musician who has ever lived or will live. In his infinite mind he conceived from all eternity all the music which this world has ever heard, and not only human compositions. A trained ornithologist, even if blindfolded, can tell what birds are about just by listening to their song. Each species has its own specific cry. God brought all this about, but He also created us with ears which could hear this music and brains which could interpret it.

Think, too, of God the artist. At this time of the year when the trees are in full leaf and the crops are growing to fruition, stand any day on top of the Downs and you will see a great variety of colours, greens of many shades, here and there a bright yellow splodge of rape and variegated dots of wild flowers. As you watch the shades of colour are constantly changing as clouds scurry across the sky and deflect the rays of the sun. A real environmental kaliedescope. God conceived all these colours and gave us eyes to see them with and minds with which to appreciate what He has created. Human artists have tried to capture such scenes on their canvas: they have tried to portray the beauty of flowers, the brilliance of birds' plumage, the expressions on a human face: to fix the fascination of a moment in the permanence of a painting. But even the finest painting of the most consummate artist is without life, whereas the landscapes and portraits of God are composed of living beings. They are alive. The live performance is always superior to the recording. As Jesus reminds us in the extract from St Luke's Gospel which Canon Collins has just read to us: *"Think of the flowers; they never have to spin or weave; yet, I assure you, not even Solomon in all his regalia was robed like one of these."*

And what of the word? The Book of Genesis tells us that God spoke the word and in the six days of creation our world came to be. John the Evangelist calls Jesus 'God's Word': *"The Word was made flesh and dwelt amongst us"*. Of all living creatures on the face of the earth only humans can verbalize. This power of the word gives us a sophisticated means of communication and enables us to express our thoughts, our emotions, or desires and our intentions in ways given to no other creature. It is the word which makes possible our literature, our drama, our poetry. Anyone who has listened to a great orator or great actor in person knows the power of speech. What power for good or evil God has given us! What verbal artistry to delight our ears and our minds! How grateful we should be! How careful and responsible in our choice of words! How compassionate to the blind, the deaf and the dumb!

The work of all creative artists – be they composers, painters, sculptors, poets, dramatists, architects, designers – is stamped with the unmistakable marks of their individual genius. How else could we distinguish a symphony by Beethoven from one by Elgar; a painting by Gaugin from one by Turner; a sonnet by Shakespeare from one by Wordsworth. In the same way the genius of God, the supreme artist, the cosmic architect, is in this work. His personality is not just stamped upon all of His creation, but all living things share his characteristics in something the same way that children of a human family share the genes and characteristics of their parents.

Now I have a confession to make. For much of my life the Holy Trinity meant virtually nothing to me. True, I learnt to make the sign of the cross at my mother's knee and to repeat the familiar words; "In the name of the Father, and of the Son and of the Holy Spirit", but wrestle as I would with the idea of three Persons in one God, I was totally defeated. My teachers told me it was a mystery. It was certainly that! I gave up but continued to mouth the words. Such understanding as I have of this great mystery which is central to the christian faith came to me one day about 15 years ago when walking along the Roman Stane Street from Eartham. The locals among you will know that after about a mile you reach a point on the Downs above Bignor where you can see for miles in most directions; to the north across Petworth to the Weald; to the south across the Manhood Peninsula to the Channel. As I stopped to take in the scene it suddenly came to me that I was surrounded on all sides by evidence of the Trinity. The grasses, the trees, the wild flowers, the crops, the birds, the insects, the animals wild and tame, human beings too, every living thing, I realized, receives its life from the fusion of two other beings, a male and a female of its own species. Pollen-flower-seedling: horse-mare-foal: father-mother-child: Father-Son-Holy Spirit. But more than this, whatever the species, the parents pass on to their offspring not only the characteristics of the species as a whole but some of their individual characteristics as well. Hence the science of genetics. If this is true of God's creatures it must surely be true of Him? As St Paul put it in his Letter to the Romans:

> *"Ever since God created the world, His invisible qualities, both His eternal power and His divine nature, have been clearly seen; they are perceived in the things that God has made."*

I had often wondered why God is trinitarian. Why could He not be a single unitary person like us? Christians believe that God existed from all eternity before time began. All sentient creatures need the company of other members of their own species. Fish live in shoals, birds in flocks, animals in herds, human beings in families, tribes and settlements. As Terry Waite and his fellow hostages have reminded us, solitary confinement is probably the worst form of punishment one human being can inflict on another. We inherit our Creator's characteristics. How solitary, how detached, how lacking in all the emotions we experience would have been a single person God, locked in his loneliness from all eternity! The fact that we have need of company, that as children we craved the love of father and mother, that as adults we need the affirmation, the encouragement and the support of friends and colleagues, above all that we want to be loved, surely this must be proof positive that these are all characteristics of the God who made us. Otherwise we should not be as we are. St John tells us that "God is love". All true love is creative; so the act of creation is as natural to God as marriage is to us. The greatest yearning of the lover is that the beloved will return his/her love. If any of you have had the misfortune to fall deeply in love with someone who proved completely indifferent to your earnest protestations and rejected your love, you will know only too well what a crushing blow such a rejection can be. This is why the rejection of God's love is so terrible, so destructive. It strikes at the very heart of creation.

"Greater love has no man than to lay down his life for his friends. You are my friends if you do what I command you. I shall not call you servants any more, because a servant does not know his master's business. I call you friends because I have made known to you everything I have learnt from my father". Jesus, the Word of God, said those words the night before He gave Himself into the hands of the torturers who put Him to death. The cross is the permanent reminder that *"God loved the world so much that He gave His only Son"*, as Jesus told Nicodemus. Unbelievably He yearns for our love in return. And the Son told us how we are to show our love for the Father – by loving our neighbour as ourselves. *"Therein lies the whole law and the prophets"*, as Jesus put it.

So, enjoy your festival, take delight in all the good things which have been prepared for you, but in the midst of your enjoyment remember to offer your praise and thanks to the Creator God who has made it all possible. Reflect on His love and resolve to respond by loving your neighbour. The organizing of festivals can be very stressful: performing in public produces nervous tension. May the audiences be supportive of the artists: may the artists be inspired: and may everyone extend understanding and patience to those who behind scenes wrestle with administration. Then, indeed, the Petworth Festival 1994 will be a huge success.

HOMILIES
ON
CHRISTIAN UNITY

SUNDAY WITHIN THE WEEK OF PRAYER FOR CHRISTIAN UNITY

CHICHESTER CATHEDRAL, 20th JANUARY 1985 at 11. 00am.

"Father may they be one in us, as You are in me and I am in You"
Words taken from St John's Gospel chapter 17.

My own interest in church unity began at quite an early age and in a somewhat unusual way. When I started studying for my School Certificate in those far-off pre 'O' level days, I took Art as one of my subjects. It comprised three papers, as I recall, one of which concerned the history of mediaeval church architecture. My home was in one of our ancient cathedral cities which had plenty of mediaeval churches, but I was a Roman Catholic and in those days protestant churches were forbidden territory to us. Our own church had been built in penal times to look like a non-conformist chapel in the hope of allaying the suspicions of the anti-papist faction in the city. Anything less like mediaeval architecture it would have been hard to find. So what was I to do? What I did was to disobey the parental ban and surreptitiously I began making sorties with increasing frequency into some of the Anglican churches where were to be found the soaring arches and groined roofs which I came to love. I can still recall the fear and trepidation with which I entered the great cathedral for the first time. Gradually I lost my embarrassment and it was there one afternoon that I heard my first choral evensong. To me the tones echoing round the great building were how I imagined the sound of the angels singing in heaven. I was enchanted. A few years later, this time with my mother, I had my first experience in the same cathedral of a major choral work with massed choirs and one of the great professional orchestras. Thus was confirmed my lifelong passion for music. Many, many years later, when I first came to Chichester, I used quite regularly to attend your choral evensong on a Sunday afternoon up there in the choir.

I am telling you all this because I want you to understand that I can identify very easily with your worship in these marvellous cathedrals, or indeed in your simpler but lovely parish churches. But I could not help contrasting the handful of people who were my companions at evensong with the crowds who thronged to the 900th Anniversary Festival events in the summer, when chairs were squeezed into every nook and cranny and all seats were sold. As Christians, ought we not to ask ourselves why people will flock in their hundreds to the House of God to hear the Royal Philharmonic or the Academy of St Martin-in-the-Fields but never darken a church door for the rest of the year? You may remember Malcolm Muggeridge's description of the last days of the British Raj in India.

He tells how the Viceroy was still making his bi-annual progress from Delhi to Simla and back again, the civil servants were still earnestly processing their files and the Works and Bricks Dept. was still busily maintaining the buildings, while all around them the real India was in a ferment and the foundations of Imperial rule were crumbling. Is there not a parallel in our devotedly conducting our age-old rituals in what are now rather inelegantly described as 'The Mainline Churches' while most of Britain treats religion as an irrelevance, and strife and violence stalk the land? We are aghast as nightly on our TV screens we watch examples of man's inhumanity to man in many parts of the world, but most worryingly in our own 'green and pleasant land'. But let us beware of seeing it all as the result of someone else's sin in which we have taken no part. If our interest in the moral collapse around us is vicarious we need to read again the parable of the Pharisee and the Publican. We are a part of the society in which we live and we cannot opt out of responsibility. I wonder if the name Corrymeela means anything to you? Corrymeela is a marvellous haven of peace on the Antrim coast in Northern Ireland. It is a truly ecumenical venture devoted to reconciliation, not only between the warring factions in the Province, but wherever there is discord and strife. The present leader of the Corrymeela Community is a man called John Morrow. In a recent book he has much to say about 'scapegoating'. Scapegoating is looking for someone else to blame. He points out that there is a perennial tendency in all of us to see violence in someone else and the ability to blind ourselves to the fact that violence in society comes from us all.

There is, I think, a danger that sometimes some of us can, if we are not careful, regard the Week of Prayer for Christian Unity rather like inviting in the dustmen for a pint of beer at Christmas time. We make our annual gesture to the lower orders and then for the rest of the year get down to the serious business of running our parishes or administering our Cathedrals. Christian unity, like worker participation, is a good idea in theory but would be much too disruptive in practice. To understand the fallaciousness of that approach, surely we have only to look about us. Even in a place as small as Chichester, there are churches which have been declared redundant and put to secular uses, churches which up to the turn of the century at least had been in constant use, some of them since they were built in mediaeval times. How many rural parishes are now lumped together under the care of a single vicar? If our practical Christianity remains parochial, then, like the Raj in India, there may be no parishes to run or cathedrals to administer by the turn of the next century. Were this to be so could those of us whose entire life-span had lain within the twentieth century say that the virtual extinction of Christianity has had nothing to do with us?

The raison d'etre for Christian unity goes much deeper than good neighbourliness. In fact it goes back to the very beginnings of creation. In the beginning

God's creation was perfect. *'He saw that it was good'*. And it was His intention that it should remain so, but in order that the explosiveness of the mighty love which caused Him to create might in some measure be returned He had to make some of His creatures free. Once you give someone freedom you run the risk that they will abuse it. If they do not have this capacity they are not free. You cannot get love out of a computer. We know that some of the angels abused their freedom, and mankind has never ceased to do so since Adam and Eve led the way. But division is not of God. Discord, strife, enmity destroy the perfection of God's creation, and nowhere more so than within His mystical body, the Church. It is Christ's intention to restore all things to the Father and, as He told us, 'to draw all things to Himself'. In so far as we persist in our denominational isolation, thus far do we frustrate His designs. In so far as we cannot bring ourselves to lay our most cherished traditions, and what to us are our deeply felt convictions, at His feet, content to let Him confirm or reject them, then we remain a scandal to the world. It is our pride which has emptied our churches. As pride was the first sin so it is the source and origin of all other sins. *'That they may be one, Father, as you and I are one, that the world may believe'*. And it will not believe so long as we remain divided. So yes, we are in some measure responsible for the increasing violence in our society which so terrifies us. We are not without blame.

To return to this morning's reading: *'The time has come; the Kingdom of God is upon you; repent and believe the Gospel'*. We cannot repent of our divisiveness one minute too soon. As for the Gospel, it is a gospel of love to all mankind. *'Jesus came into Galilee proclaiming the Gospel'*, St. Mark tells us. That was the work given Him by His Father. That is still the first aim and object of His Church – to preach the Gospel to all men. It is, therefore, our first duty as Christians. Until we burst forth from our parishes, from our cathedrals, as God's people working in full communion and with obvious love for each other, to carry the Gospel to those who neither know or care about God, though like us they were made for Him, so long will the body of Christ continue to waste away, while unbridled sensuality will continue to sap the moral fibre of the body politic and the lust for power will escalate the level of violence until man in his pride might even destroy the earth God gave him to live on.

So, my dear Brothers and Sisters, let us pledge ourselves this morning to work unceasingly for that unity for which Christ prayed. As a start, however meagre my talents and however imperfect my love, I offer them to you as an earnest sign of my continuing endeavour for the cause of full communion between our churches.

Finally, a postscript: One cannot say everything in a twelve minute sermon. No doubt you will wonder, in view of what I have said, why I shall not join you at your Eucharist in a few minutes time. If you want to find out you will have to come to the Church of St. Paul and St. Peter the Great on Friday evening at 7.30 p.m.

THE WEEK OF PRAYER FOR CHRISTIAN UNITY, 1985

CHURCH OF ST PAUL & ST PETER THE GREAT, CHICHESTER. FRIDAY 25th JANUARY AT 7.30pm

"He must grow greater: I must grow smaller"

The words of John the Baptist as recorded in St John's Gospel, Chapter 3.

Pride was the first sin; the sin committed by Lucifer and his companions. It is also the deadliest of sins because it opens the way to most of the others.

At the root of most disagreements between individuals, of divisions and strife between groups of people, is pride: the refusal to admit the possibility of being wrong; perhaps even the refusal to admit it when we know in our heart of hearts that we are wrong or in a false position. Pride leads to the stance of 'My country, right or wrong'; 'My church, right or wrong'. Most heresies and divisions within the Church, like most wars between nations, have arisen because people could not bring themselves to pocket their pride, to forgive an injury, to try again to live in peace and harmony even if total agreement was not possible.

The antidotes to pride, its contrary virtues, are humility and obedience, accompanied always by true love which is essentially unselfish. But in this brash, self-centred, self-opinionated, technological world of 1985, which thinks it can solve its problems without God, humility and obedience are not popular, to put it mildly. Though the world may have no use for them, they are, however, essential to anyone who is seriously concerned about Christian unity.

If we are genuinely seeking the reunification of Christendom, then we have to bring ourselves to the point of being able to face the possibility that our Church may have got some things wrong and that another Church may have got them right. With John the Baptist we must grow smaller, more humble, in order that God may grow greater within us. We have to try to be so unselfish, so objective in our approach, that we can actually lay at His feet all our most cherished traditions, all the things we have believed and held dear for perhaps fifty or sixty years, and say to Him: 'Lord, take from me everything which is not in accordance with your will and pleasure; give me back only those things which are true; help me to understand, cherish and hold fast any things which hitherto I have not understood, or believed, but which you want me to'. You see, in the final analysis the only thing that matters is His truth: and God is truth. *'I am the Way, the Truth, and the Life'.*

Unity, if it is to be genuine and lasting, must be rooted in truth, but it is important here I think to make a distinction between unity and uniformity. If we look at the world of nature we cannot fail to be amazed at the variety of God's creation. Moreover, it is not all neat and tidy but gloriously higgledy-piggledy. So I do not believe that the reunification of Christendom implies that we must all act in unison like soldiers on parade. Nevertheless, there are certain fundamentals of Christian belief and certain moral laws which are not negotiable. God is not a mental contortionist who can espouse complete opposites simultaneously. Truth is indivisible. So, for instance, Christ was either true God and true man, or He was not. Moral acts like abortion and divorce are either right or wrong; they cannot change their acceptability according to circumstances. For our part what we always can, and must, do is to refrain from judging other people and be ever ready with compassion and forgiveness, but what we must not do is to compromise on principle. Our Lord readily forgave the woman taken in adultery, and rounded on her accusers, but He was uncompromising on the commandment; in fact He tightened up the interpretation of that particular commandment. So it is truth we must seek without fear or favour, but we shall not succeed in finding it unless we are humble to the point of self-abnegation.

I mentioned also obedience. Obedience has been one of the great religious principles all down the centuries. This is hardly surprising because Christ Himself told us that obedience to His Father was the mainspring of His life. St Paul tells us that *'Jesus emptied Himself, taking the form of a servant ... and being found in human form He humbled Himself and became obedient unto death, even death on a cross'*. Last June at my ordination I placed my hands in the hands of my Bishop and promised obedience to him as my father in Christ. Kneeling within a few feet of me was my dear friend, the Anglican Bishop of Lewes, who also has priests and deacons who have promised obedience to him as their bishop. I knew that when it came to the reception of Holy Communion he was suffering agonies of humiliation and the pain of division, as indeed I am sure, were my other non-catholic friends who paid me the singular honour of being present on that occasion. In spite of the great joy I experienced it was as though a harsh rusty file had been drawn across my soul by the knowledge that friends I value greatly could not share with me the great mystery of our faith. Tonight I must again suffer that pain and frustration because, you see, I believe that this is a true cross which has been sent us. A cross is not something we choose for ourselves but something Jesus gives us. Those of us who feel deeply about these things must hang on our several crosses beside Him, as did the two thieves on Calvary, until He sees fit to release us. He did not get down from His cross, so neither must we chicken out in order to achieve some easy incomplete solution. As for myself I believe it would be presumptuous of me to think that I am better qualified to judge these matters than Bishop Cormac or Pope John Paul and that I must be humble enough to submit my judgement to theirs. I only know that genuine and lasting unity is not to be won by cheap compromise but by submitting oneself to God's grinding mill in which the soul is ground into the form He wants between the twin grinding stones of relentless prayer and frequent penance. In foretelling his death, Jesus said that when He was lifted up He would draw all men to Himself. By humbly accepting the pain of our own personal crucifixions we, too, shall be lifted up and drawn together in Him. But this I can promise you: when or if, no when, Bishop Cormac gives the green light I shall be the first at your altar rails and the first to invite you to our altar at St Richard's.

But while theologians and church leaders are sorting out the doctrinal problems there is much we ordinary folk at the grass roots can do together; indeed must do together. If we understand the full implications of the Incarnation we must believe that Christ is to be found in our neighbour. *'If you do not love your neighbour whom you see'*, says St John, *'how can you love God whom you do not see?'* And he goes on, *'He who says he loves God but hates his brother is a liar'*. Strong words. It is because we have failed so signally in that that we are failing to be the salt of the earth. Even in my lifetime I have seen many churches made redundant or pulled down. I have seen parishes which, when I was a lad, each had a vicar and a full Sunday congregation, amalgamated two, three, even four at a time under one over-worked vicar with but a handful of people at each service. I have seen house churches and fellowships spring up all over the place because people said that what have become known as the 'mainline' Churches no longer provided the spiritual nourishment they were looking for. There is a great hunger for the life of the Spirit, a great need to find a meaning to life. 'Our heart is restless until it rests in Thee', said Augustine. Reliable statistics reveal that barely ten percent of the adult population of this country have any connection with a Church of any kind. The most recent figures published at the new year show the main Christian churches still losing ground. One of the principal reasons for this sad state of affairs is that people are scandalized by the disunity and division among those who profess to be Christians. *'You are the light of the world'*, He said. *'You do not light a lamp and hide it under a barrel, but put it on a lampstand that it may light up the whole house'*. Are our lamps lighting up the houses of Chichester? *'You are the salt of the earth'*, He said, *'but if the salt becomes tasteless, what can make it salty again?'* Non-Christians, and even some Christians, it would seem, find our salt tasteless. So how can we make ourselves salty again? We can do so by repenting of our stubbornness, our pride, our unwillingness to allow that we might have been wrong all along; by repenting of our self-righteousness. And then in their place substituting humility, obedience, a willingness to learn, to listen to what He is telling us with that still small voice in the quietness of our souls and in the fellowship of our Christian brothers and sisters. Above all by seeing in our neighbour the person of Christ Himself, for it is on this that He will judge us. *'So long as you did not do it to one of these my least brethren you did not do it to Me'*. To take two extremes, that means nothing less than Ian Paisley being willing to see Christ in the person of Pope John Paul, and Pope John Paul being willing to see Christ in Ian Paisley. Christ chose the Samaritan as His example of our neighbour because the antipathy between the Jews of Judea and the Jews of Samaria was extreme, akin to the hostility between Protestants and Catholics in Northern Ireland. *'It is by their fruits you shall know them'*, He said. The world is not drawn to the fruits hanging on our trees because it sees those who tend God's orchard arguing and fighting among themselves.

In restoring unity to the Body of Christ the first step is forgiveness, so let none of us leave this church tonight without forgiveness in our hearts for those Christians of other traditions whom we may think have offended against us or our Church. We can try to make the second part of the Lord's Prayer especially real. But more than that. When we reach the sign of peace in the liturgy let our handshake not be a bit of perfunctory ritual, but let it demonstrate our belief that the person standing next to us is for us at that moment the person of Christ Himself. We are close here, you see, to the mystery of the Incarnation. To Philip He said, *'To have seen Me is to have seen the Father'*. Join that to: *'So long as you did it to one of these My least brethren you did it to Me'*, and you will see what I mean.

'He must grow greater: I must grow smaller'. All this requires great faith and much humility. Christ said of John the Baptist 'there is none greater born of woman', yet the Baptist found it necessary to fast and to do penance. The plight of the world we live in is too perilous to allow of half-heartedness in those who believe in the Saviour of Mankind, in the brotherhood of all people in Christ.

The reunification of Christendom is an essential element in the conversion of the world; the drawing together of all people in Christ, which alone can avert that cataclysm referred to in Mark, Chapter 12 and 2 Peter Chapter 3. Until our day men could only guess how the destruction of the world could come about. We know.

My Brothers and Sisters in Christ, let us pledge ourselves tonight to work unceasingly for Christian unity, however great the problems may at times appear. Let us ask for strength to follow St Peter and St Paul, the feast of whose conversion we are celebrating. Like their Master they were obedient unto death. Our martyrdom may not be at the hands of violent men (though we should never rule that out) but every true Christian must be willing to be immolated on the cross chosen for them by Jesus Christ. He wants nothing less of us. For my part, however meagre my talents, however imperfect my love, I offer them to you that together we may go forward hand in hand to work for the salvation of the world by offering ourselves on the altar of the cross where hangs the Sacred Victim, the Perfect Sacrifice. He gave His life for our salvation and in return He wants the total dedication of our lives to His service, but particularly He wants our love. *'How can we say we love God whom we cannot see, if we do not love our neighbour whom we see?'* My Brothers and Sisters, let us love one another.

THE WEEK OF PRAYER FOR CHRISTIAN UNITY 1986

EUCHARISTIC SERVICE AT ST RICHARD'S, CHICHESTER

Those of you who are not Roman Catholics or Anglicans are probably wondering why we are dressed up in funny clothes. I'll let you into a secret: I sometimes wonder too! But the fact is that every human group or organisation from the very early days of its formation begins to develop some kind of ritual, something to establish its identity. Our teenagers whom we see around the town with coloured hair, tight trousers and the other things we are all familiar with are merely conforming to the mores of their peer group. Religious groups have always had their rituals, their liturgies, some elaborate, some simple. In the same way some people like candles. If you go to Scandinavia you will find that people there light candles at all the main meals be it spring, summer, autumn or winter. The only difference is that the colour of the candles changes according to the season. Orthodox Christians, Roman Catholics and Anglo-Catholics have long been partial to a little incense. Some of the Eastern religions burn joss sticks. Traditions and tastes vary as people do, but usually traditions are significant and symbolic for those concerned; so it is with us. At all events I hope we can disregard the externals for a few minutes and concentrate on the inner significance of what we are about.

We Christians believe that the God we worship is infinite and eternal and that we could not know Him unless He had first revealed Himself to us. We believe that He reveals Himself to us in different ways but primarily through the Sacred Scriptures. We refer to the Bible as God's 'Word'.

In biblical times the Jews believed that God's word was so powerful that its effect was instantaneous, and so they often fused the two as it were. *'God said: "Let there be light", and there was light'*. In a way this is true of us too. If in a moment of anger when I am off guard I say something hurtful to a friend, the wounding effect of my words is instantaneous. Having said them I may bitterly regret my foolishness, but there is no way in which I can take back those words, try as I might to mitigate their effect.

In the same way I am sure we can recall a time when we were distraught and feeling lonely. Someone, perhaps a complete stranger, notices our anguish which evokes their concern. The few kind understanding words they say are like balm on a wound. We feel we could fling our arm round their necks because we realize there is someone who cares. The effect of their words is instantaneous. In the New

Testament Christ the Son of God is referred to as 'The Word'. *"In the beginning was the Word: the Word was with God and the Word was God".*

I expect you have noticed how Jesus often identified Himself, and sometimes his followers, with the everyday things He mentioned in His discourses. *"I am the vine, you are the branches".* He does not say *"I am like a vine, you are as it were the branches".* No, He identified Himself completely in order to bring home to us what to Him was the reality, that His life runs through us and ours through Him. And He goes on, *"If you remain in Me and My words remain in you".* His word is the lifeblood of our life together, His and ours.

"I am the light of the world", He says. He does not say, *"I am like a light"*, but *"I am the light".* And He says to His apostles, *"You are the light of the world".* Once we are baptized and have the life of the Spirit in us we are a light because we share in His life which is light. And He tells us why we are lights, *"so that men seeing your good works, may give praise to your Father in heaven".* If you have ever been at sea at night trying to navigate your boat into an unfamiliar harbour you will know how easy it is to mistake lights on shore for navigation lights. You are looking for a light on a buoy or on the harbour wall but there are lots of lights in the town or village behind. It is very easy to mistake a street light, or the lights of a stationary car perhaps, for a leading light, especially if there is a tree in between which is waving in the wind so that the light appears to be flashing. If we follow a false light we may easily end up on the rocks. In the same way we are lights, for better or worse. If we give a false lead others may end up not with God but in trouble.

"I am the gate", He said. *"Anyone who enters through me will be safe".*

So at the Last Supper He took some bread and when He had said the blessing He broke it and gave it to His disciples. *"Take it and eat"*, He said *"this is my body".* Then He took a cup, and when He had returned thanks He gave it to them. *"Drink all of you from this"*, He said, *"for this is my blood".* Notice again He did not say *"This is a kind of representation of my body"* or *"This wine can be used to remind you of my blood which will be shed".* No, He again identifies Himself with the object He is talking about. I am not a scholar, either of scripture or of ancient languages, but I am told by those who are that in the original Aramaic or Greek in which the gospels were written there is no possibility of mistaking the meaning of the words. He said, *"This is my body"* But there was a difference this time from the other examples I have given. He added something: *"Do this in memory of me".* He tells His Apostles to do as He has done at the Last Supper, and at that supper He identified Himself with the bread He held in His hand.

Down the ages theologians have tried to probe this great mystery and have coined words and phrases in an attempt to explain how this could be. The result has been that people get hang-ups about words like 'transubstantiation' and 'consubstantiation'. Those words and other theological dicta certainly were unknown to the apostles. St Peter would not have known what you were talking about if you had asked him what transubstantiation was. But all the apostles understood what He said in its awesome simplicity and it was from them that Paul received the word, the Word that was made flesh and dwelt amongst us.

My Brothers and Sisters I can only tell you what I believe, that what we can all see in that golden monstrance is without a shadow of a doubt the true body of my Saviour Jesus Christ. (This will probably be my last sermon as Chairman of the Chichester Council of Churches. If you remember nothing else about me I would like you to remember what I have just said.) I believe that the best of any person is the faith in them which gives rise to their integrity as people. So I believe that you and I by virtue of our baptism are integrated into the living body of Christ. St Paul tells us that together we make up the body of Christ. I believe it is His life which courses through us, so that your life is in me and mine in you. We are one vine; we are the light. At baptism we entered through Him who is the gate and we are therefore safe in His fold. In His presence therefore let us recognise each other as true brothers and sisters. If we have anything to forgive let us do so now, so that we can then bring the gift of ourselves to His altar and be united in the Word of God which is life itself.

The Churches and Fellowships to which we belong may differ on point of doctrine, but where charity is concerned there can be no divisions St John says: *"If you do not love your brother whom you see, how can you love God whom you do not see?"* Writing to the Romans St Paul says, *"Owe no one anything, except to love one another; for he who loves his neighbour has fulfilled the law. Love does no wrong to a neighbour therefore love is the fulfilling of the law"*. In the parable of the Good Samaritan Jesus told us how to recognise our neighbour. The orthodox Jews of His time regarded the Samaritans as heretics. And in St Matthew's gospel Jesus tells us how the Just Judge will differentiate between the blessed and the damned – *"So long as you did it to one of these my least brethren you did it to Me"*.

WEEK OF PRAYER FOR CHRISTIAN UNITY JANUARY 1989

SERMON PREACHED AT THE PARISH CHURCH OF ST MARY MAGDALENE, MIDHURST

Cardinal Hume in his latest book, "Towards a Civilization of Love", says: 'Increasingly it has become obvious that the Age of Enlightenment is now psychologically and morally bankrupt. The underlying consensus of values which held society together no longer exists in any effective way'. Indeed it is so. We find that man is not after all superman. By any standard which is measurable christianity in Britain has been in decline for at least half a century. Whether through apathy, intellectual conviction or unreasoned hostility the christian religion is now openly rejected by a large proportion of the population. The results are apparent for all to see. As Jesus Christ put it: *"By their fruits you shall know them"*.

Chief constables in their annual reports have for some years been warning Government of the remorseless rise in violent crime, of which perhaps the most distressing development is the violation of the defenceless - the very young and the very old.

Dishonesty and theft, often euphemistically referred to as 'fiddling the system', is now perpetrated on a vast scale – the police estimate is an annual total in excess of £2 billion – from shoplifting worth a few pounds at one end of the scale to massive commercial frauds involving millions at the other. And this does not take into account forms of dishonesty which are now so common that few people consider them dishonest any more – like doing one's private telephoning (especially long distance calls) from the office without asking the boss's permission.

Sexual permissiveness is now socially acceptable and virtually taken for granted. You may have read in the press recently of a research project undertaken by Exeter University among students. 50% of those interviewed were young women. Most admitted to sexual intercourse by the age of 17. 20% took the so-called 'recreational' view of sex. Only 6% held the view that sexual intercourse should be confined to marriage. I suggest it might not be far from the truth to aver that of the previously unmarried couples who present themselves at the altar for marriage nowadays those who are still virgins are very much the exception.

And what about usury – a word seldom heard nowadays. Do you not think our forefathers would have considered usurious the interest rates charged today by some well-known commercial companies and credit firms? 20-30% is common; 40 and even 50% by no means unknown.

As for the affirmation to tell the truth in a court of law, well, that would be a joke were it not a manifestation of a widespread public disregard for the truth.

You see, once a person, or a section of society, abandons an objective moral code the only criterion left is self-interest – what best serves me as I perceive my needs at any particular moment. But there's more to it than that. Because we humans are both body and spirit, if the spirit fails to comprehend the distinction between right and wrong and loses control of the body, then the animal in us takes over. Brutalized humanity is more dangerous that the brutes of field or forest because human beings have intelligence which they can use for evil ends. So it is not just a matter of having any moral code. If we are to work towards a better world, towards what Cardinal Hume calls "a civilisation of love", the only moral code which will do, the only way of life which leads to true peace and happiness is the one given us by Jesus Christ who alone is the way, the truth and the life.

So, what are the Churches doing to arrest the decline of christian living in our land? As you know, this is a question much under discussion at the present time. The Prime Minister wants the Churches to proclaim the moral values which she believes underlay Victorian society and led to its prosperity. She expects the Established Church in particular to support the State in its efforts to improve, as she sees it, the lot of its citizens. The liberation theologians, on the other hand, want the Church to identify itself with the poor and rejected and take their part against, what they see, as oppressive regimes. If that means entering the political arena, then so be it. So there are those who think churchmen have become too liberal and failed to uphold traditional values, and there are those who think that church leaders have failed to adapt the christian gospel to the 20th century and are not liberal enough. One way or the other, can it be said with any truth that the Churches are fiddling while the world burns, as once t'was said Nero did on his palace roof while Rome burned around him?

I am sure we are all familiar with the aphorism which states that 'evil triumphs when good people do nothing'. I am sure this can be so, but in my experience it would be truer to say that evil triumphs when well-meaning people concentrate their energies on the wrong things. Satan is very accomplished at convincing us that we are doing God's work when in fact we are doing his. For instance, people can, with the best of intentions, join an organisation devoted to a good christian cause, but end up by being thoroughly unchristian. Just for the sake of illustration let's suppose it's the Red Cross – a thoroughly reputable cause. The Red Cross committee of Much-Binding-in-the-Marsh has been chaired for many years by Colonel Bloggs, the local squire. Mrs Hacker, who has been a committee member of one of the big thrusting London branches, comes to live in the district and immediately joins the local branch. Within a week she has decided the Much-Binding branch is moribund and inefficient, so she starts gathering a like-minded group about her, determined to oust the Colonel and his cronies at the next AGM. By the time that takes place internecine war is well advanced and much more energy is being put into canvassing for membership of the new committee than into what the Red Cross is meant to be all about. Both factions are absolutely convinced they are fighting for the future well-being of the Red Cross whereas in fact they have done nothing but disrupt the harmony of the local community and bring the Red Cross into disrepute.

Could the cause of Christianity's decline in the West be due to the devil's success in getting christians to concentrate their attention and effort on matters of theology, doctrine, canon law and scriptural interpretation to the neglect of neighbourly love and charity, and forgetfulness of mission and evangelization? Might it be that churchmen, from parish clergy to the upper echelons of the hierarchy, have fallen prey to the disease which has afflicted much of British commercial and industrial management?

Two of the reasons why the Japanese have been so successful as industrialists and entrepreneurs is because they take infinite pains to find out the precise needs and aspirations of potential market populations, and because their managers spend much time on the shop floor, whereas in this country we have too often adopted a take-it-or-leave-it attitude to our customers, and too many of our managers have remained desk-bound, cocooned in a boardroom world of their own. It is perfectly possible today for a clergyman to convince himself that he is doing great pastoral work even though he seldom leaves his rectory, and when he does, more often than not it is to attend a meeting or conference. He finds himself bombarded by a daily postal mountain and incessant telephone calls. So management becomes the name of the game. In almost every sphere of life today vast amounts of time, energy and money are spent in organising, conducting, minuting and evaluating conferences, seminars, meetings and discussion groups. To this meleè of incessant verbiage and masterly inactivity the Church is no stranger.

When the time came for Jesus to start his public ministry He left His home at Nazareth. Pagan lands have never been won for Christ by those who stayed at headquarters but by those who ventured forth into the field. Those of my generation must surely have learnt from the Second World War that a Maginot Line mentality is no recipe even for survival let alone victory. Moreover, when an army advances it may well have to accept pockets of enemy resistance in its rear to be mopped up later on. To hold up the advance until there is no enemy in sight might well mean never advancing at all.

Christians are at war with the powers of evil. We know that on the authority of Christ Himself. If we delay taking the fight into enemy territory until all the doctrinal differences between the so-called mainline Churches are resolved we shall still be losing ground fifty years hence as we have been doing steadily for the last 50 years. No, we must join hands and take the gospel to the people. Clearly they are not going to come to us. Take a look around 90% of the churches and chapels in Sussex on any Sunday other than Easter or Christmas.

It is not fashionable to mention social class, but we have to face the fact that the christian religion is in danger of being largely a middle class activity. Until about 50 years ago the strength of the Free Churches, the Roman Catholic Church and the Anglo-Catholic wing of the Church of England was among working class communities. No longer so. As for young people, to a distressing extent they have said a plague on all your houses. Christ preached in simple language which could be understood by all, and his illustrations were contemporary and easily identifiable within the everyday experience of His listeners. From the earliest times, on the contrary, there has been a temptation to intellectualize religion, to make it cerebral and ethereal. Gnosticism and Manachaeism are still alive and kicking. The gnostics taught that knowledge of God belonged to an exclusive group of initiates: manachaeism is the belief that matter is inherently evil and that the purpose of religion is to free the spirit from involvement with material things. But it seems to me that God has always acted in exactly the opposite way. The Book of Genesis assures us that when God had created the world and all its creatures He surveyed it and saw 'that it was good'. From then onwards the story of His dealings with mankind is that He comes among His people. In the Old Testament we find Him taking an active part in the lives and history of His chosen people. In the end He sent His Son who took our flesh so as to be not just with us but one of us. He brought the gospel to us. We must do likewise.

Pope Paul VI in his encyclical letter of 1975 on Evangelization wrote that the essential mission of the Church is to evangelise. "Evangelization is the special grace and mission of the Church, a task which the great and fundamental changes of contemporary society make all the more urgent", he said. The present Pope, John Paul II, speaking to the Catholic bishops of Europe in January 1986 urged them to undertake afresh the evangelization of their ancient continent.

At the Swanwick conference in August 1987 Cardinal Hume said: "First I hope that our Roman Catholic delegates will recommend to members of our Church that we move now quite deliberately from a situation of cooperation to one of commitment to each other. By 'commitment to each other' I mean that we commit ourselves to praying and working together for Church unity and to acting together, both nationally and locally, for evangelization and mission".

The Roman Catholic Church, then, is committed to working with all baptized christians for the evangelization of the world. That is our mission. For us in the UK that means to advance the cause of Christ in what is now a neo-pagan country. Why is it that the only significant growth in the christian community is in that part of it represented by the house churches and charismatic fellowships? It is because they are uninhibited in talking about their christian beliefs and are prepared to go out and about and ask people to join them. They also make a great effort to look after their members in all sorts of ways other than the purely spiritual. I am not suggesting that we should all go off and join charismatic groups, but I do think we can learn a good deal from their dedication and enthusiasm. And age need be no handicap. Everyone can pray: everyone can be kind and helpful and welcoming: everyone can share their faith. Anyone who is really happy and bubbling over with good news finds it impossible to keep it to themselves. Enthusiasm is infectious. If each of us here this afternoon could bring just one person to Christ during 1989 Midhurst would be a much better and happier place by this time next year. And you know that is possible. And why? Because that is what Jesus came for - "to draw all things to Himself". It is the work of the Holy Spirit to bring about love, peace, harmony and unity. That is why we can be certain that the ecumenical movement is of God, and that is why we can be sure that He will be with us if we go forward together to do His work of spreading the Good News and of bringing all the sheep into His sheepfold.

THE WEEK OF PRAYER FOR CHRISTIAN UNITY 1990

SERMON AT ST MARY'S CHURCH, LITTLEHAMPTON

SUNDAY, 21ST JANUARY

I am what in the Roman Church we usually refer to as 'a cradle catholic', i.e. I was born into a devout Roman Catholic family (have you noticed that whenever the media refer to a practising Roman Catholic he or she is always devout'?). My parents I think could fairly claim that sobriquet. I am not so sure about myself. However, apart from a few wobbles earlier in life, I still profess the faith of my fathers. What has this to do with Christian Unity? Just this. When I grew up it was commonly held among Roman Catholics that outside the Catholic Church there was no salvation. Amongst other things this was a powerful incentive to missionary endeavour. Equally it is, I understand, commonly held among evangelical protestants, and certainly among many of the born-again christian sects, that unless a person is baptized and confesses Jesus Christ to be the Son of God he or she cannot be saved. In other words there is no salvation outside the baptized christian community.

In my old age I have to say that I cannot subscribe to either of these beliefs. To hold the first would mean that all of you listening to me would be on your way to perdition: to hold the second would mean that people living in Outer Mongolia or in the forests of Borneo, or wherever, who had never met a christian missionary or heard the name of Jesus Christ, but who within the parameters of their society try to lead a good life, would also be destined for perdition. To write off good intentioned people who try to serve God and their neighbour as best they can, would seem to me to run counter to everything Jesus told us about His Father and everything He Himself did and taught.

I say this because Jesus announced in very clear simple language what was to be the main thrust of His public life. At the outset of His campaign He told the people gathered in the synagogue at Nazareth that He had come to *"bring good news to the poor, to proclaim liberty to captives and to the blind new sight; to set the downtrodden free; to proclaim the Lord's year of favour"*. Later on John the Baptist sent some of his disciples to ask Jesus if He was the true messiah the Jews had been waiting for. Although he had baptized Jesus in the Jordan and had had that vision of the heavens opening and had heard a mysterious voice, he had obviously had time in Herod's prison to think back over his life and he was still not entirely sure that he had got the right man. So Jesus is asked a direct question about His authenticity. Jesus replies by pointing out that He is doing what at Nazareth He said He would. He does not mention any of the things we might put under the heading of 'religion'. He did not say, for instance, "Go and tell John that we have built 20 new synagogues, that we now have a college of theology and a biblical institute, we have started 200 prayer groups and a couple of monasteries". No, practically everything He mentions concerns the physical needs of those among whom He was working. He does include preaching but specifically mentions the poor for it is to them that His words bring Good News. Finally near the end of His life He again spelt out in very clear simple words the criteria by which God will judge all mankind, ourselves included therefore. We have his words in Matthew 25.

Am I saying that the only thing that matters is charitable work and that the only qualification for being a good christian is to be some sort of social worker? Am I saying that there is no particular point in being a christian: that to be a Buddhist or an atheist will do just as well? No, I am not. Jesus spent long hours in prayer and put obedience to His Father at the top of His priorities. Moreover, the first commandment is to love and worship God, but Jesus tied the second to it. His apostles, reflecting on His teaching after His death, understood His message very clearly. St John, the disciple whom Jesus loved, had a lot to say about love of neighbour in his First Letter (1 John 3). His brother James lays emphasis on the same point in his Letter (Jas 2). As regards the importance of christianity we need only recall that Christ commissioned His apostles to *'Go and teach all nations, baptizing them in the name of the Father, and of the Son and of the Holy Spirit'*.

So what I am suggesting is that many christians down the centuries, and some in our own day, have failed to understand the importance of the Second Commandment in the practice of their faith. Many cruelties have been perpetrated on individuals, and even wars have been fought by people who called themselves christians but who disagreed with other christians about scriptural interpretations or theological doctrines, or believed that military force should be used to compel non-christians to accept christian beliefs. In our own country, in this very county, in penal times Protestants subjected Catholic priests to horrifying tortures and death, while the cruelties meted out to Protestants during the reign of 'Bloody Mary' need no rehearsal. For a hundred years continental Europe suffered a permanent state of war in the name of religion. The barbarities of the mediaeval crusades and of the Spanish conquest of the Americas make terrible reading. I have never, however, read of cruelties or wars resulting from people squabbling over who should help the poor, the sick, the lonely, the disabled, the prisoners. Usually the problem is to find enough people to lend a helping hand to meet all the local needs.

Today, thank God, the Christian Churches all subscribe to the desirability of christian unity, some with more enthusiasm than others, it is true, but the principal effort is again going into sorting out theological and doctrinal disagreements. So we have an interminable series of conferences, seminars, commissions, synodical debates, etc. What wonder that the ecumenical enthusiasm of the 60s and 70s has run into the sand in the 80s. Yet, we do now speak to each other and we know more or less the theological positions of the various denominations, but unity seems as far off as ever, indeed in some cases it seems to be receding.

Why am I saying this? Because I believe that armchair holiness is an illusion. It is of little avail to prepare lovely liturgies in church and spend much time on one's knees if we are beastly to those among whom we live and are selfishly unconcerned about our fellow human-beings who are much worse off than ourselves. The holy people are those who sacrifice themselves and their possessions for others. Who is recognized by christians of all persuasions, and by non-christians alike, as the authentic voice of the Gospel in our day? Surely it is Mother Teresa of Calcutta. Her example and simple words continue to inspire women from all walks of life to leave their homes to work among the poor. Her Order has a long waiting list while most others languish. Even the great and the powerful recognise her authenticity.

I think that the christian unity we pray for today will come about not through the Convocation of Canterbury, not by carefully prepared statements following a meeting between the Archbishop and the Pope, not by the doctrinal discussions of ARCIC, good though these things are in their own way, not by pious hopes or charismatic junketings, but by the likes of you and me rolling up our sleeves and working together to house the homeless, to take into our own homes the lonely, the sick and the depressed, to visit the imprisoned (how many of us have ever set foot inside Ford Prison?), to reduce, if necessary, our standard of living that we might together raise enough money to bring to Sussex one or two families of the wretched Vietnamese boat people held like animals in those dreadful compounds in Hong Kong, to give a break to young families holed up in single rooms in bed & breakfast accommodation in London, for example. I have a feeling that when we die God will judge us by our response to needs like these rather than by how much time we have spent in and around the church. When I referred to you and me rolling up our sleeves, I should perhaps have left it at 'I' because you probably do these things already. I know my record is pretty poor, but I suspect that I am not alone in this respect. Every working day hundreds of people from this area crowd the commuter trains to London where they earn very good money in many cases. I wonder how much of that money and how much of their leisure time goes towards helping the needy either in London or down here?

You see, God and justice are inseparable; so justice is at the very heart of Christianity. When Jesus told the Jews "to seek first the kingdom of God and His justice" He was echoing what the prophets had said in the Old Testament. (Isaiah, Amos). If we go quietly about serving God in His little ones we shall find that two things happen: firstly, our own spiritual life will blossom and God will reveal Himself to us increasingly; secondly, the world and those who follow its godless philosophy will see Christ in action and be drawn to help and so find Him, as many have done through the example of Mother Teresa. People will begin again to pray and the churches will start filling up instead of emptying. *"Seek you first the kingdom of God and His justice, and all these other things will be added unto you"* – including Christian unity. Let me end with a quotation from the 33rd General Congregation of the Society of Jesus::

"The way to faith and the way to justice are inseparable ways. It is up this undivided road, this steep road, that the pilgrim Church must travel and toil. Faith and justice are undivided in the Gospel which teaches that 'faith makes its power felt through love'. They cannot therefore be divided in our purpose, our action, our life."

ADDRESS GIVEN DURING THE WEEK OF PRAYER FOR CHRISTIAN UNITY

AT THE CHURCH OF THE SACRED HEART, PETWORTH, ON SUNDAY, 23RD JANUARY, 1994

I think it true to say that over the past 5-10 years a good deal of the steam has gone out of the ecumenical movement in this country. The excitement, the expectations and the euphoria which gripped many of us in the sixties, around the time of the Second Vatican Council, has in the longer term proved to have been over-optimistic and to some extent unrealistic. We expected too much too quickly. When a supertanker, or a large container ship, is ploughing through the ocean at 20 kts it cannot be stopped and turned round in 5 minutes: it's too big and heavy. Likewise the Christian Churches carry heavy cargoes of tradition and ingrained misconceptions and antipathies. It takes a long time for the whole body to alter course. In the past 30 years we have jettisoned a lot of rubbish and are now more or less on the right heading for the Harbour of Unity, but there is still some way to go, and the nearer you get to the coast the more tricky navigation becomes. As the depth of water lessens so the underwater hazards become more apparent. In our search for unity we have sailed merrily over many things which once seemed insuperable, but as we draw closer together we are having to face the very bedrock of belief - and that has slowed us down. The time has come to take the inshore pilot on board. I suggest we need to make a re-assessment of the situation and take account of the realities of where we are before proceeding. It is better to anchor for a while and await a favourable tide than to enter an estuary unprepared.

May I remind you of two passages from Scripture which I am sure you know well. The first is from Psalm 48:

> *"Go through Zion, walk round her,*
> *counting her towers,*
> *admiring her walls,*
> *reviewing her palaces;*
> *then tell the next generation*
> *that God is here,*
> *our God and leader,*
> *for ever and ever."*

The second is from the Book of Revelation, 21_9-22_5:

> *"One of the seven angels that had the seven bowls full of the seven last plagues came to speak to me, and said, 'Come here and I will show you the bride, that the Lamb has married.' In the Spirit he took me to the top of an enormous high mountain and showed me Jerusalem, the Holy City, coming down from God out of heaven. It had all the radiant glory of God, and glittered like some precious jewel of crystal-clear diamond. The walls of it were of a great height, and had twelve gates; at each of the twelve gates there was an angel, and over the gates were written the names of the twelve tribes of Israel; on the east there were three gates, on the north three gates, on the south three gates, and on the west three gates. The city walls stood on twelve foundation stones, each one of which bore the name of one of the twelve apostles of the Lamb.*
>
> *The angel that was speaking to me was carrying a gold measuring rod to measure the city and its gates and wall. The plan of the city is perfectly square, the length the same as its breadth. He measured the city with his rod and it was twelve thousand furlongs in length and in breadth, and equal in height. He measured its wall, and this was a hundred and forty-four cubits high – the angel was using the ordinary cubit. The wall was built of diamond, and the city of pure gold, like polished glass. The foundations of the city wall were faced with all kinds of precious stone: the first with diamond, the second lapis lazuli, the third turquoise, the fourth crystal, the fifth agate, the sixth ruby, the seventh gold quartz, the eighth malachite, the ninth topaz, the tenth emerald, the eleventh sapphire and the twelfth amethyst. The twelve gates were twelve pearls, each gate being made of a single pearl, and the main street of the city was pure gold transparent as glass. I saw that there was no temple in the city since the Lord God Almighty and the Lamb were themselves the temple, and the city did not need the sun or the moon for light, since it was lit by the radiant glory of God and the Lamb was a lighted torch for it. The pagan nations will live by its light and the kings of the earth will bring it their treasures. The gates of it will never be shut by day – and there will be no night there – and the nations will come bringing their treasure and their wealth. Nothing unclean may come into it: no one who does what is loathsome or false, but only those who are listed in the Lamb's book of life.*

Then the angel showed me the river of life, rising from the throne of God and of the Lamb and flowing crystal clear down the middle of the city street. On either side of the river were the trees of life, which bear twelve crops of fruit in a year, one in each month, and the leaves of which are the cure for the pagans.

The ban will be lifted. The throne of God and of the Lamb will be in its place in the city; his servants will worship him, they will see him face to face, and his name will be written on their foreheads. It will never be night again and they will not need lamplight or sunlight, because the Lord God will be shining on them. They will reign for ever and ever.

What you see of a city or village depends on the vantage point from which you view it. From a distance, certain prominent features, like Chichester's cathedral spire, or Petworth's church tower, can be seen from most angles, but many buildings can be seen from only one position when you are down in the street, and then only one side of them. If you look at "The Angel" next door from the road you see only its attractive inviting facade; from the back you see the kitchens and the dustbins. But they are both part of the same building, and who is to say which is the more important? Now it seems to me that the great truths of the Christian religion are rather like this. Take, for instance the Trinity, the Incarnation, Baptism or the Eucharist. View them through the eyes of someone brought up in the tradition of the Eastern Orthodox Churches (in Constantinople, or Moscow or Athens); then view them through the eyes of the Protestant reformers (in Zurich or Geneva); then through Roman Catholic eyes (in Rome or Westminster); or through Anglican eyes (in Canterbury or York); or through Baptist eyes (in the Bible Belt of the USA): each person is looking at the same truth but they see different aspects of it and so emphasize different points.

I believe our first aim must be to seek the truth, because, as John the Evangelist tells us, "God is truth" and "The truth will set you free", he says. We have come a long way in the past 30 years. Many of the old prejudices have gone: the members of most churches and fellowships are on friendly terms: we meet to pray together: we work together to alleviate the great social problems of the moment. The Christian Care Association in Chichester draws volunteers from 66 Churches, Chapels and Fellowships within a radius of about 15 miles. Perhaps we have come to take all this too much for granted. It should be a matter for our daily thanksgiving and praise. Corporate unity, however, eludes us, but we must not give up the search. While the navigators plot our next moves on the bridge, the engineers must be getting up steam in the engine-room.

There is only one God and His truth is indivisible. If we look back over the history of christianity there are certain periods which stand out above the general level like a church spire on a misty morning: periods when the Church developed and expanded in spectacular manner; when it was so obviously alive and vibrant. Among the distinguishing marks of these golden periods was a burning desire to get at the truth: there was intense theological discussion. First there was the so-called "patristic age", those first centuries of the christian era when christians focussed on the person of Jesus Christ and the nature of the very godhead itself. Some of the great theologians of that time, the "Fathers of the Church", are household names to this very day – Justin, Irenaeus, Cyril, Athenasius, John Chrysostom, Augustine. Another high point occurred between the 11th and 13th centuries which produced such towering personalities as Thomas Aquinas, Gregory, Bernard, Francis, Dominic and Anselm. Nearer our own time in this country there was an explosion of religious interest in the middle of the last century. I have just been reading two of David Newsome's books: "The Parting of Friends" about the leading figures of the Oxford Movement – Pusey, Keble, Newman, the Wilberforces, the Sargents who, as you will know, used to congregate at the Rectory at East Lavington just down the road – and David's most recent work "The Convert Cardinals", Newman and Manning. All these people in their different periods were passionate seekers after God's truth and generated great theological debates, inspiring others with their own enthusiasms. We must follow their example. We must not be content with just good fellowship: we must not settle for the lowest common denominator of religious belief. That is the easy way out. We must get at the truth.

So we must go together as a group of pilgrims, humble and willing to learn, and allow ourselves to be conducted by the Angel of the Apocalypse around Mount Zion and the Heavenly Jerusalem. We must not be afraid to look at its towers and its palaces, its streams, its houses and its gardens from every vantage point. We must not refuse the invitation and remain rooted to the spot where we were brought up. If we accompany the Angel in a spirit of adventure, with open minds, leaving our prejudices and preconceived ideas behind us, we shall discover with growing excitement the whole truth, not just parts of it, and in doing so shall reach "the throne of God and of the Lamb". That is where true unity is to be found. As Paul puts it in his letter to the Colossians: *"This is the new man which God, its creator, is constantly renewing in His own image, to bring you to a full knowledge of Himself. As a result, there are not Gentiles and Jews, circumcised and uncircumcised, barbarians, savages, slaves, or free men* (or we might add Anglicans and Roman Catholics, Protestants or Orthodox), *but Christ is all, Christ is in all".*

I will end by reading an excerpt from a contemporary author, Eusebius of Caesarea, written about the time of the Edict of Constantinople in AD 313, which brought to an end three centuries of persecution of the early Christians. Let us hope and pray that the time is not far off when we shall be able to enjoy a situation similar to the one he describes and be able to echo his words of joy and thanksgiving:

> *Then indeed, a bright and splendid day, with no over-shadowing cloud, shone with heavenly light on the churches of Christ which are spread throughout the whole inhabited world. Even those outside our religious community were allowed to enjoy, if not an equal share, at least some part or overflow of the good things that God had granted us.*
>
> *But for us especially, who put all our hopes in the Christ of God, there was happiness beyond belief. There was a sort of heavenly joy in everyone as we saw every place, which a short time before sacrilegious tyrants had reduced to ruins, come back to life as from a long and mortal destruction. Once again places of worship rose from the soil to lofty heights adorned by a splendour far exceeding that previously destroyed.*
>
> *In addition, we witnessed a sight we had longed and prayed for, the feasts of dedication in every city and the consecration of newly-built places of worship.*
>
> *Along with this came the assemblies of the bishops, throngs of pilgrims from far distant places, the charity and goodwill between different peoples, the union of the members of the body of Christ gathered together in one harmony.*
>
> *As the prophet had said, foretelling what was to happen by means of an imagery full of hidden meaning, 'bone to bone, joint to joint'. All that had been prophesied in mysterious words happened.*
>
> *There was one power of the Spirit of God flowing through all the members and one soul in all. All had the same eagerness in the faith. All were united in harmony in one song of praise to God.*
>
> *Yes, now there were the liturgies of our leaders performed with full solemnity, the holy rites of ordained ministers and the sacred ceremonies of the Church: here the psalms might be heard and the other divine utterances; there the divine mysteries were celebrated. Now too there were the awe-inspiring symbols of the Saviour's passion.*
>
> *Together, people of every age, men and women alike, gave themselves with all their minds, with joyful hearts and souls, to prayer and thanksgiving, as they praised God the author of all good."*

TO
"MY FRIENDS PICTURED WITHIN"

(Edward Elgar – Dedication of 'Enigma' Variations)

SISTER ANNE TERESA

In the Armed Forces men and women in the ranks are awarded the Long Service and Good Conduct Medal after twenty-two years service to Queen and Country. We have come together today to celebrate a much greater achievement, a record of long service to our heavenly King. Sister Anne Teresa was clothed in the Carmelite habit on the feast of St Mary Magdalene fifty years ago last July. The same feast this year will mark the Fiftieth Anniversary of her profession. Sister, we praise and thank God for you, for all the graces and blessings He has bestowed on you, and through you on us, and we thank you for inviting us to share with you this your jubilee Mass.

This convent has, I guess, witnessed a good many jubilees but those who were present at any of them will have noticed something different about this one. Not only are there no medals in evidence, but there is no carpet of flowers, no prie-dieu set apart, nothing to mark out our jubilarian from her sisters. This tells us something about her. Sister Anne Teresa is a retiring, humble person who shuns any form of notoriety which might single her out. In a world which avidly seeks publicity and is desperate for attention and praise we pay tribute to one who so closely resembles her divine Master who, St Paul tells us, "emptied Himself, becoming as a slave", who made Himself so like one of us that His contemporaries failed to recognise who He was. We marvel at one who mirrors in her life our Blessed Lady who throughout the gospel story stays in the background, scarcely mentioned by three of the four evangelists, content just to serve her Son, happy that in the good times all the glory should be His, and in the bad staying faithfully by His side to share His sufferings. We should be hard put to find another person as gentle, as kind, as sweet natured as Sister Anne Teresa. She has, what St Peter in his first letter describes as, "the ornament of a sweet and gentle disposition" which, he says, is precious in the sight of God. But her life of seclusion within these convent walls has much more to teach us.

When fifty years ago, turning her back on the world, she said goodbye to her family and the front door of the cloister closed behind her, she had already made her commitment to spend the rest of her mortal life in poverty, chastity and obedience for the praise and glory of God and for the redemption of the world. Jesus told us that the whole law and teaching of the prophets is summed up in the first two commandments, "To love the Lord your God with your whole heart, your whole mind, your whole strength, and your neighbour as yourself". It is by the love of our neighbour that we prove the sincerity of our love for God; as St John says:

"for she who does not love her sister whom she has seen, cannot love God whom she has not seen"; and nowhere is love of neighbour more thoroughly tested than in a small, closed community. Jesus also told us that "Greater love has no man than to lay down his life for his friends". The sisters here have done precisely that; they have laid down their lives for the salvation of others.

There are two kinds of martyrdom. There is the one we are familiar with, the martyrdom which consists in one concentrated act, or series of acts, of terminal physical heroism, like the death of St Margaret Clitheroe or St Maximilian Kolbe. The other is less spectacular because it extends over a much longer period and is paid out in farthings not fifty pound notes, but cumulatively it is just as heroic. Dear Sisters of Carmel, we acknowledge the sacrifice of your lives and we ask for a share in your prayers.

The modern world is very volatile and people are subject to a great many pressures. Young people in particular, I think, find themselves battered by forces they do not fully understand. But whatever the cause, people nowadays find it very difficult to make even short-term commitments, let alone permanent ones. This affects marriages, priestly and religious vocations and a whole range of human relationships. You have noted this phenomenon, I am sure, in some of your postulants. In such a world the example of lifelong commitment which we are here to celebrate is of paramount importance. That world may totally misunderstand your vocation, Sisters, may even deride it (indeed it may not be properly understood by many Catholics) but you are witnessing to a profound truth. The stability of your vocation is a rock to which the rest of us can cling when the storms of life break and the raging seas wash over us. Though there may be few to appreciate what you do, as indeed there were few who appreciated the life of our divine Master, "your heavenly Father who sees in secret will reward you".

And in this paschal season it is on the subject of reward that I wish to close.

I should like to take your minds back, if I may, to the retreat we made together last August. You will remember that we reflected on the gospel story of Mary Magdalene, the subject of today's gospel reading. When the story begins she was, as all the world knows, a naughty girl. At that time her life revolved around men, and it would have been out of curiosity in the first instance that she went to listen to this new preacher everyone was talking about. We can imagine her going to one of His meetings with some of her friends for an evening's entertainment. They would have stood on the edge of the crowd giggling and joking, not paying much attention to what He was saying. For the other girls that was probably as far as it went. But Mary had felt the charisma of His presence and realised there was something about this man different from all the other men she knew. She could not get Him out of her mind, though doubtless for a time she continued to join in the jokes about Him. Eventually she will have gone back to listen to Him again, this time by herself, and she will have eased herself nearer the front of the crowd. She found herself drawn irresistibly to Him, at first no doubt with a certain sexual infatuation, but as her visits to His meetings became more frequent infatuation was transmuted into love. There is a difference between flirtation and falling in love. When people fall truly in love they become serious about each other, and at some stage Mary's friends will have noticed a change in her. She was no longer willing to joke at Jesus's expense. And so there came the point when all the pent up passion and impetuosity of her nature forced her "to go public", as the saying is, and she paraded her feelings for all to see in the house of Simon the Pharisee. After that she was committed and joined the small band of those who followed Jesus around in His ministry. And her love was returned. It is clear that Jesus had a special affection for this convert of His "from whom He had cast out seven devils". From today's gospel it would seem, too, that He had allowed her a certain intimacy, for He tells her now not to touch Him, indicating, surely, that she had been in the habit of doing so before.

And so, therefore, we come to this wonderful scene outside the tomb on Easter morning.

Mary is all worried and agitated at finding the body of her Lord missing. She is grief-stricken and desperate, and her spinning mind is much too occupied with what to do next to realize who the person is who has just arrived on the scene. How often this is true of us! We are certain that Our Lord cannot be in this place, or in this circumstance, or in this person. Our minds are disorientated and full of other things, so we search for Him in the wrong place.

> *"But the Lord was not in the wind;*
> *And after the wind an earthquake,*
> *But the Lord was not in the earthquake;*
> *And after the earthquake a fire,*
> *But the Lord was not in the fire;*
> *But after the fire there came a still small voice."*

You remember, too, that lovely passage in the Song of Songs:

> *"Upon my bed by night*
> *I sought him whom my soul loves;*
> *I called him, but he gave no answer.*
> *I will rise now and go about the city.*
> *In the streets and in the squares*

I will seek him whom my soul loves.
I sought him but found him not.
The watchmen found me as they went about in the city.
"Have you seen him whom my soul loves?" I cried.

All good things come from God. Sometimes, I think, we tend to forget that among them is a sense of humour. Your holy mother, St Teresa, certainly had one, so why not Our Lord? Lovers often play with each other, pretending to be cross, forgetful, or off-hand, or forgetful just for the pleasure of seeing the reaction and relief in the loved-one when the truth is revealed. So it is that for a few moments Jesus played with His Magdalene and let her go on thinking that He was the gardener.

There follow just two words; two words which sum up the whole of scripture, which encapsulate the concept of love in its entirety. "Mary!" "Rabboni!" Once the lover has established that the beloved is present no further words are necessary. Communication between the two of them is intimate and complete. In that moment of recognition there is a whole eternity of bliss. It is this total absorption of the lovers in each other, of the soul in God, way beyond any need for the normal means of human communication, which is at the heart of Teresian contemplation, the very core and centre of the Interior Castle. It is this union we long and pray for, but experience only fleetingly, if at all, in this world (most of us), that union which will form the motionless peace, fulfilment and ecstacy of heaven. This is to be our reward THE reward.

"Scarcely had I passed them (the watchmen)
When I found him whom my soul loves.
I held him and would not let him go.
Until I had brought him into my mother's house,
And into the chamber of her that conceived me."

When our mortal life comes to an end and Jesus beckons us forth, there will be no need for more than one word. For the first time we shall hear Him call us by the name we were given at our baptism, when first His life flowed into our souls. Oh, the joy and the ecstacy of realising that our faith is fulfilled and now no longer necessary. No more as through a glass darkly but for the very first time we shall see face to face Him for whom our soul has thirsted and our body pined. But what must it be like to hear Him call us by our very own name, to know even as we are known. "Lilian!" – "Rabboni!"

The Chichester Carmel 7th April 1986

PETER FAUVEL-BENTLEY

In 1940 when France was overrun by the German armies, Peter Fauvel came to England and joined the Fleet Arm of the Royal Navy. He subsequently took the name 'Bentley' as a cover for clandestine operations in his occupied homeland. Among his colleagues in the Fleet Arm he was famous for his courage, his daring and his panache. He was the embodiment of what most foreigners think of as 'the dashing Frenchman'. But eventually he was shot down and spent three years as a prisoner of war.

After the war he went to Kenya. The wildness of Africa captured his adventurous spirit. He loved the freedom of the wide open spaces: the bush, the sea and the sky. He and his wife, Wynne, lived very close to the spirit of that mysterious continent.

But in the words Shakespeare attributed to one of his characters, *"Nothing in life so became him as the leaving of it"*.

Those of us who ministered to Peter in various ways during his last illness, are aware that we were vouchsafed a singular privilege. There was about him a tranquillity, an acceptance of his fate, a deep inner peace and joy which were certainly not of this world. There was a light which shone from his face, and the strange thing was that the weaker his body became the brighter the light shone. It instantly attracted to him everyone who came into contact with him. They could not help but love him. Even the cat at St Wilfrid's Hospice, where he died, took a shine to him and insisted on lying on his bed until he died. And when the end came his soul passed quite peacefully from this world to the next as if it were going to its natural metier. I am sure we have another brother in heaven now who is with us as we celebrate his requiem Mass.

So now all our care must be for his widow. During this last long harrowing year Wynne has had to watch helplessly as her husband slowly slipped away from her. Her courage matched his every step of the way. In the middle of the road to her own personal calvary, Canon Collins and I had the immense joy of receiving her into the Catholic Church. Wynne, we offer you our condolences, our support, our prayers and our love. May the God who is full of mercy and compassion, and who mourned for His friend Lazarus, bless you, console you and strengthen you. Amen.

St. Richards
Chichester

18th February 1987

MURIEL UNIACKE

THE DARK SEED

I plant a small dark seed
In the spring-warmed earth,
And I'm planting two small miracles:
The loveliness of the flower that now I see
In my mind's eye,
And the flower that soon will grow,
Beautiful in colour, form and scent.
So I plant the small dark seed
With gratitude – and wonder at
These two small miracles.

LATE SNOW

The calm solemnity of snow at sunrise
Enfolds the land where yesterday was Spring;
It comes as a gentle admonition,
A sudden soft rebuke to frenzied speed.

The snow's purity drains the bright
effulgence
Of the sky, reveals the still naked beauty
of the trees;
There is no colour, save in the pastel
clouds,
And in the small birds' wings
As they fly like spoken words.

Such muted hesitance floats on the crisping air
That now we are compelled to pause,
– And in the silence, contemplate
This awesome natural eloquence.

Those two short poems written by Muriel seem to me in some way to contain the essence of her, rather as Edward Elgar wrote on his manuscript of his Violin Concerto: "Herein is enshrined the soul of ...." For Muriel had a remarkable empathy with nature. She loved the wild things of the meadows and woods: she exulted in the wide sweep of the heavens and the freedom of birds on the wing.

She had a finely trained intellect nourished by years of reading the great classical authors, particularly the poets, and her incisive mind was always questing, not content with the appearance of things but seeking the great realities beyond. In her long life she had scaled the heights and plumbed the depth of human emotion. There were periods when she was ecstatically happy and others when life seemed full of anguish, sorrow and bitterness.

When she came to live at Walderton she was touched by Martin's deep faith and his generous commitment to the Catholic Church. She longed to share his faith and so it was that Canon Francis received her into the Church. About a year later I came into her life. It was a year of anguish for her with Corrine's death and the first signs of her own failing health.

I used to take Holy Communion to her most Fridays and over the years we became close friends. We discussed all manner of things. She told me about her early years and her marriages. We discussed the Gospels and the warp and weft of the spiritual life. In those last years, as you know, she suffered from a particularly nasty attack of shingles, worse, I suspect, than most people realised. She was never without pain, yet, certainly when I was there, she was always cheerful and dismissed her own problems with that characteristic little chuckle and wave of her hand and concerned herself with those of others. Her family were always uppermost in her mind for she loved you all dearly.

She was born into the Church of England and belonged to what in Anglican terms, is, I believe, called the 'Broad Church' which is fairly eclectic in its theology. Coming late in life to the Catholic Church she struggled to adapt herself to our ways and I don't think she ever felt completely at ease with our liturgy. But that did not matter for she was always close to God and longed to do what He wanted of her. I always thought of her as the 'anawim' of the Old Testament, that handful of faithful souls, among them Anna and Simeon, who waited patiently and in peace for the coming of the Messiah. Muriel longed for her Lord, and I am certain that when He finally came for her, last Friday morning, she will have given herself joyfully into His embrace. I can picture her now (can't you?) busily pottering about in heaven, as she used to potter about her garden, delighting in the discovery of the solutions to all the questions which exercised her mind on earth but the answers to which eluded her. What a thrilling time she will be having!

As we gather round her coffin to celebrate Mass I am sure she is present with us and through these sacred mysteries will accompany Jesus to comfort and strengthen us who mourn her passing. How fortunate you are that the matriarch of your clan was a woman of such faith!

St. Richards
Chichester

25th March 1988

SAM JAYE

When at the beginning of his public life Jesus was gathering His disciples together, He saw Nathaniel coming towards Him and said those famous words: *"Behold, here is an Israelite in whom there is no guile"*.

Audrey, your Dad; Lesley, your Grandad; Clare, James and Danny, your Gransie; for the rest of us, our Sam, belonged, like Nathaniel, to that rare and very select group of people who are without guile; of whom it can truly be said that throughout their lives they never did anything mean or underhand or dishonest or cruel. It is just unthinkable to link Sam's name with anything of that sort because he was so transparently good. He was, in fact, a living example of that simplicity and childlikeness (not childishness) of which Jesus spoke; *"Unless you become as little children you cannot enter the kingdom of heaven"*. Today we live in "The Achievers" culture, in which people only receive recognition if they go from success to success as the world measures success. True goodness (and holiness) are not reckoned of much account. How false that world is! For *"God does not see as man sees; man looks at appearances but God looks at the heart"*, and in the beatitudes Jesus tells us who the people are whom God values – "the meek, the gentle, the poor in spirit, the merciful, the pure in heart, the peacemakers". Sam was all of these. In a word, he was a gentleman in both senses of that word. He let people be and was not critical or judgmental. He was just happy to be himself. He was not ambitious and, unlike so many people who are, he found satisfaction in each phase of his life: in his youth as a junior clerk in a shipping office; as a young man in the Royal Navy; later as a messenger with Thames Board Mills; and latterly in his garden and greenhouse. He was content with what he had. Contentment is a richness unknown to our modern restless world which is always seeking something new, never satisfied. Above all he loved his family. He was immensely proud of his granddaughter and her husband, and their children were a constant source of delight to him. For you, Audrey and Joe, he had the deepest love and undying gratitude for the long years of companionship and care.

So what lessons are we to learn at his passing? Clare, James and Danny, he would have you learn to value people for their goodness and not for what you can get out of them. He would want you to be generous, kind and loving as he was generous, kind and loving. If from him you can learn contentment you will have a happy life.

Secondly, we must all learn that each one of us will have to pass this way. Death is as much a part of the human condition as is birth. Sam passed peacefully from this world to the next without fuss or drama, just as he would have wished. He has proved to us that death is not something to be afraid of. For the christian death, is not the end but the entrance to the promised land for which we have all been made, a land of peace and eternal happiness in the presence of our loving Father. By his example of goodness Gransie has taught us that a life well spent leads to a peaceful death and thence to that fantastic reward which Paul tries to describe in his letter to the Corinthians: *"The things that no eye has seen and no ear heard, things beyond the mind of man, all that God has prepared for those who love Him".*

The Crematorium
Stratton St. Margaret

28th September 1992

MICHAEL HUGHES

Introduction

Because Mike was the most tender-hearted of men he would understand our grief and our need to mourn, but he would not want this gathering of his loved ones and friends to be a gloomy affair. Were he here he would have that impish look in his eye and a ready quip to make us laugh, so we must try to raise our spirits for his sake, for we are here to honour and celebrate the life of a man whose outstanding characteristic was love – love from him for all mankind, and the ability to evoke love in return from all who knew him. His close family have agreed that we should concentrate our thoughts for a few minutes on three aspects of Mike's life and character.

Mike's Humanity

Mike was a lover of children and children loved him in a way given to few adults. He could make each one feel special. It was this gift, as much as anything, which right to the end kept his mind open and inquiring and interested in all that was going on around him. It was said of J M Barrie, the author of "Peter Pan", that he was that very rare person who "by some divine grace can express the childlikeness that is in him". Like Barrie, Mike was able to see the world through the eyes of a child because he had a boundless imagination which enabled him to soar above earthbound concerns to 'The Land of Never-Never'. It was this same quality which enabled him to extract the spiritual from the material and project what he saw into his paintings. He used to joke that one day a "Hughes" would rival a "Picasso" at Sotherbys, but he was too humble a man to harbour illusions about his ability as an artist, yet this very humility drove him constantly to improve his technique, and the paintings which adorn his house testify to his development as a portrayer of the Universal Soul. And Mike's humanity was universal. It went far beyond his love of children to encompass all mankind. He detested violence in all its forms, and he had a deep political conscience which caused him to cry out against injustice wherever it showed its ugly head. He was incensed equally by the exploitation of Third World peoples by the economic might of multi-national companies as by the exploitation of Labour by Capital in his own country. He had an instinctive sympathy for the underdog, whether the cause of vulnerability was economic poverty, social disadvantage or a person's mental or physical handicap. For much of his adult life he was a tireless supporter of and fund-raiser for the Camphill Communities.

Mike's Love of Nature

Mike's affinity with and passionate concern for nature derived, I think, from his early years in Devon. Although for most of his working life as an innovative and successful journalist he was based in the City and suburban London, he was at heart a countryman. His concern for the natural world involved amongst other things a love affair with animals. I like to think that he and his beloved Sadie are now reunited and enjoying their morning walks in paradise as they used to beside Chichester Harbour. Mike loved his walks in the countryside, but the sea vied with the countryside for his devotion, and it was in that context that I first met him. He had put an advert in the 'Chichester Observer' for someone to crew his boat, and I had the temerity to reply. We met over a drink in the now defunct 'Birdham Inn' and he signed me on – or at least I thought he had. It was only at the end of our first voyage together that I realised I had been on probation. After we had moored up to our buoy, I was standing on the foredeck coiling a length of rope when I became aware that he was watching me intently from the cockpit. As I finished he said: "You'll do. You can always tell whether a chap knows what he's doing on a boat by the way he coils a rope". Thereafter we sailed together for many seasons, first on his boat 'Tamu', then on my boat 'Corantella' and her successor 'Flame Lily'. We had lots of fun and our own private fund of jokes. At one point Olive was trying to get him to give up smoking, but somehow 'Corantella' always seemed to have just the odd cigarette in her locker. "Just one, Larry old man," he'd say. "Just one won't hurt me, will it? – but not a word to Bessy", he'd add as he drew in the first gorgeous draught of the demon weed. I don't know if Bessy knew, but I never split on 'Corantella'. However, later I was paid back in my own currency when Bessy was trying to wean him off caffeine and coffee. I had to share some foul herbal concoction he used to bring on board. We kidded each other that it was delicious – and blessed Bessy!

Mike's Sense of Humour

Now a word about Mike's humour and the touch of the rogue in him. He had an inveterate attachment to his MG. It made him feel he was back in the 30s roaring along the pre-war English roads in an open-top sports car with a gay young thing by his side, the wind rushing through her flying locks and he in scarf and cap at a jaunty angle. He even wore the regulation gloves when driving. He never quite grew out of those early carefree days and he had an eye for the girls which, I gather, was not quite dimmed even in the heart unit at the hospital when he was on the last lap. He used to make all sorts of outrageous remarks but, in fact, never was there a more loving and devoted husband, father, grandfather and friend than Michael Hughes. He loved to tease and shock, but always kindly, nicely and with a twinkle in his eye. He was horrified if ever he thought he had hurt someone.

And so to my final remark. Mike was a true gentleman, and he never abandoned the old world courtesies which the brash modern world so sadly lacks. He managed to combine in his person the best of the old and the best of the new.

Final Commendation and Blessing

God, our Father, Creator of the Universe, of the sea and the sky and the countryside, we thank you for Mike, for his life and his love, and we thank You for the privilege of knowing him. You are the author of love, and love all that You have made. Send Your angels to accompany Michael on his last voyage to paradise, where he will find eternal peace and happiness. We ask this through Your Son, Jesus Christ. Amen.

May the blessing of God's Spirit come down upon us all and remain with us for ever. Amen.

> "And all I ask is a merry yarn from a laughing fellow-rover,
> and quiet sleep and a sweet dream when the long trick's over."

The Crematorium
Chichester

10th February 1994

NICOLA HUE AND MARK BENNETT

A wedding is always a lovely, happy occasion because it centres around a man and a woman deeply in love, whose love has reached the point at which they decide to commit themselves to each other in a lifelong union. There's something special about people in love; an aura of happiness surrounds them and spills over onto everyone who has contact with them. The flowers, the fine dresses, the music, the bells, the feast are all expressions of that happiness which marks the celebration of marriage, in which we know Jesus Himself once joined at Cana in Galilee. But christian marriage is much more than the external frills, nice and good though these are. This morning we are here about serious business.

In the first place, christian marriage is about the building and sustaining of communities. Mark and Nikki have invited us to witness their marriage because we are their relatives and friends who represent either the communities in which they were born and reared or to which they have belonged at different stages in their adult lives. Marriage, you see, is not a purely private affair affecting only the bridal couple. At its heart is the family, and the family is at the heart of society. A bride and groom, hopefully, will become a mother and father and start their own little community. But a wedding also brings together in a special way the parental families from which they sprang and which henceforward should become a single extended family. The traditional music-hall jokes about mothers-in-law are, in my experience, neither helpful nor justified. The sustaining and nourishment of happy peaceful communities is essential for progress in human affairs. This is why marriage breakdown is such a disaster: it shatters communities.

But for the bride and her groom the christian marriage ceremony has a very personal and intimate meaning. Nikki and Mark are here to make promises, to take vows. It is one thing to make promises to each other, and to make them before witnesses in public: it is quite another to make them in the presence of the living God to Whose church you have come. I ask you, therefore, to reflect for a moment on what you are about to do. You are about to enter into a lifelong commitment which you will express in words which are very well known, but which too often nowadays, it seems, are spoken glibly and their implication taken lightly.

You will say that you take each other "*to have and to hold from this day forward; **for Better, for Worse***". We all hope and we pray that for you it will always be "for better", but what happens in cases where, for instance, after two, three, four years of marriage, the new wife discovers she has married a philanderer who cannot keep his eyes or his hands off other women? What happens if after two, three, four years of marriage the new husband discovers that his wife has become an alcoholic? Does the one disillusioned and deceived continue to "love and cherish" the one in trouble "till death do them part"? Please God nothing like this will happen to either of you, but to hold your marriage together in spite of such eventualities is what you are about to promise.

For Richer, for Poorer. At the moment you both have good jobs and can look forward to fulfilling careers and a prosperous future, but we live in an uncertain world. What happens if in two, three, four years time Mark is made redundant and, despite his best efforts, cannot find further employment, by which time, let us suppose, Nikki has a brand new baby and perhaps cannot work? According to statistics from the divorce courts the No. 1 cause of marriage breakdown is bickering over money. Let us hope misfortune does not overtake you, but if you should fall on hard times, will you continue to "love and cherish" each other "till death do you part"? Because that is what you are about to promise.

In Sickness and in Health. We all hope and we pray that you will always enjoy good health, but I know a couple, now in their 70s, whose marriage was hit by sickness after barely 8 years. The wife was struck down by polio and paralysed from the waist down. Ever since she has lived most of her waking hours in a wheelchair. For close on 40 years her husband has cared for her and tailored his life to her needs. If, which God forbid, one of you was to contact a crippling long-lasting disease, or be permanently injured by an accident, would the healthy one "love and cherish" the sick one "till death do you part"? Because that is what you are about to promise.

As you hold hands and make your promises, you will end with these words: *"and this is my solemn vow"*. No promise could be more binding than that. May God bless you both; may He give you the grace and the strength always to honour your promises; and may you live in love, happiness, health and peace to see your children and your children's children to the third generation.

St. Paul and St. Peter the Great
Chichester — 30th April 1994

JOHN EVANS

How can one encompass in a few minutes a spirit as free, and a personality as engaging, as those of John Evans? But such is my task.

John inherited from his grandparents a natural musical talent of quite exceptional brilliance. As a boy he discovered that just by ear he could play almost any stringed instrument, and as an adult he knew he had a fine tenor voice. He received no formal musical training, but such was the determination with which he honed the musical gifts which he recognised had been given him by God that in due course he was not only accepted as an equal by professional musicians, but in 1979 he and Rozanne were offered a contract by the recording giant EMI. He would not have got that far on musical talent alone. It was the combination of talent with a charismatic personality that brought him success. He could not only entertain; he could also inspire others with his own enthusiasms.

We males are not noted for our modesty - or so the women tell us - but one thing we do recognise is when we are in the presence of one of our own sex who has us beat. When John was on form and in good voice he had a glint in his eye which felled the heart of every woman within range. It was his own good fortune to fall in love with and to marry a young woman who was not only beautiful and madly in love with him, but who was artistic and talented like himself. John's and Rosanne's strengths and weaknesses and the variations of their talents fitted each other exactly. They made the perfect pair, maritally and professionally. Rozanne said to me the other day: "John was more than a husband: he was a real friend, a mate, a colleague as well". Because of a somewhat unhappy childhood John wanted above all else in life to create a happy and secure home for Rozanne and the children he hoped they would have. In due course Sam and John arrived. Nurtured in such a home their own talents developed to the point where they could join their parents in some of their professional work. The "Sailmakers" were not only a brilliant act but a close-knit family unit as well.

On leaving school John spent 12 years in the Medical Branch of the Royal Navy. It was while serving at the Royal Naval Hospital Haslar, at Gosport, that he met Rozanne who had gone there to train as a physiotherapist. Although he had begun to make an alternative career for himself as an entertainer before he had actually left the Navy it took some time for him, once he had left, to establish himself as a full-time professional. So for about 18 months he took an unskilled job on a building site to supplement his income. Now John was never one to waste an opportunity. He got the various craftsmen – bricklayers, plasterers, plumbers and the like – to show him the secrets of their trades. He did nothing by halves, for he was a perfectionist in all things. He watched, he thought, he read, he practised and he succeeded in becoming a competent jobbing builder which our Carmelite Sisters, among others, have reason to remember with gratitude. It was these same skills, of course, which later on gave him the confidence to undertake the renovation of the French farmhouse at Emet where he and Rozanne made their home on leaving England.

There was a depth to John's character which was not immediately apparent to those who knew him only as an entertainer or a craftsman. From his Irish mother he inherited a deeply-rooted Catholic faith. Knowing what the world of entertainment was like he realised that if he accepted the EMI contract I referred to it would mean selling his soul to big business and putting his family life at risk. So on the very threshold of fame and fortune he and Rozanne turned down the offer and elected to retain their independence – at very considerable cost. Thus it was that the Evanses came to Chichester.

Shortly after their arrival a copy of the Vatican II documents came into their hands and the Decree on the Sacred Liturgy fired their imagination with the almost limitless possibilities which it opened up for the development of a new musical genre within a fresh liturgical vision. They started to attend liturgical courses and workshops: they met other Catholic professional musicians: in the Society of St Gregory they found a musical and spiritual home. At the same time they took an increasingly prominent part in the liturgical life of this parish and in the mid-80s the eucharistic liturgy in this church, particularly at the 11.00 a.m. mass each Sunday, achieved an eminence which was recognized well beyond Chichester. It was during this period that the Mass for the Feast of the Purification was televised from here and broadcast live on the national network; that the choir undertook a tour of Canada and recorded the tape "Breath of Dawn". But apart from the parish liturgies the Evanses were much in demand for weddings, funerals and other special occasions within the parish. They gave of their services generously and unstintingly. With hindsight I think some of us took too much for granted the professional and liturgical expertise we had in our midst and failed to understand the personal cost involved, for the truth was that because of their commitment to the Church John and Rozanne turned down many professional engagements which, at one point, reduced their income to a dangerous level and threatened to disrupt their family life. It was only John's expertise as a builder which enabled him to keep the family finances afloat. John, for the lack of recognition which you felt so deeply, we ask forgiveness.

I think Rozanne would agree that while he lived in Chichester I was probably closer to the real John than most people outside the immediate family circle. I want to say that what I admired most about John was his openness of heart and soul. He was incapable of dissembling and was as honest as the day's long. Because he said what he thought he did not always make himself popular, and he would not lower his professional standards merely to keep the peace. Integrity mattered to him. It was the same with his faith. When he talked about God and spiritual things he disclosed an almost childlike innocence. I found in him a living embodiment of those words of Jesus: "Unless you become as little children you cannot enter the kingdom of heaven". It was because his relationship with God was so direct and uncomplicated that at times he was bewildered by some of the goings-on among some of God's representatives on earth. His spirit always wanted to be free and to soar. What he saw as the rigidity of some of the Church's structures and laws he found as difficult to cope with as what earlier he had felt to be the pettiness of certain aspects of naval discipline. But like the Lord he aspired to follow he was deep within humble of heart. Having passed through a dark night he found peace of soul. In France he felt free and had an outlet for his restless energy which was concentrated on restoring the near-derelict farmhouse. His periodic visits to the UK with Rozanne reassured us that he was his old, gay, generous, enthusiastic self, still dreaming dreams, still finding mountains to climb, still determined to succeed right up to his very last breath. I am sure he is now entertaining the angels in heaven with songs and jokes they have never heard before, and helping St Joseph, a fellow craftsman, to build the New Jerusalem. Thank you, John, for bringing us light and laughter, for a liturgy which touched our hearts, and for revealing to me the simple love of God in your heart. May you rest for ever in peace and from the heights of heaven care for Rozanne, John, Sam, Rudy, Jamie and David with even greater love and protection than was possible when you were here on earth. Amen.

St Richard's
Chichester

26th July, 1994

FRANK WALSH

Frank Walsh was a fine catholic gentleman with an irrepressible sense of humour. He was born into a London family and spent his childhood at the family home at Southfields near the Wimbledon All England Tennis Courts.

He belonged to that rapidly diminishing generation of Catholics who were brought up and educated in England during the first three decades of this century, when the Catholic Church in this country reached the zenith of its post-Reformation development. The Catholic Emancipation Act of 1829 marked the official end of three centuries of persecution and repression. It made possible the re-establishment of the hierarchy in 1850 which was followed by an expansion probably unique in European ecclesiastical history, what Cardinal Newman described as "The Second Spring". From a Catholic population of a few thousand at the beginning of the 19th century, mostly the families and employees of the old Catholic gentry, Catholics were numbered in hundreds of thousands by the beginning of the 20th century. During the second half of the 19th century Catholic churches and presbyteries were built in every town of any size across the land. The old Religious Orders returned and close on their heels some of the newer Religious Congregations which established schools (parish primaries, grammar schools and what we nowadays call independent schools), orphanages, nursing homes and refuges for the poor. By the time Frank came on the scene English Catholics had regained their self-confidence and were once again making a significant contribution to the life of the nation. Today we live in an age of debunkers when writers, journalists and commentators delight in exposing the shortcomings of our predecessors. The Church at that time was not perfect, but Catholics knew who they were, what they stood for, what the Church taught and they received from their parents and schools a grounding in the faith which was to remain with them throughout their lives, no matter how far short at times they might fall below the ideals the Church had put before them. It was in this tradition that, when they were old enough, Frank and his brother Denis were sent to be educated by the Jesuits at Wimbledon College and his two sisters to the Notre Dame Convent at Battersea.

It was at Wimbledon College that Frank developed his lifelong love of rugby football, but he also did well enough at his studies to qualify for a career in Lloyds Bank. Like many of his contemporaries he also joined the Territorial Army, in his case the Westminster Dragoons. When the Second World War broke out he soon realised that promotion was likely to be slow in the infantry so he volunteered for armoured cars with which he went to France with the British Expeditionary Force. So it was that in May 1940 he was caught up in the German blitzkrieg. By the skin of his teeth he managed to reach Dunkirk harbour, which by then was under intense bombardment, just in time to get aboard a Royal Navy destroyer which was the last ship to leave before the port fell. On return to England he was commissioned into the RASC and sent to Northern Ireland to a company commanded by an alcoholic CO. Frank's experiences there provided him with a string of humourous stories with which he enlivened the company at many a bar in later life. On promotion he was given command of a unit whose job it was to ferry tanks overland from the northern ports ready for the D Day invasion, and then keeping the front line supplied as it moved forward across Western Europe. On demobilization Frank returned to Lloyds Bank and spent the rest of his career in the Foreign Exchange Department in the City.

It was in retirement that he and his wife, Bobbie, came to Sussex and settled in their bungalow at Singleton. Having no children they were all-in-all to each other and Bobbie's untimely death dealt Frank a blow which he never really got over. But like all good rugby players he loved his pint and his pubs, and with one or two of his mates made a serious study of the hostelries hereabouts. It was in a pub, needless to say, that I first met Frank in the course of one of my Downland walks. Ironically and sadly it was in a pub that Frank's last illness effectively began. Being on his own Helen and I thought it would be a nice idea to give him a Christmas dinner at the pub of his choice. He chose the 'Royal Oak' at Lavant. He arrived in great form, but as he entered he went forward to greet his friends behind the bar, caught his foot on a loose mat and fell heavily on the tiled floor, breaking his leg. The ambulance was called and he was taken to hospital.

There followed several years of declining health and unremitting pain. Latterly, when he was no longer able to look after himself, he was cared for by lady care attendants from the local Social Services Department. I want to take this opportunity to thank them publicly. I cannot praise them too highly, in particular Shirley who, sadly, predeceased Frank, and Jenny who took over from her. For these two ladies nothing was ever too much trouble whether in or out of duty hours. It was during the last pain-filled year of his life in particular that his deep-rooted Catholic faith enabled Frank to carry his cross beside his Lord with incredible patience and humility. He believed himself to be an unworthy sinner and was touchingly grateful for the least kindness done for him. Despite having been somewhat delicate as a child, as a man he had great strength, and almost to the end his handshake was a rock-crusher, but like many strong, good men there was a transparent, almost childlike, honesty and conscientiousness about him which was touching in its simplicity.

I loved Frank as an elder brother, and with his sister Kathleen, her sons and the other members of the family I mourn his passing, but I know that I have now another brother in heaven. So as we mourn we can also celebrate the victory of a Christian soul. We must also remember that in due course we shall all follow Frank through the gates of death, and it behoves us to clear our consciences and set our lives in order so that we may have nothing to fear at the judgment seat of our Redeemer but may pass swiftly from death to eternal life in our heavenly Father's home, where we shall be welcomed by the whole court of heaven, including our loved ones who have gone before us.

St Richard's
Chichester

21st November 1994

VALERIE BRADY

Val Brady has been a name to conjure with in this parish for many years. Whether you have been here a long time or whether you are a comparative new-comer, we all owe a great deal to her whose Funeral Mass we are here to celebrate. I want to suggest that Val's contribution to the life of God's people in Chichester was on two levels.

First were the many christian works in which she engaged. Some had a fairly high profile and were thus well known such as her ministries of Reader and Eucharistic Minister, her key role in the Renew Process and in the organisation of the small groups which resulted, her work as a RCIA catechist, and her devoted support of the Carmelite Sisters when they were at Hunston. Other things she did were less visible and more routine but nonetheless essential to the life of the parish. I refer to her secretarial work for the priests, her care of the presbytery garden, earlier on her weekly work for the football pool syndicate and, of course, her unrivalled knowledge of the parish which was always at the disposal of the parish priest. But then again there was her discreet, pastoral work mostly known only to those who benefited. In talking with people around the parish since the onset of Val's final illness I have been impressed and edified by the number of people who have told me how her advice, her prayers, her teaching and her companionship opened to them a new vision of the faith, and in some cases saved them from spiritual disaster. Finally, there was the work lovingly done in her home. When it became clear that, due to age and infirmity, her parents needed constant care, she gave up her job in London and bought the house in New Park Road where she cared for them until they died. She then took in her Aunt Mary and cared of her until she met with a fatal accident. Only then did she move to a newer house in Juxon Close.

But what of the second level I referred to? I believe Valerie's life was prophetic and that her greatest work may yet to be made manifest. We live at a time and in a culture which has lost its moral bearings, particularly regarding human sexuality. Virginity is scorned and those who live chaste lives are ridiculed. It is assumed in secular society that a person who does not have an active sex life is either physically defective, psychologically damaged or fatally frustrated. There are many single people in the world. A few have deliberately chosen to remain single, but there are others for whom the opportunity to marry has never occurred: there are widows and widowers and there is an increasing number of people whose marriages have broken down and who are separated or divorced (a couple of

Sundays ago we had an appeal here from representatives of the separated and divorced in this parish). Just recently homosexuality has been prominent in the media. In all of these categories there are Catholics struggling to keep God's commandments and live up to the Church's teachings. What single people, the young and the not-so-young, need is the role model of a single lay person who has chosen virginity deliberately and has lived a chaste life without any of the ill effects the world would have us believe to be inevitable; someone who is manifestly normal, sane, well-balanced and fun to be with. Val was just such a lay person.

She felt herself called to a life of prayer from her earliest years. At the age of five she was discovered praying before a statue she had placed in a secluded corner of her parents' garden, a grotto which came to be known within the family as "Valerie's Garden". To this grotto she was wont to invite some of her little friends. The ability to attract people to pray with her was a charism which was to mark the rest of her life. Val was highly intelligent and carried off many of the top prizes at school. She was also blessed with good looks, enhanced during the War by her WRNS uniform, and she did not lack for suitors. It could be said that as a young woman the world was her oyster, but she felt a higher calling. Some people wondered why, if she did not marry, she had not become a nun. Anyone who was bold enough to put that question to her got a dusty answer. She said she had not the least desire to be a nun and would not have lasted five minutes if she had tried. Val's spirituality was not of the sugar piety variety. She was full-blooded and a person of strong views. When she thought something needed to be said she did not mince her words, no matter who was on the receiving end. She was broad-minded and loved company. Allow her to absorb some alcohol at a social gathering and she would become the life and soul of the party with a string of funny stories, some of them quite risquèe. And she retained her sense of humour to the end.

Although on occasions she could criticize her priests, she loved them all and was loved by them in return, as is demonstrated by the number around the altar this afternoon. She had a deep respect of and loyalty to the priesthood. She was also devoted to our Carmelite Sisters and is to be buried next to the graves of those who died while the community was at Hunston. But she saw her own place in God's Church as a lay woman, with emphasis on both words – 'lay' and 'woman'. Hence her importance. The example of her life fits exactly some of the crucial moral and spiritual needs of contemporary society. In the Church the roles of women and of the laity are undergoing a revolution; and in society as a whole the need has never been greater for people to understand the value of chastity and to have living proof that it is attainable with God's help. People need examples of living prayer, of devotion, of fidelity, of unselfish care for others. They need to see with their own eyes that these qualities produce happiness, serenity and peace, and to understand that what the world says about them is bunkum.

Val told me that her spiritual life was lifted into a higher gear when Canon Collins invited her to take an active part in the preparation for Renew and in the groups which resulted. She described this experience as a second conversion. Those of us who were near her in her last years were, I think, aware of her closeness to God. As one of the few people outside the immediate family privileged to visit her in the hospice, I shall always remember her face - beautiful, serene and smiling. To the end she thought constantly of other people and uttered not a word of complaint or anguish about her cruel illness. A couple of Saturdays ago at evening Mass I tried to explain how thin is the veil which hides from our human eyes our God and His heavenly court. Emmanuel, our God is with us. Anyone who visited Val's room at the hospice cannot but have been aware of this. A week ago last Sunday night God drew back the veil for Val and she slipped peacefully and silently to Him whom her heart loves, as the reading from the Song of Songs so beautifully expresses it. Our Lord's analogy of the vine and the branches was her favourite gospel reading. We also are grafted into that same Vine. This is why Val is not lost to us; why her influence can still affect us. St Thérèse of Lisieux, after whom Val was thirdly named, said that she would spend her heaven doing good on earth (in her case especially helping missionaries); I believe Val will also spend her heaven doing good on earth (especially caring for single people). So those of you who are single, those of you who are struggling with your sexuality, those of you who live alone, and those of you who are, well, just lonely, take heart. Lift up your eyes and your hearts and know that you have a new advocate at the throne of God; an advocate who is one of us and who understands our modern world.

Pat and Michael, Celia, Andrew and Lou, and Val's cousins, we offer you our heartfelt condolences and prayers, but also our congratulations, because God has raised up from your family a very special holy soul. As in our humanity we mourn the passing of a dearly loved sister, aunt and friend, let us in spirit rejoice and sing in our hearts the Easter anthem: *"This is the day which the Lord has made: let us be glad and rejoice in it"*.

St Richard's
Chichester

22 March 1995

JERRY AND SHEILA LYONS

One might think that because people in general are living longer than in times past that Ruby Weddings would become increasingly commonplace, but since at the same time divorce is becoming increasingly prevalent my guess is that Ruby Weddings will remain a rarity and the cause of special celebration. At all events I am sure I speak for all of us in thanking you, Jerry and Sheila, for inviting us to this your very special Mass. We are delighted and privileged to be here.

Statistics apparently indicate that marriage breakdown, divorce and re-marriage are now as prevalent among Catholics as the rest of the population in Western Europe and North America, so a Ruby Wedding Mass would seem a suitable occasion for reminding ourselves of the essentials of christian marriage which we are here to celebrate.

At the heart of Christian marriage is a promise. A man and a woman promise before their chosen witnesses, before an official representative of the State, before an official representative of the Church, and most importantly before God that they will love and cherish each other until death do them part. It's the "till death do them part" bit that's the problem. No less a person than the Son of God Himself, Jesus Christ our Lord, has said in plain language that no human person can dissolve the union created by that promise – not the couple themselves, not the State, not the Church. So the promise made at a wedding is meant to be kept. Now if society decides otherwise and authorizes the State to dissolve that marriage and permit the couple to disavow their promise, then, I suggest, one of the primary pillars on which a civilised society is built is undermined. The reason why God "made them male and female", as the Book of Genesis puts it, was so that other human beings might be produced. The family is the basic unit of society, and the stability of the family depends on the stability of the marriage which begot it. Life is the one thing human beings cannot make. Life is the province of the Creator God alone. Therefore there is a sacredness about the procreation of children which is why the Catholic Church teaches that marriage is a sacrament of divine origin. If you reject its sacredness and tamper with the marriage bond, allowing couples to disavow their promises, and worse still allowing them to make new promises to new partners in new marriages which they may also disavow, then you devalue the whole idea behind the making of a promise. It can no longer be taken for granted that a person's word is their bond, and this devaluation spreads like a sinister disease throughout society. It infects family life and relationships first of all, but it does not stop there. It finds its way into schools, into the professions, into commerce, into politics, into international affairs. If you cannot rely on people to keep their promises, you cannot rely on them to speak the truth. I suggest you only have to look around you at today's world to see abundant evidence of this. There are broken promises, dishonesty, deceit, deception and lies on every hand. Moreover, the disease, unless checked, passes to the next generation. It is a good thing to remind ourselves from time to time of the Word of God in the Book of Exodus, Chapter 34:

Moses called on the name of Yahweh. Yahweh passed before him and
proclaimed, "Yahweh, Yahweh, a god of tenderness and compassion,
slow to anger, rich in kindness and faithfulness; for thousands
he maintains his kindness, forgives faults, transgressions, sin;
yet he lets nothing go unchecked, punishing the father's fault
in the sons and the grandsons to the third and fourth generation."

Today's mass media claim the right to portray contemporary life as it is. Thus when children watch contemporary productions on television they watch people telling barefaced lies and witness deceit, broken promises, divorce, casual sexual couplings portrayed as the norm. No society can tolerate this situation indefinitely. Eventually it will collapse through its own corruption. The stability of the State depends upon the stability of the society of which it is composed: the stability of society depends upon the stability of the family: the stability of the family depends upon the stability of marriage: the stability of marriage depends upon the keeping of a promise. Allow the promise to be broken and sooner or later you will bring the State crashing down on top of you.

So how can the process be reversed? Only by speaking the truth "in season and out of season", as St Paul has it. In St John's Gospel, Chapter 8, Jesus is recorded as saying to the Jews who believed in Him:

If you make my word your home you will indeed be my disciples.
You will learn the truth and the truth will make you free.

To speak the truth requires courage and persistence, because a degenerate society does not want to hear the truth, for the way of truth includes some rocky paths and some hard sayings. In this country every couple who marry in a church make the same promise: "I call upon these persons here present to witness that I N.N. do take thee N.N. to be my lawful wedded wife/husband, to have and to hold from this day forward, for better for worse, for richer for poorer, in sickness and in health, to love and to cherish, till death do us part." Because there are so many divorces I can only assume that a great many couples are not made to think seriously about what they promise on their wedding day. To make such promises with the intention that if things don't work out as you want you will get a divorce and consider yourself free to marry someone else would surely be hypocrisy of the most cynical kind, would it not? "For better for worse" means that if, for instance, your husband turns out to be a philanderer or your wife an alcoholic you will hold the marriage together as best you can nonetheless. Statistics from the divorce courts indicate that quarrels over money are the number one cause of marriage break-up. Even if a couple start their marriage in good jobs with good prospects it is by no means certain in this topsy-turvy world that that happy state will continue. "For richer for poorer" means that if poverty overtakes you, you will stick together and share what little you have. "In sickness and in health" means that if your partner is struck down by a long-lasting disease, like multiple sclerosis or Alzhimers, you will stand by them to the end. Of course, everyone on their wedding day hopes that it will for them always be "For better", "For richer" and "In health", but they promise to take the rough with the smooth.

It is because we live in times such as I have described that the example of couples like Jerry and Sheila is not only praiseworthy and a just cause for celebration, but a vital witness to those who come after them. Not everyone is capable of sustaining the christian ideal of marriage but everyone is capable of recognizing that ideal when they see it. It is when you reject the ideal that the rot sets in. None of us who, with God's help, have held our marriages together would claim, I think, that married life has been a bed of roses all the time. We are all fallible; we all have our weaknesses; we all fail from time to time; and, let's face it, there have been occasions when we have driven each other up the wall. But as Christians we believe that on our wedding day God gave us enough grace, special to each individual marriage, to see us through till death do us part. This has enabled us to take the rough with the smooth, to enjoy the happy times and not to lose heart during the storms. With Jesus as our pilot, even if at times He seems to sleep as He did on Peter's boat on the Sea of Galilee, we can navigate a reasonably steady course, secure in the knowledge that He will see us safely home to the heavenly harbour.

It is important that we who believe in the ideal of Christian marriage should demonstrate by our lives and in our speech the joys and benefits of lifelong loyalty and be ready to defend the principle against all comers. So in conclusion may I remind you of what St Paul says in his Second Letter to Timothy, chapter 4?

> *Before God and before Jesus Christ who is to be judge of the living and the dead, I put this duty to you, in the name of his Appearing and of his Kingdom: proclaim the message and, welcome or unwelcome, insist on it. Refute falsehood, correct error, call to obedience - but do all with patience and with the intention of teaching. The time is sure to come when, far from*

being content with sound teaching, people will be avid for the latest novelty and collect themselves a whole series of teachers according to their own tastes; and then, instead of listening to the truth, they will turn to myths. Be careful always to choose the right course; be brave under trials; make the preaching of the Good News your life's work, in thoroughgoing service.

Our Lady of the Assumption
Bosham

5th August, 1995

A POSY

OF

POEMS

THE VICTORIA FALLS

JANUARY 1948

'The Smoke that Thunders', your brothers called you;
The smoke that has thundered a thousand years.
A thousand, did I say? Aye, seventy times seven thousand,
Before the dawn of created man.

What tale, what story lies bound, spume-chained,
Casketed in your jewelled waves?
What day was it that saw your stream-tied waters
Loosed by God's creative hand?

He fashioned the earth and loosed the waters,
Those seven days He made our world;
And beholding His work from Heaven's dream heights
"He saw that it was good".

He watched your cataracts come hurtling down;
And in your spray-spangled depths
Beheld, in mirrored form, His majestic Self:
The glory of unutterable power.

In time predestined in Eternal Mind
Man was made, and from his rib a woman formed;
Theirs was the earth as a garden home,
Its beauty, its intrinsic loveliness.

Man sinned, cast forth, died a putrid death:
Nature stopped; venom, hate within her realm.
Adam's fall from Eden's peace, from placid life to death,
I here behold in your tremendous fall.

Your glory waters, your mesmeric roar,
Your spray flung cloud-tossed to the sky
Holds within those rocky heights
A wonderment too great for man.

Man, who can but gaze enraptured,
May learn of you unspoken truths,
May see in symbol where great errors end:
With gathering speed he's rushing to his doom.

And still through wars and peace, midst death and life,
You flow on to the end of time.
Kings may die and kingdoms fall
But your fall is endless, proud, defiant.

THE SOUL OF MAN
1955

The air was heavy that summer's night;
Thunder rumbled round the distant hills.
No living thing betrayed its presence:
And the soul of man was restless.

Past his cottage that very day
More armed men had straggled by,
Their faces grey and drawn and grim,
Their end uncertain, their faith distilled.

Their faith? How well the Soul of Man
Remembered those grievous days
When faith in oneself and in one's cause
Was the common possession of men.

Those days, not so very long ago,
When men were satisfied with life;
Bright were their faces and open their minds
And they laboured well to gain their bread.

Their hands were gnarled with sterner toil;
They worked long hours for smaller pay.
Yet, though life and discipline were hard,
The Soul of Man was happy.

This still and sombre summer's night
The Soul of Man was restless.
The portents of his world were evil
And, as he lay, he wondered why.

These latter years so rich in pleasures,
So fruitful in discoveries,
Had raised the hopes of men on high;
Their leaders promised peace and plenty.

How foolish then they all had been;
How lulled by vain and empty words!
This science, what riches had it brought?
This creed, what peace of mind?

"Fool, idiot, sot that I am",
So the Soul of Man chastised himself.
"Deceived, betrayed, beguiled, bewitched
I sold my faith for an ounce of gold."

In my comfortable chair I leaned back
While music was brought to me on the air.
I saved my body with surgery;
I abandoned my plough to snatch my pen.

It was easy to sit and be carried by car;
It was cosy to lounge in the picture house;
But at home my piano and my plough
Rusted, neglected and forgot.

SUNDAY AFTERNOON - INKUDSE BAY

LAKE NYASA May 1959

Rumble, tumble, smithereen,
The waters roll upon the shore;
Sparkle, jazinth, silver sheen
The droplets glisten in the sun.

Sway, weigh, suck and splash
The gentle waves roll in and out;
Roll, scroll, lift and crash
To break exhausted on the beach.

Soothing sighing in the trees
(As I lie upon my bed)
The soft air blows among the leaves
And puffs the cottage smoke away.

Peace, sleep, sweet content,
The bay is drowsed and drunk;
Work, school, bank and rent
Too far away to think about.

Fish, swish, swim and leap
In their freedom - great expanse
Plunge, lunge in the deep,
Their watery homes and mates to seek.

Love, dove are often linked,
The latter flies untrammeled;
As if at humans he had winked
He's free to fly where fancy wills.

God's rod and rule are here,
The Maker and the made;
Balance, poise and symetry,
A world unspoilt and primitive.

To
SIR EDWARD ELGAR

ON THE MALVERN HILLS
SEPTEMBER 1963

Of English composers the greatest,
Who taught you the magic of your art?
Unfold to me the secrets of your heart –
I who have known the same fields and orchards.

You genius was born in my own Worcestershire.
You grew up among the same sights and sounds:
The same streets, the same houses surrounded you
During those most impressionable of years.

You worshipped in the same church,
You wandered through the same cathedral,
Its ancient grandeur seeping the while
Through your eager maleable soul.

The same river threaded its even way
Through the youthful dawn of your life;
By its willowed banks and rushing weirs
You have heard, as I, the music of the stream.

You have leant, as I too, against a stile
And from across those silent snow-deep meadows
Have felt the spirit of Winter pass by
As the chill wind cut your burning cheeks.

Your soul sated with the countryside's peace
You, too, have returned to the glowing cottage hearth,
Have shaken the snow from off your shoes
And thoughtfully munched chestnuts before a roasting fire.

On these hallowed hills you have sat,
Some drowsy summer's evening,
And watched the hay carts roll home
To the distant sound of farmers' voices.

The swallows weaved around the chimney tops,
The skylark shrilled his lofty evensong,
The crows chattered querelous in the elm tops,
The lone seagull followed the river's course.

Bredon still looks benignly over his busy valley;
Behind the Cotswolds, blue in their distance,
Still tell of nestling Broadway and of Moreton-in-Marsh,
Of Chipping Norton and of Oxford beyond.

Do you remember those golden harvests?
Those ruddy apples on the laden orchard trees?
Can you recall the falling Autumn leaves?
The horses toiling afore their lumber wagons?

Those villages and hamlets and market towns,
Each so individual and separate, and yet
All bred of the self-same womb and speaking
The same rolling roisterous tongue?

But above all, the dear loved ancient City,
Proudly clustering around its eternal pile
With its pinnacled tower and majestic nave,
Its haunting cloisters and homely green?

It stands there now keeping guard
By the Severn, as it has done for
Nigh on a thousand years.
It links my days to yours, and yours to the centuries beyond.

Yes, dear Master, you have breathed the same air
And seen the same familiar sights,
And heard the self-same voices of nature
And caught the spirit of departed ages.

These were the rich food on which your genius fed,
These the inspiration of symphonies and sonatas,
The life-blood of oratorios and concertos;
Your pen weaving the Severn through the staves.

When you stood with baton in hand
Conducting your works in foreign shires and lands
You listened across the dividing space to catch
The voice of Worcestershire and to interpret,
As only you have done, the mystic strains
Of Worcester's soul, which is England's heart.

THE NIGHT WATCH
AT
MY MOTHER'S DEATHBED

WORCESTER - DECEMBER 1963

The mellow bell
A-dong booms
From cloistered tower;
On frosty air,
'Cross muddy river,
Flood-meadows green,
Over clustered roof-tops comes its sound.

And down stairs
In my Mother's hall
The old grandfather ting-chimes.
The hour has passed.
Beside me a little old lady,
All a-dying, shriven and a-shrunk,
labours to catch her breath.

The old city lies a-yonder.
Father and Mother loved it.
All our childer memories cluster,
And she was here.
To school and back again
And she was always here.
War, peace, overseas, a-wandering
But she was always here.

The hour passes.
An odour, a sweet gentle odour
Hangs still on the frosty air,
A-fire warmed, slightly.
A death odour, but a white death,
All angel waved.
It is the odour of sanctity.

For this little old lady,
All a-dying and at peace,
Is my own Mother.
This old body gave me life;
And we're all here now,
All flesh of her flesh
This little old bag of bones.

Gerontius music
Filled that cloistered tower
Where the mellow bell booms.
She took me once.
Now her soul 'on its journey goes forth,
A christian soul'.
And the mellow bell
A-dong booms
The passing of the hour.